RWANDA AND THE MORAL OBLIGATION OF HUMANITARIAN INTERVENTION

RWANDA AND THE MORAL OBLIGATION OF HUMANITARIAN INTERVENTION

Joshua James Kassner

EDINBURGH
University Press

For Stephanie, Mackenzie and Abigail

First published in hardback in 2013

This paperback edition 2014

Edinburgh University Press Ltd
The Tun – Holyrood Road
12(2f) Jackson's Entry
Edinburgh EH8 8PJ
www.euppublishing.com

Typeset in 11/13 Palatino Light by
Servis Filmsetting Ltd, Stockport, Cheshire,
and printed and bound in Great Britain by
CPI Group (UK) Ltd, Croydon CR0 4YY

A CIP record for this book is available from the British Library

ISBN 978 0 7486 4458 2 (hardback)
ISBN 978 0 7486 9627 7 (paperback)
ISBN 978 0 7486 4459 9 (webready PDF)
ISBN 978 0 7486 7048 2 (epub)

CONTENTS

ACKNOWLEDGMENTS

This project has consumed my intellectual life for more than a decade. The initial idea was formed in the spring of 2002 during a course I took in conjunction with the University of Maryland's Committee on Politics, Philosophy, and Public Policy. We were reading Philip Gourevitch's detailed account of the Rwandan genocide, *We Wish to Inform You that Tomorrow We Will be Killed with Our Families: Stories from Rwanda.* In one particular class Joseph Oppenheimer raised a provocative question regarding the occurrence (and recurrence) of genocide; and from that day I have spent much of my time and intellectual effort pondering one question that grew from the discussion that day – what moral obligations, if any, did the international community have to act?

My initial thoughts were met with invaluable skeptical and constructive criticism; some of which no doubt remains. The project was too large, too ambitious, and slightly wrongheaded; but, other than that, it had promise. The project could not have been completed without the guidance, criticism, and time so many were willing to give. There are a number of individuals in particular to whom I owe thanks.

First, despite his schedule and even with his frustration at my less-than-concise writing style (still a work in progress), Christopher Morris has been a constant source of guidance on this project and others. He suggested that I should adjust the goals of the project as the initial idea would have required volumes to complete. Since then, he has always found time to chat, challenge, and point me in the right direction. Judith Lichtenberg has also played a central role in my development as a philosopher. Without her I may have never attended the University of Maryland. In fact it was a discussion with her that had a determinate influence on my decision to attend Maryland for my doctoral studies. She has always been kind and supportive, even when expressing her concerns about my work. As to this project in particular, she helped me to see objections that I had initially overlooked. I would also like to acknowledge the impact Samuel Kerstein has had on this project and the lasting impression he has had on me. As to this project, his analytic scrutiny made the supporting arguments much stronger than they would have been, and in the initial phases of the project he recommended an entire shift in methodology. Without that change, the end product may have been interesting, but not likely as compelling. I would also like to thank Mortimer Sellers for his guidance and mentorship. He has been a tremendous influence on my development as a philosopher from the time I spent in his class on Jurisprudence, and his influence continues to the present day.

In addition, I want to thank David Lefkowitz, Matt King, and Craig Derksen for allowing me to bend their ears and pick their brains about the many ideas that were, at any given moment, racing through my mind. There are also a number of other individuals who have provided me with various forms of support, criticism, and opportunity. My colleagues at the University of Baltimore and especially in the Division of Legal, Ethical, and Historical Studies have been a steady source of support. In particular, I would like to thank Michele Cotton for her invaluable input regarding the style of my writing. I would also like to thank James Pattison and the University of Manchester for inviting me to give a talk on Chapter 4 at a time when I was in need of, and they were more than able to supply, constructive criticism regarding my suggestions about the transition from theory to practice. I would also like to thank Thom Brooks, who has helped me shepherd this project from proposal to publication. In that vein, I owe many thanks to Michelle Houston for her patience, and to Edinburgh University Press for the opportunity to share my ideas.

Lastly, I would like to thank my wife Stephanie, who never blinked when nearly fifteen years ago I told her I was going to leave the practice of law to study philosophy. Her support has never waned.

INTRODUCTION: BRIEF HISTORY AND OVERVIEW

In 1994, approximately 800,000 Rwandans were sought out and killed simply because they were Tutsis or Tutsi sympathizers. The tragedy of the Rwandan genocide has since caused many to question the international community's choice not to intervene. Much of the discussion over the moral nature of humanitarian intervention has revolved around the moral *permissibility* of humanitarian intervention and the right of sovereign states to be free from outside interference in their internal affairs. In the discussion that follows, it is argued that not only are there circumstances under which humanitarian intervention is morally permissible, but that in Rwanda there was a moral *obligation* of humanitarian intervention. The existence conditions for such an obligation are identified and a reconstructed normative framework to govern the practical deliberations of states is offered in which the lessons learned from the moral critique inform the institutionalization of the reconstructed normative framework; completing the transition from theory to practice.

THE RWANDAN GENOCIDE

Before turning to the substantive discussion, it is helpful to start with a brief account of the Rwandan genocide. Between April and July of 1994, approximately 800,000 Rwandan children, women, and men were slaughtered because of their ethnic ties.[1] Lt-Gen. Romeo Dallaire and Philip Gourevitch add to that number countless others who were forced into refugee camps where they were subjected to violence, starvation, and disease.[2] Most of the killing was carried out, not by the military, but by citizens in machete-wielding mobs. Individuals were betrayed, and often sought out and killed, by those they knew. For example, in one particularly egregious instance, a physician, Dr Gerard, betrayed the Tutsis under his care.[3] Dr Gerard led a Hutu militia to his Tutsi patients, knowing and intending that his patients would be killed.[4]

In August 1993, nearly a year before the genocide, the Hutu-led Rwandan government and the Rwandan Patriotic Front (RPF)[5] entered into a power-sharing agreement known as the Arusha Accords.[6] The Arusha Accords were intended to bring an end to a bloody civil war.[7] On 5 October 1993 the United Nations approved a mandate for the deployment of a peacekeeping force (UNAMIR) to aid in the implementation of the Arusha Accords.[8] UNAMIR never received the support necessary to accomplish its mission. While the implementation of the Arusha Accords dragged on, Hutu extremists consolidated their power.

By April 1994, UNAMIR had received numerous warnings from an informant within the interahamwe (a civilian militia with close ties to Hutu extremists in the Rwandan government) that a campaign of violence against the Tutsi was about to begin.[9] One particularly relevant piece of information provided by the informant was the identification of hidden caches of weapons being stockpiled by the interahamwe. Dallaire contacted the United Nations seeking permission to raid the weapons caches, the very existence of which was a violation of the Arusha Accords. Permission was denied, and Dallaire was chastised for "even thinking about raiding the weapons caches."[10]

On 6 April 1994, a plane carrying Rwanda's president exploded in mid-air over the Rwandan capital Kigali. Almost immediately, violence broke out throughout Kigali. The Hutu extremists used this event and its chaotic aftermath as an excuse to seize control of the government and put the implementation of the Arusha Accords on hold. The interahamwe put the weapons they had hidden and that Dallaire had sought to confiscate to their intended use – the eradication of Tutsis.

At the request of the United Nations, Dallaire outlined a plan to halt the killing. With a force of about 5,000 well-equipped soldiers Dallaire believed that he could stop the violence, and put the implementation of the Arusha Accords back on track.[11] However, even after the killing had begun, the United Nations refused to give the peacekeepers the support necessary to protect the Rwandan people. Though many at the United Nations expressed shock at what was happening in Rwanda, they did nothing to halt the killing.[12]

Numerous reasons were offered for the refusal to intervene. One reason pressed by the Hutu-led interim government was based on the claim that Rwanda, like any other sovereign state, was presumed to enjoy the right of nonintervention. The international community could justifiably interfere in the internal affairs of Rwanda only under certain narrowly prescribed circumstances. The interim government claimed that the violence was an *internal* matter, and that it would soon be under control.[13] This argument against intervention was pressed in the United Nations Security Council, where Rwanda held one of the rotating seats at the time.[14]

Humanitarian crises are not generally recognized as providing the necessary justification for violating a sovereign state's right of nonintervention; however, under the Convention on the Prevention and Punishment of the Crime of Genocide 1948 ("Convention"), intervention is, at the very least, *permitted* to prevent or stop genocide.[15] Despite this legal permission, while Tutsis died, those in the international community argued over whether the violence in Rwanda counted as genocide.[16] In fact, in an intentional effort to avoid the possible demands of the Convention, the United States avoided use of the word "genocide" in describing the events unfolding in Rwanda.[17]

Eventually, the violence in Rwanda was recognized as genocide.[18] This, however, did not result in an intervention; rather, many claimed that recognition of genocide merely made intervention permissible, but did not require action. This position was captured in PPD-25, under which the United States would only intervene if the national interests of the United States were at stake.[19] While the international community dithered, the killing of Tutsis continued.

By July 1994 the RPF had gained control of Kigali and most of Rwanda, and had put an end to the slaughter in the areas under their control. At about that same time, under a mandate from the United Nations, the French deployed a sizeable military force, known as "Operation Turquoise," to provide secure areas for refugees.[20] The Hutu extremists and the genocidaires fled to the French safe areas, where, owing to failures on the part of the French to screen the incoming refugees, making no distinction between victims and genocidaires, the violence would continue.[21]

Additionally, the justifications for Operation Turquoise were not based on the genocidal actions that had resulted in the deaths of hundreds of thousands of Rwandans. Rather, it was the danger to international peace and security caused by the resultant refugee crisis that the French and the United Nations relied upon to justify Operation Turquoise.[22] In addition, rather than protecting refugees, the intervention had the effect of protecting the genocidaires as they fled.[23]

In considering the Rwandan genocide, it is easy to get lost in the sheer enormity of the tragedy. The senseless and brutal murder of an individual is swallowed by the effort to slaughter an entire ethnic minority. It is important, however, to be conscious of the plight of the individual victims. In Rwanda, there were no gas chambers, no machinery of death to kill large numbers at a single time. Instead, most of the victims were "murdered, not by automatic weapons but by machetes and clubs wielded by soldiers, mayors, police, and neighbors."[24]

MY PROJECT: THE INTERNATIONAL COMMUNITY'S FAILURE TO INTERVENE IN RWANDA

In 1948, in the aftermath of World War II and with the horror of the Holocaust known to the world, the United Nations sponsored the Convention on the Prevention and Punishment of the Crime of Genocide, which states,

> The Contracting Parties confirm that genocide, whether committed in time of peace or time of war, is a crime under international law which they undertake to prevent and to punish.[25]

Yet, less than fifty years later, the international community allowed nearly a million men, women, and children to be brutally killed.

In some cases it wasn't the commitment of troops or direct military action that was at issue. For example, in May 1994, the United States military contemplated jamming the radio signal of Radio RTLM (AKA Radio Mille Collines) – a radio station broadcasting anti-Tutsi propaganda, identifying specific individuals by name and address, and exhorting the civilian population to kill their Tutsi neighbors.[26] Jamming the radio signal would have involved little more than flying a US military plane over Rwandan airspace. The United States, however, decided against such action, claiming it would be too costly, and that such action would violate international law.[27] If jamming a radio signal was outside the range of appropriate action, it is not clear what commitment to the Convention meant, or required.

I share the visceral reaction many have had to the vile acts that make up the Rwandan genocide; however, as an intellectual matter my interest in this project is motivated by my interest in global justice and the role it should play in the practical deliberations of states and the international community. In seeking insight into this subject, focusing on a particular historical event has a number of advantages. First, it allows for a discussion of the major issues in, and questions associated with, global justice and its relationship to the normative framework of international relations (the principles and institutional structure governing the practical deliberations of states), without having to provide a complete account of either. Second, specifically with reference to the critical assessment of the normative framework of international relations, using a past event is advantageous because historical study renders the practical deliberations by the relevant actors more open to assessment. In recent years, there has been much written about the Rwandan genocide. These accounts paint a sufficiently clear picture of the genocide, as well as the deliberative processes engaged in by those in the international community deciding what ought to be done in response to the violence.

Another reason for evaluating the moral obligations that states and the international community owed to the Rwandan people is directly related to my belief that there are circumstances under which humanitarian intervention is not only permissible, but obligatory. The Rwandan genocide presents an interesting case because there is a growing consensus that the choice by the international community not to intervene in Rwanda was morally wrong. Since judgments of wrongness are appropriate only if there was an obligation to have done otherwise, the consensus indicates a belief that the international community was under an obligation to intervene. Consequently, it would seem that if we are ever to have obligations to distant others that give rise to an obligation of humanitarian intervention it would be to prevent and protect against the mass violation of the basic right to physical security.

OVERVIEW

In the end, the discussion that follows is a defense of a number of simple propositions: that the international community ought, all things considered, to have intervened in Rwanda to stop the genocide; that the normative framework of international relations was and is unjustified; and that the institutions and principles that make up the normative framework of international relations ought to be reformed. Though these propositions can be stated in simple terms, their defense is complicated, and the argument in support unfolds in four steps.

The first step (Chapter 1) is focused on a critical assessment of conventional thinking regarding the moral nature of humanitarian intervention. In particular, the contemporary debate has – as noted above – consistently focused on determining whether humanitarian intervention is morally *permissible*; and, if so, under what conditions. These discussions have tended to center on a small number of themes. For many the debate is about whether the potential moral hazards (futility, the possibility of perverse results, and the pretextual use of the justification, and so on) associated with military interventions are too great to merit the risk.[28] For others, the debate is over the moral value of the right of nonintervention held by sovereign states.[29] Since the Peace of Westphalia (1648) the relations between states have been an increasingly rule-governed arena. The state system is built around the right of nonintervention, under which sovereign states are protected against outside interference in the affairs of the state because respect for the right of nonintervention is taken to be crucial to providing international peace and security.

Still others challenge the possibility that *humanitarian* intervention is conceptually consistent; in fact, in *The Responsibility to Protect* the International Commission on Intervention and State Sovereignty refused to use the phrase "humanitarian intervention," in part because of the controversy over the phrase itself. Yet despite the seemingly intractable nature of the disagreements over the permissibility of humanitarian intervention a widely shared consensus has emerged that in the case of Rwanda the international community's choice not to intervene was a moral failure.

Despite the fact that I have already employed the phrase, a discussion over the moral nature of humanitarian intervention must begin with a working definition of "humanitarian intervention". As Stephen A. Garret has pointed out,

> The terms "humanitarian" and "intervention" are typically imbued with such a variety of nuances and differing interpretations that to join them together into a single concept almost inevitably produces ambiguity and perhaps even tension, especially since both words inherently carry a lot of emotional baggage.[30]

For this discussion I will accept J. L. Holzgrefe's definition of humanitarian intervention as:

> the threat or use of force across state borders by a state (or group of states) aimed at preventing or ending widespread and grave violations of the fundamental human rights of individuals other than its own citizens, without the permission of the state within whose territory force is applied.[31]

It is important to note that the definition offered does not require that the only motivation for intervention is humanitarian. It would be disingenuous, however, to call an intervention humanitarian if humanitarian considerations were not determinative of the choice to intervene.

If it can be demonstrated that under certain circumstances not only is humanitarian intervention morally permissible, but is in fact morally *obligatory*, this would move the debate over the moral nature of humanitarian intervention past the issue of permissibility. In that case, thinking of a right or responsibility to intervene as the basis for its moral permissibility misses the mark. What we ought to be seeking are the conditions that morally obligate the international community to act.

There are others who defend a moral obligation of humanitarian intervention. For example, Jovana Davidovic offers an alternative defense of the existence of moral obligations of humanitarian intervention.[32] Though sympathetic to her view, I find her argument lacking. The obligation she defends is one that is isolated from the real-world circumstances under which such an obligation would have to be applied. I am concerned with defending a moral obligation to intervene as an operative principle governing the practical deliberations of states and the international community. As such, the obligation must be explored as an *all-things-considered* reason for action, and not merely as a conceptually possible obligation that gives us *a* reason for action that may or may not be determinative of how the international community ought, all things considered, to act.

In defense of the proposition that there are circumstances under which there is an all-things-considered moral obligation of humanitarian intervention, the conceptual possibility of international morality must be defended. In that vein, various skeptical accounts made by international relations scholars, and political and moral philosophers are subjected to critical scrutiny and I argue that none of the arguments addressed precludes the possibility of international morality. Second, a weak moral principle in support of the moral obligation of humanitarian intervention is developed. The principle is comprised of the set of conditions under which no one could reasonably deny that an obligation of humanitarian intervention exists. The principle developed is weak in the sense that it takes into account and accommodates the major moral objections that might be raised by those who accept the possibility of international morality, but who reject the notion that humanitarian intervention could be morally justified.

The second step (Chapter 2) addresses various arguments raised against the moral permissibility of humanitarian intervention. I contend that none of the objections considered demonstrate that humanitarian intervention is always impermissible. This does not, however, imply that the reasons upon which such objections are based could not support the rejection of a claimed obligation to intervene in a particular instance. For example, under a consequentialist view, the fact that an intervention might require massive military force to save the lives of a small number of people would provide a reasonable basis for claiming that the moral obligation to intervene has been outweighed. Neither, however, does this imply that no action should be taken. It merely implies that military intervention is not a morally defensible option in that case. Such circumstances are incorporated as additional conditions that must be met if there is to be an *all-things-considered* moral obligation of humanitarian intervention.

I argue that the Rwandan genocide fulfilled the conditions identified; and, as a consequence, that there was an all-things-considered moral obligation to intervene in Rwanda. Providing a convincing argument for a moral obligation of humanitarian intervention is no small task; however, without more, such an accomplishment would simply be an intellectual exercise with little chance of making a practical difference. We will have gained a greater understanding of the moral nature of the world in which we live, but such a limited argument would fail to provide practical guidance.

Making the transition from theory to practice involves two additional steps. As such, in the third step (Chapter 3) I assess the role that moral demands do and should play in the practical deliberations of states and I offer a reconstructed normative framework of international relations. Chapter 3 begins by recognizing that questions of intervention have largely been determined by the right of nonintervention held by sovereign states. The right of nonintervention precludes other states and the international community from considering reasons for action that would require intervention. In which case, moral reasons for action based on the internal affairs of another state are irrelevant to the practical deliberations of states and the international community; rendering action by the international community unlikely. Against this position, I argue that the right of nonintervention and the role it has played in the practical deliberations of states were /are unjustified. In the alternative, I argue that we ought to adopt a rebuttable presumption in favor of nonintervention.

Defending this position, I begin with an explication of various justificatory arguments for the right of nonintervention. None of the arguments put forward is capable of supporting a principle with such a preclusive effect on the practical deliberations of states. Instead, the best argument for the right of sovereign states to be free from intervention is an instrumental one. Instrumental justifications, however, carry with them inherent limitations. The principle being defended is only as strong as the degree to which it serves the goal(s) that justify the principle.

I contend, however, that from the perspective of the practical deliberations of states and the international community this does not mean that humanitarian intervention should be treated as an open question. It is not the case that our deliberations about possible humanitarian interventions should begin with an assumption that each option is normatively equal. I argue instead that we ought to adopt a *rebuttable presumption* in favor of nonintervention; thus privileging the option of nonintervention. Such a rule would serve the same goals as the right of nonintervention, but without the unjustified preclusion of moral reasons for action.

The fourth and final step in the substantive argument (Chapter 4) is focused on completing the transition from theory to practice. In addition to assessing the implications to be drawn from Chapters 1–3, Chapter 4 is focused on identifying the reforms to the normative framework of international relations that are necessary if we want to avoid future Rwandas, as well as future failures on the part of the international community to respond appropriately. To do so we must take steps to advance principles and create institutions that more effectively influence the practical deliberations of states and the international community.

To date, the most significant change in the institutional landscape has been the emergence of the responsibility to protect principle. Within contemporary thinking on the nature of sovereignty and the responsibilities of states and the international community, the responsibility to protect represents the most progressive mainstream view. As such, it serves as the basis for my critical analysis of our current normative framework. As an approach to dealing with crimes against humanity and other violations of basic rights, it suffers from a fundamental flaw. Namely, it is intended to be consistent with accepted views of sovereignty, basic principles of international relations, and the Charter of the United Nations. In proposing an alternative institutional framework, I do not assume that existing institutions and underlying principles are justified. Rather, I begin with an explication and critique of the responsibility to protect; highlighting how even the most progressive view of our current institutional framework fails, and I offer a more aspirational but attainable institutional structure guided by the principle of subsidiarity, and a commitment to effectiveness and political legitimacy.

CONCLUSION

The discussion that follows includes a number of significant implications for our understanding of the moral nature of humanitarian intervention and the role that moral reasons ought to play in the normative framework of international relations. Despite the importance of these theoretical implications, one of the primary objectives of the arguments presented is to provide a framework for a cross-disciplinary discussion focused on reforming the normative framework of international relations with the goal of insuring that the principles governing the international community's response to grave humanitarian crises conform to the demands of global justice.

If we are committed to doing all that is reasonable to insure that the international community will not yet again stand idly by while men, women, and children have their basic rights violated, then we must reform the principles and institutional structures that constitute the normative framework of international relations. In short, we must change the way basic moral principles are dealt with by the institutions that govern the actions of the international community.

Chapter 1

THE GROUNDWORK FOR A MORAL OBLIGATION OF HUMANITARIAN INTERVENTION

INTRODUCTION: AN ALL-THINGS-CONSIDERED REASON FOR ACTION

Are there any circumstances under which the international community has an all-things-considered moral obligation of humanitarian intervention? This threshold question must be answered before turning to the critical evaluation, reconstruction, and reform of the normative framework of international relations that governs such decisions. Providing an answer to this question is the focus of Chapters 1 and 2.

First, it must be determined whether such a principle is conceptually possible. The defense that follows proceeds in two steps. First, there are a number of oft-cited skeptical arguments from political realists, constructivists, and moral relativists that are intended to demonstrate that international morality is impossible. If these skeptical arguments are true, then there aren't *any* moral obligations states owe to distant others; nevertheless a moral obligation to risk blood and treasure to protect the basic rights of distant others. Thus, it is necessary to demonstrate that international morality is not precluded by such arguments before addressing objections specific to humanitarian intervention.

Having demonstrated the conceptual possibility of international morality, the next conceptual hurdle to the defense of a moral obligation of humanitarian intervention is to be found in various arguments intended to demonstrate the moral *impermissibility* of humanitarian intervention. Since the moral permissibility of an action is normatively prior to any moral obligation to act, if humanitarian intervention is morally impermissible, then a discussion of a moral obligation is moot. None of these arguments, though based on reasonable moral concerns, justifies the preclusion of the possibility of a moral obligation of humanitarian intervention.

The next step in the argument, to be taken up in Chapter 2, is the identification of the conditions under which no one could reasonably deny that a moral obligation of humanitarian intervention exists. The argument and methodology employed are not unlike that used by Ernest J. Weinrib in his defense of a duty of easy rescue; wherein Weinrib sought to demonstrate that under certain circumstances an individual would be under a duty to perform a rescue.[1] The strength of this approach is found in the weakness of the principle defended. With respect to the moral obligation to intervene, if we are ever to have an all-things-considered moral obligation of humanitarian intervention it will be under the conditions identified. If successfully defended, the principle would have implications for what states can be morally obligated to do in the international arena, and provide a moral justification for the development or reform of institutions intended to render the obligation practically effective. Additionally, it would serve to broaden the debate over the moral nature of humanitarian intervention.

MAKING CONCEPTUAL ROOM: RESPONDING TO THE SKEPTIC

The skeptical arguments to be addressed rest on the proposition that morality does not apply to states or the international community, or at least not in the same way it applies to individuals. If such arguments are correct, then discussion of the moral permissibility (or obligation) of humanitarian intervention is meaningless. To make the needed conceptual room, it is not necessary to demonstrate that the reasons upon which such arguments are based are false. I need only demonstrate that there is no implication from these reasons to the ultimate claim that international morality is impossible.

Since many of the skeptical arguments to be considered preclude the possibility of any principles of international morality, these arguments should be addressed first. The descriptive political realist presents the most skeptical perspective on the relevance of moral rules to international relations; consequently, it makes sense to begin with this version of the realist argument. The skepticism of the descriptive political realist is based on the proposition that all forms of prescriptive normative theory are inapplicable to the relations between states.[2] The philosophical foundations for descriptive political realism are found in Thucydides' "Melian Dialogue" where it is claimed that the relations between states are defined by each state's desire for power and promotion of its self-interest. It is the hierarchical relations of power that determine what *will* or *will not* happen in the international arena.[3] Thus, international relations are not governed by normative principles but are instead the result of power relationships and the behavior they cause; what states *ought* or *ought not* to do is irrelevant.[4]

Since the skepticism of the descriptive realist is based on the claim that normative theory is irrelevant to understanding international relations, if states are capable of acting on normative judgments, the skepticism fails. The actual behavior of states in the international arena would seem to indicate that states can and often do engage in practical deliberation and act on normative judgments. The realist bears the burden of explaining why normative theory is irrelevant to our understanding of this phenomenon.

It may be claimed that this apparent capacity to act on the outcome of practical deliberation is nothing more than epiphenomena – the babbling of the brook – and that states are *directed* by the imperatives of power. For the descriptive realist to be correct, however, it must be the case that states are incapable of doing anything but acting in accordance with the imperatives of power. Failures to do so are an indication that states are capable of acting in ways other than in accordance with such imperatives. The fact that states do often fail to act according to the imperatives of power undermines the claim of the descriptive realist.

In addition, for the skepticism of the descriptive realist to be correct, the imperatives of power must govern the actions of states much like the laws of physics govern the interactions of physical objects.[5] However, the actions of states are the actions of governments that control such states, not natural forces. Governments are comprised of individuals making decisions.[6] The actions of governments are based upon those decisions involving the weighing and balancing of reasons for action. Thus, to the extent that individuals are capable of acting for reasons, so too are governments. It may be the case that more often than not states do act according to the imperatives of power, but they only do so after it has been determined that this is how they *ought* to act. The stringent skepticism of the descriptive realist fails.

It should be noted that what I am arguing for is not a matter of determining preferences. The importance of this disclaimer is derived from the strength of Kenneth Arrow's "Impossibility Theorem."[7] Arrow's theorem demonstrates the impossibility of devising a method of aggregating individual preferences into a social preference. If the determination of a preference is required for an agent to act, one might contend that our inability to identify the preference of a state undermines the claim that states can act and deliberate in ways similar to individuals. I am not, however, making the claim that states act and deliberate just like individuals; rather, decisions to act by a state are made by individuals, and as such, are capable of being influenced by normative considerations. Consequently, it makes sense to assume that states act on normative reasons even if such reasons are not based on the determination of a *social* preference.

Unlike the descriptive realist, the normative realist concedes that normative theory has an important role to play in the relations between states.[8] However, the normative realist argues that, since international relations is like a Hobbesian state of nature, the demands of morality do not apply to states in the international arena.[9] For Hobbes, the state of nature is a pre-societal condition in which the inhabitants are in a constant state of war.[10] Individuals would do better by adhering to the demands of justice; however, it would be irrational for *any single* individual to act on such demands without assurance that others would do so as well.[11] What is needed, according to Hobbes, is a common power to enforce the demands of justice.[12] Without such a common power each individual's right to self-preservation is paramount,[13] and the fundamental prescriptive norm in the state of nature is prudence; and the demands of justice are inapplicable until a common power is established to define and enforce such demands.[14]

Since there is no world sovereign to enforce the demands of justice, it is argued that the international arena is like a Hobbesian state of nature.[15] As Hobbes notes in his discussion of international relations, "The notions of Right and Wrong. Justice and Injustice have there no place. Where there is no Common Power, there is no Law, no Injustice. Force and Fraud, are in warre the two Cardinall Vertues."[16]

Two conditions must be met for the normative realist's skeptical argument to succeed. First, it must be the case that the Hobbesian argument about the role of morality in the state of nature is correct. Second, for the analogy to hold it must be the case that states in the international arena are analogous to individuals in the state of nature. The normative realist fails on both accounts. First, the Hobbesian argument is supposed to demonstrate either that the demands of justice don't exist in the state of nature, *or* that such demands are perpetually ineffective without the assurance of a common power. Regarding the former claim, the possibility that the demands of justice *might* conflict with the right of self-preservation does not demonstrate that such demands don't exist. All that can be claimed is that self-preservation trumps or outweighs such demands when they conflict.

As to the argument that Hobbes has demonstrated the demands of justice to be perpetually ineffective in the state of nature, this argument is based on the proposition that for the demands of justice to be effective one needs to be assured that others will also adhere to the demands of justice. For Hobbes, the fundamental right of nature is the right of self-preservation – "By all means we can, to defend ourselves."[17] It is this right that, depending on the circumstances, leads to or trumps the fundamental law of nature, "to seek Peace, and to follow it."[18] For Hobbes, what needs to be assured before the demands of justice are practically effective is self-preservation. If such assurance is required, for it to be the case that morality is ineffective in the state of nature it must be the case that such assurance cannot be attained in any instance in which the demands of justice would arise, and that the *only* way to have such assurance is through the establishment and maintenance of a common power.

Regarding the former condition, the assurance required is too demanding. It is highly unlikely that even a common power could provide such assurance. However, if Hobbes means something less, it does not follow that such lesser assurance could *never* be had in the state of nature. It is certainly possible, and reasonable to expect that on at least one occasion in the state of nature two individuals could meet and be assured that neither was a threat to the self-preservation of the other. As to the latter condition, Hobbes's argument demonstrates how a common power might be good at delivering the requisite assurance, but Hobbes fails to demonstrate that a common power is necessary or sufficient for such assurance.

Lastly, even if the Hobbesian argument regarding the role of justice and morality in the state of nature is correct, for the skepticism of the normative realist to be justified the analogy between individuals in the state of nature and states in the international arena must hold. Charles

Beitz has identified four criteria that must be met for "this analogy to be acceptable."[19] Specifically, Beitz claims:

1. The actors in international relations are states.
2. States have relatively equal power (the weakest can defeat the strongest).
3. States are independent of each other in the sense that they can order their internal (i.e., nonsecurity) affairs independently of the internal policies of other actors.
4. There are no reliable expectations of reciprocal compliance by the actors with rules of cooperation in the absence of a superior power capable of enforcing these rules.[20]

For the analogy to hold, the four conditions identified by Beitz must be met as a matter of empirical fact; it is not enough that they *could* be met.

Beitz notes that the

> radical individualism of Hobbes's state of nature helps to make plausible the prediction of a resulting state of war because it denies the existence of any other actors . . . that might mediate interpersonal conflict, coordinate individuals' actions, insulate individuals from the competition of others, share risks, or encourage the formation of less competitive attitudes.[21]

States, however, are not the only actors in the international arena; consequently, the first condition is not met.[22] Beitz points out that the second condition is also unsupported by empirical facts.[23] Even the proliferation of nuclear weapons has failed to render the power states have sufficiently equal.[24] Beitz points to the economic interdependence of states to demonstrate how the third condition is not fulfilled, and specifically to the fact that the domestic economy of one state can be drastically affected by the domestic, economic, and political affairs of another state.[25] Lastly, regarding the condition that there must be "no reliable expectations of reciprocal compliance by the actors with rules of cooperation in the absence of a superior power capable of enforcing these rules," Beitz notes that international relations are "characterized by high degrees of voluntary compliance with customary norms and institutionalized rules."[26] Such compliance and the expectations that underlie it are had without a common power. The skeptical argument of the normative realist fails.

A more moderate form of skepticism over international morality is found in the work of David Hume. If we assume that the normative realist is correct, and international relations is like a Hobbesian state of nature, then Hume would likely agree with the claim that in international relations there is no justice and no moral obligations borne by states.[27] Justice for Hume is instrumental and conventional.[28] Like Hobbes, Hume contends that there is no justice or injustice in the state of nature.[29] However, for Hume, justice does not require a sovereign or common power; rather, justice requires a conventional agreement providing protection for private property, and the stability of possessions.[30] The agreement is binding because having such stability of possessions is better for everyone involved.[31]

Hume, however, denies that the international arena is like a Hobbesian state of nature. Rather, Hume contends that the international arena is a society governed by its own set of conventional rules,[32] and the moral demands implied by justice in the international arena are weaker.[33] Specifically, as Marshall Cohen states,

> Since the mutual interest in abiding by the fundamental rules of justice is weaker, the moral obligation arising from it must partake of this weakness and we must necessarily give greater indulgence of a prince or minister who deceives another than to a private gentleman who breaks his word of honor.[34]

Thus, Hume allows for global justice; however, the scope of justice under Hume's understanding is determined by the convention upon which justice is based. Justice in the international arena, according to Hume, is based upon a conventional agreement amongst sovereigns. Even if Hume is correct in claiming that justice in the international arena is not as stringent as in domestic society, this fails to preclude the possibility of international morality.

There is one additional position that lies somewhere between the skepticism of the realists and the moral objections to be considered next. Specifically, there are those who accept the *possibility* of international morality and global justice; but, contrary to Hume's beliefs, deny that the necessary conventions upon which such a moral system depends exist. The position referred to is known as constructivism.

Constructivists like Thomas Nagel and Saladin Meckled-Garcia challenge the existence, though not the possibility, of global justice.[35] Nagel and Meckled-Garcia argue that systems of justice only exist within an institutional context in which those bound by justice are "fellow participants in a collective enterprise of coercively imposed legal and political institutions."[36] Constructivists argue that whatever international legal and political institutions exist, they fail to provide the institutional context necessary to support a system of justice.

There are a number of reasons for not engaging with this objection. First, the constructivist is not arguing that global justice is not possible; nor is the constructivist arguing against a moral obligation to engage in humanitarian intervention. In fact, even though most constructivists are committed to the proposition that there is no extant system of global justice, many also defend the idea that intervention may be morally justified as a matter of *humanitarian* concern.[37] It is my contention that the moral obligation of humanitarian intervention is a matter of global justice; in which case, there is an interesting philosophical/conceptual disagreement I have with those who defend the constructivist view. However, I am concerned with defending an all-things-considered reason for action. If, in the end, that reason is based in fundamental humanitarian duties rather than global justice, it would not alter the conclusion that the reason for action exists, though it may have some impact on the nature of the demand.

MAKING CONCEPTUAL ROOM: RESPONDING TO THE MORAL NONINTERVENTIONIST

The fact that neither the skeptical arguments addressed nor the arguments of the constructivist do not preclude the conceptual possibility of international morality merely provides the conceptual space for international morality (and global justice); not for the moral justifiability of humanitarian intervention. As such, the question of whether humanitarian intervention is ever morally justified must be addressed directly. The moral noninterventionist argues that there are moral considerations that weigh decisively against intervention. This is not to say that moral noninterventionists deny that an injustice is being done, nor do they claim that no action should be taken. Rather, the position of the moral noninterventionist is that even if an injustice that demands action is occurring, intervention is impermissible.[38]

As such, the defense of the possibility of a moral obligation of humanitarian intervention requires that these objections to the moral permissibility of humanitarian intervention be addressed. The first argument to be addressed is based on the proposition that states have a legal obligation to refrain from interfering in the internal affairs of other states; and since there is a moral obligation to obey the law, there is an obligation to refrain from humanitarian intervention. There are three distinct arguments upon which this contention may rely. Two of these arguments will be addressed in this section, and discussion of the third will be bracketed until later as it is an example of a type of instrumental argument that will be discussed below.[39]

The first argument is one alluded to by Fernando Teson, but not fully explored in his discussion.[40] The argument is based on the claim that there is an inherent obligation borne by the subjects of a system of laws to obey the laws of that system.[41] The obligation to obey in this instance is not a moral obligation, but a legal one. Legal obligations claim to be second-order exclusionary reasons.[42] The implication is that legal obligations are content-independent and that "they require the subject to set aside his own view of the merits and comply nonetheless."[43] If this is true, then, since international law prohibits humanitarian intervention, states should abide by the legal demand that they obey the law and refrain from considering reasons for action that would require intervention rather than consider each case on its own merits.

There are a number of reasons for rejecting this argument. First, as Leslie Green points out, that legal obligations should supplant the reasoning of the subjects of the law is a *claim* of the law.[44] This merely begs the question, however, as to the justification for the law's claim. To answer this question one must engage in an evaluation of the merits of the law's claim that it ought to be followed simply because it is the law. In so doing, one evaluates the underlying substantive bases for the law's claimed authority, thus undermining the claimed content-independence of legal obligations. Assuming this argument is correct, and being a legal obligation necessarily includes a claim to being pre-emptive, it is a descriptive fact about what existing laws claim; not a justification for this claim.

Second, the question of the *moral* justifiability of humanitarian intervention is left unaddressed. Under this argument from legal obligation humanitarian intervention is only *contingently legally* impermissible. Law is an artifact of human construction; consequently, if the law were otherwise, then humanitarian intervention might be permissible. Additionally, if in particular cases there is a moral obligation to intervene for humanitarian reasons then the law should be changed.[45]

Lastly, for the argument to succeed it must be the case that the law is clear on the matter of humanitarian intervention. This is far from the truth. Looking first to treaty law as a source of international law, though the Charter of the United Nations and other instruments of international law express a prohibition on intervention, many other treaties and conventions – the Universal Declaration of Human Rights and the Convention on the Prevention and Punishment of the Crime of Genocide – emphasize the importance of human rights and expressly permit action for humanitarian reasons. More recently, the International Commission on Intervention and State Sovereignty (ICISS) report on the responsibility to protect principle challenges the notion that the law governing humanitarian intervention is clear.[46] In fact, the ICISS contends that the responsibility to protect is consistent with international legal norms.

The second argument is based upon the claim that states have a *moral* obligation to obey international law and that international law prohibits such intervention. As Teson notes, this argument "locates the obligation to obey the law outside international law itself: there is a moral reason to comply with international law where doing so leads to sometimes undesirable or even immoral outcomes."[47] Here the moral obligation to obey the law is grounded in political authority and political obligation.

This argument depends on the claim that states are obligated to obey international law as a matter of political obligation. One might contend that states are under such obligations in much the same way individuals in domestic society are. The most widely discussed accounts of political obligation can be divided into two categories; voluntarist and non-voluntarist theories.[48] Non-voluntarist theories share one common feature that makes them an unlikely source of political obligations for states in the international arena. As Green notes, "[a] theory of political obligation is non-voluntarist if its principles justifying legal authority do not invoke the choice or will of the subjects among its reasons for thinking they are bound to obey."[49] The normative force of international law is grounded in the express or tacit consent of states – the laws themselves depend for their existence on consent to the demands of particular laws or the expression of such consent through the treatment of custom and practice as law. As such, it would be difficult to see how a non-voluntarist argument could ground authority in the international arena.

Alternatively, voluntarist theories are based on the proposition that political obligations are grounded in the subjects' voluntary assumption of such obligations. Two of the most prominent theories are the consent theories of Hobbes[50] and Locke.[51] The common feature of such theories is that the subject agrees to give up its rights – through agency or alienation – to a sovereign for regulation and adjudication. It is this aspect of consent theory that renders it inapplicable for international law. There is no such sovereign of the appropriate sort in the international arena.

A more promising approach would be one based upon H. L. A. Hart's claim that,

> when a number of persons conduct any joint enterprise according to rules and thus restrict their liberty, those who have submitted to these restrictions when required have a right to a similar submission from those who have benefitted by their submission.[52]

As Leslie Green points out, however, this is not enough to give rise to an obligation, for it may be the case that the beneficiary was either an unwilling beneficiary or unaware of the enterprise, in which case it would be unreasonable to require that the beneficiary adhere to the rules of the enterprise.[53] For this reason, Green notes that such benefits must be accepted if they are to give rise to an obligation.

Assuming that states in the international arena are engaged in a joint enterprise governed by rules, that the enterprise provides states with benefits that they accept, and that one of the rules governing the enterprise is a prohibition on intervention; the argument fails to demonstrate that humanitarian intervention is morally impermissible. Even if states do bear political obligations to adhere to the demands of international law as a matter of fairness, this again assumes that the law on humanitarian intervention is clear. Second, fairness would only seem to demand adherence to those rules related to the benefit provided. The ostensible benefit provided by international law is international order. At first glance, it may seem that nonintervention is related to the provision of international order; however, if one of the reasons for seeking international order is that it is necessary for individuals to enjoy their basic rights, refraining from intervening in cases where mass violations of basic rights are occurring would undermine, not promote, that goal.

Third, unlike the argument from legal obligation discussed above, the political obligation from fairness is but one moral obligation amongst many. It does not supplant the agent's evaluation of the overall merits of the case; rather the moral obligation to obey the law is merely *an additional* reason to be taken into consideration by the agent in its practical deliberations. For it to be the case that such an obligation renders humanitarian intervention morally impermissible, it must be the case that such obligations exhaust the moral space, or that they always outweigh other competing moral obligations. It is doubtful that obligations of fairness that arise between states exhaust the relevant moral space; especially when it comes to the treatment of individuals. Consequently, such an obligation does not implicitly preclude from consideration countervailing moral considerations weighing in favor of humanitarian intervention.

In addition, the strength of the obligation to which the principle of fairness gives rise depends on the value of the goal of the enterprise. A conspiracy to commit murder *arguably* provides each member of the conspiracy with *some* obligation owed to others in the conspiracy who have already carried out their obligations under the conspiracy, but the strength of that obligation is weakened by the very purpose of the enterprise. So, even if we assume that international order is the benefit to be provided by international law, the strength of the obligation to obey the law will depend on the value of promoting international order in any particular instance.

In the end, one can concede that states can have political obligations and that they are demands of fairness; yet it is not the case that such demands render humanitarian intervention morally impermissible. The question of the moral permissibility of humanitarian intervention cannot be circumvented by arguments defending the claim that there is a legal obligation borne by states to obey international law.

Turning now to an explication of the objection of the moral relativist to the permissibility of humanitarian intervention; the relevant notion of relativism is based upon the proposition that there are no moral principles accepted by all cultures (cultural relativism), and the further proposition that the validity of moral claims is dependent on cultural acceptance.[54] From these two premises the relativist concludes that there are no universal moral principles, and that morality is simply what the relevant society or culture says is right or wrong, good or bad.

The relativist objection would run as follows: humanitarian intervention involves an external moral judgment about the immoral or unjust nature of certain internal practices being engaged in by the institutions of a state. Therefore, to avoid unjustified moral imperialism, humanitarian intervention can only be justified by moral principles that are (at least) culturally neutral. This condition could be fulfilled by principles that are based on an overlapping consensus, or it could be fulfilled by principles that are universally valid. According to the moral relativist, however, cultural relativism is true. Thus, as there is no universal overlapping consensus upon which culturally neutral principles could be found, and since validity for the relativist depends on cultural acceptance, the possibility of universal validity is precluded. As a consequence, humanitarian intervention will necessarily involve moral imperialism and cannot be justified.

There are numerous reasons for rejecting the claims of the moral relativist. The implications of the relativist argument are uninviting. There would be no basis for cross-cultural dialogue about the morality of particular practices. Provided the underlying practices are culturally accepted, there would be no basis for moral judgments regarding violations of basic rights. And, more pertinent to this project, it seems absurd to think that cultural acceptance could make genocide or the violation of the basic right to physical security morally permissible.

In addition there are numerous conceptual problems with moral relativism, many of which the reader is no doubt familiar with. Here I will mention only one. It is unclear what counts as cultural acceptance. It cannot be enough that the practices engaged in by the state, and/or the empowered are not met with open resistance. If that were the case, a brutal dictator with a small but efficient military could terrorize a people into submission through violent oppression, and such coercive actions would morally justify themselves. But what does count? In a pluralist society, is a single individual's choice of what is moral or immoral, right or wrong, sufficient? Does the acceptance have to be informed or rational? At the very least, it would seem to be necessary that all affected by the practice are informed, uncoerced, and maintain an internal perspective with regards to the practice – meaning that they acknowledge the rightness of the practice and that they would criticize others for not adhering to the practice.[55]

In addition, both premises upon which the moral relativist objection is based are open to criticism. Cultural relativism, the claim that there are no universally accepted moral values, is not uncontroversial. One might point to the fact that the Universal Declaration of Human Rights was passed without a single dissenting vote. Others claim that the relativist position is often raised by those in power who benefit from the very practices being scrutinized, and that there is much greater consensus than the oppressors would have us believe. Lastly, cultural relativism is an empirical claim about the comparative situation of various moral codes throughout the world. Cultural relativism fails to preclude the possibility of shared moral beliefs.

The second premise is also highly suspect. It is a claim about the nature of morality and justice. Unlike cultural relativism which is either true as a matter of descriptive fact or not, the claim that moral validity depends on cultural acceptance requires an argument. Simply relying on the descriptive fact of cultural relativism, assuming it is true, is not enough. The argument for the second premise is based upon the general proposition that agreement is necessary for validity. We would never accept such a claim in the sciences. For example, string theory is either true or it is not. Neither agreement nor disagreement on its validity settles the issue. The relativist might object that science provides us with a method for determining the truth or falsity of the claims made by those in the field, but that there is no such analog in moral discourse. Such a claim, however, would rely on the very conclusion the relativist is seeking to prove – that there are no universal moral truths, only culturally valid moral truths, and thus no possibility of cross-cultural criticism and dialogue. It is through the proffering, criticism, and defense of moral judgments that we test our moral judgments. The relativist cannot rely on the truth of relativism to *prove* the truth of an underlying premise.

But what can we learn from relativism? There is diversity amongst the moral codes of the world. The fact that such disagreement exists is relevant because it raises doubts about the correctness of our moral judgments. However, it would be impractical and inappropriate to require certainty in such matters. Rather, in cases of disagreement over a moral principle we should test the principle's validity by assessing whether anyone could reasonably reject the principle at issue.[56] In the end, this may not lead to an extensive account of global justice or international morality and will likely provide an account of the moral minimum that we owe to one another.[57]

Turning now to the communitarian objection, there are a variety of communitarian arguments, but they share at least two things in common. First, communitarians contend that the emphasis of liberal theorists on individual liberty as the paramount moral and political concern is misplaced, and that the value of community and communal rights should be given greater weight in our moral and political reasoning.[58] Second, the value of community is based on the proposition that community is necessary to individual human flourishing.[59]

Michael Walzer presents us with a classic communitarian argument. He contends that the "state is presumptively, though by no means always in practice, the arena within which self-determination is worked out and from which, therefore, foreign armies have to be excluded."[60] The argument for the presumption is based on Walzer's contention that individuals have a right to develop or determine the community in which they live,[61] and that for the purposes of international relations the state should be presumed to fit with the community and thus be a result of the exercise of the rights of individuals.[62] The presumption of fit between the state and the community is justified, because foreigners have "no direct experience" of the development of the community.[63] Walzer further contends that this presumption leads to another principle which weighs against intervention – that if an intervention were attempted those residing in the state would feel obligated to defend the state.[64]

As Walzer admits, his argument does not support an absolute prohibition on humanitarian intervention.[65] Humanitarian intervention is generally impermissible, according to Walzer, owing to the presumptive fit between the people as a community and the government. If there is no fit then humanitarian intervention could be morally permissible. However, since the international community lacks "direct experience" of the cultural, moral, and historical development of the community, we must presume that such a fit exists unless it is "radically apparent" that it does not.[66] For Walzer, such a lack of fit is radically apparent when any one of his three "rules of disregard" are applicable.[67] Most relevant to the debate over humanitarian intervention is Walzer's rule that "interventions can be justified whenever a government is engaged in the massacre or enslavement of its own citizens or subjects."[68]

David Luban has pointed out many problems with Walzer's argument, as well as the problematic nature of Walzer's empirical and historical assumptions.[69] Luban, however, agrees with Walzer that "the lack of fit between government and people should be 'radically apparent' to justify intervening, because intervention based on misperception is horribly wrong."[70] In short, Walzer and Luban agree that community is important, and that if there does exist a fit between the individuals as a community and the government then this is a weighty, if not pre-emptive, reason weighing against intervention. They further agree that the lack of fit that might permit humanitarian intervention has to be known with a great degree of certainty.

Walzer and Luban disagree, however, over Walzer's epistemic justification for the presumption that the requisite fit exists between the community and the government. Walzer contends that the international community must presume the fit exists. Luban accepts that in circumstances under which we do not have access to information about a particular community and its relationship to its government we should give the government the benefit of the doubt, but this is not the same as a general presumption that we are always ignorant.[71] As Luban points out, in most cases we do have access to the information relevant to the determination of fit, thus Walzer's presumption is unjustified. For that reason, whether or not such fit exists should be treated as an open question.

The last objection to the moral permissibility of humanitarian intervention to be addressed is instrumental in nature. The argument is based on the proposition that achieving and maintaining international peace and security requires a rule against intervention. To understand this objection, one must first understand what is meant by *international* peace and security. Understanding that international relations are concerned with the relations between states helps to understand the relevant notions of peace and security.[72] As such, the relevant notion of peace presumes that the only relevant actors are sovereign states, and threats to international peace are threats to the peace between states. Similarly, international security refers to the security of a state from aggression or intervention. A state is secure if other states, individually or collectively, refrain or are prevented from engaging in either aggressive action toward the state or intervention into the internal affairs of the state.

So understood, it becomes apparent how a rule of nonintervention is instrumental to achieving and maintaining international peace and security. In light of this understanding, the instrumental argument such as that found in Kant's claim that peace between states requires that "[n]o state shall forcibly interfere in the constitution and government of another state"[73] seems incontrovertible. Intervention into the internal affairs of another state simply *is* a threat to the peace between and the security of the states involved.

This argument is institutionalized in the Charter of the United Nations. Article 1 identifies as one of the purposes of the United Nations the maintenance of international peace and security.[74] Article 2 identifies as one of the principles which serves the purpose of maintaining international peace and security a rule requiring each state to "refrain in their international relations from the threat or use of force against the territorial integrity or political independence of any State" – a rule of nonintervention.[75]

There are a number of questions begged by the instrumental argument. First, are the only relevant actors in the international arena sovereign states? If not, then international peace and security ought not to be limited to the peace between and security of states. A second question arises because there are at least two possible interpretations of the argument, one strong and one weak. Is the relationship between the rule of nonintervention and international peace and security one of necessity or efficacy? The strong claim, which seems to be implied by Kant's statement, is that international peace and security requires a rule against intervention. The weak claim is that a rule against intervention makes international peace and security more likely.

But, no matter how we answer the second question there are a number of questions related to the value of international peace and security. The rule of nonintervention, assuming that it is either weakly or strongly instrumental to international peace and security, is justified by the instrumental role it plays in achieving and maintaining the goal of international peace and security. Thus, the value of the rule of nonintervention is dependent on the value of international peace and security.

It is unlikely that either the weak or the strong interpretation of the instrumental argument will support an absolute moral prohibition on humanitarian intervention. Under the weak interpretation, there may be instances in which the goal of international peace and security could be served, or at least not be hindered, by intervention. Consequently, if it is more likely than not that a choice not to intervene will undermine international peace and security in a particular case and there are other moral considerations weighing in favor of intervention, under the instrumental argument it would be morally permissible to intervene.

On the other hand, if the strong interpretation is correct it needs to be demonstrated that international peace and security precludes from consideration all countervailing reasons for intervention. This could be demonstrated either by defending international peace and security as the sole moral consideration in the international arena; or by defending the claim that international peace and security will invariably outweigh other moral considerations. Neither understanding of the relative value of international peace and security is likely correct; nonetheless, to be successful those who would defend the instrumental view need to provide a defense. In the end, it is far more likely that international peace and security is itself instrumental to other values such as the provision and protection of basic rights, individual human flourishing, and communal rights. Nonetheless it would be wrong to fail to recognize that there is some value in the state system and its commitment to international peace and security.

The underlying moral claim of this project is that there are circumstances under which no one could reasonably deny that a moral obligation of humanitarian intervention exists. However, for there to exist a moral obligation of humanitarian intervention it must be the case that humanitarian intervention is not morally prohibited. The arguments addressed fail to preclude the possibility of such an obligation. However, there are lessons to be learned from each of the arguments considered which will serve as the basis for the identification of considerations to be taken into account in the identification of the conditions under which no one could reasonably deny that a moral obligation of humanitarian intervention exists.

METHODOLOGY: WHY A STANDARD OF REASONABLE DENIABILITY?

In the discussion that follows, the defense of the existence of a moral obligation of humanitarian intervention is built around a standard of reasonable deniability. As this discussion is intended to be accessible to those from other disciplines, it is necessary to discuss the nature of and reasons for employing a standard of reasonable deniability. First, it must be understood that the standard of reasonable deniability has both a weak and a strong implication for the resolution to a matter of moral disagreement. If we adopt the perspective of an individual defending his or her position, one need only be sure that one's position is not unreasonable. If this can be accomplished then one need not give up his/her position. However, to be justified in rejecting another's position as unreasonable, one must demonstrate the unreasonableness of the interlocutor's position, a much more difficult task.

One might contend that very little is gained by employing a standard of reasonable deniability. Specifically, it could be argued that a standard of reasonable deniability is merely a "stand-in" for a standard of wrongness, and that there is nothing that distinguishes one from the other. There is certainly some truth to this charge as reasonable deniability is intended to serve as a standard for the justified rejection of a position held by another. Thus, reasonable deniability could be understood as a standard for determining when we are *justified* in claiming that another's position is *wrong*.

There are important differences, however, between a standard of wrongness *simpliciter* and a standard of reasonable deniability. If what we mean when we employ a standard of wrongness is that our interlocutor is objectively wrong, such a standard requires too much. It is no doubt the case that if we *know* the other to be wrong, then we are justified in rejecting or ignoring their objection. However, we rarely have such epistemic certainty about a disputed matter of morality. Thus, if we were to employ a standard of wrongness *simpliciter*, we would rarely be justified in rejecting another's position.

Reasonable deniability, on the other hand, focuses on whether one's interlocutors are entitled to hold the position they do *for the reasons they do*. Such a standard does not require that we discern substantive wrongness to be justified in rejecting our interlocutor's position. A standard of reasonable deniability is a matter of assessing the justifiability of a claim; not objective truth. The fact that a standard of reasonable deniability is broader than a standard of wrongness does not undermine its strength. If an individual is not justified, for reasons of theoretical rationality or intersubjective justification, in holding the beliefs s/he does, we are justified in rejecting his/her position. In other words, if one does not have good reason for believing X or for believing in certain implications one takes X to have, then we are justified in rejecting his/her belief in X; or his/her position based on X.

There are two reasons for the decision to employ this standard, one rhetorical and the other philosophical, both of which derive from the following considerations:

1. That reasonable disagreement over the rightness or wrongness of humanitarian intervention exists; and,
2. That one of the core purposes of this project is to make a case for an all-things-considered moral obligation to intervene which would convince skeptics who doubt the possibility of such an obligation.

Though not an analytic reason for employing a standard of reasonable deniability, there are good rhetorical reasons for employing such a standard. As noted, one of the goals of this project is to justify the existence of a moral obligation of humanitarian intervention to those skeptical of its existence. How the discussion over the existence of such an obligation is framed can have a dramatic impact on the nature of the dialogue. To claim that those who disagree with me are simply wrong because they disagree with me about certain fundamental matters turns the discussion into a confrontation; undermining the possibility of a constructive dialogue.

The philosophical reason for employing a standard of reasonable deniability is grounded in the justificatory aspect of the project. It is apparent that there is significant, and often reasonable, disagreement over matters of morality. Recognizing the existence of such disagreement does not commit one to moral relativism, but does heighten the importance of the burden of justification. In the case of actions that interfere with the lives of others, the intervener must be able to justify their action to those who would deny its moral permissibility, and to those affected by the intervention.

This standard may simply beg the question as to what is reasonable or what counts as an unreasonable objection. That question cannot be fully answered fully here. However, the following skeletal outline of the standard of reasonable deniability is offered to remove as much ambiguity as possible. First, though related, reasonable is not the same as rational. Rationality is a matter of understanding. In other words, to act rationally or be rational in one's beliefs, there need only be the right sort of relationship between one's reasons – whatever they happen to be – for those beliefs or actions and the beliefs or actions themselves. Reasonableness, on the other hand, is a standard of evaluation that applies to both the beliefs that one holds and the implications that one takes those beliefs to have, including actions based on such beliefs. Whereas rationality is a matter of understanding others *given* their beliefs, reasonableness is a matter of justification that applies even to those beliefs that serve as the starting point for one's theoretical and practical deliberations. This is not to say that rationality does not have a role to play in assessing reasonableness. One way in which one can fail to be reasonable is if s/he fails to be rational.

In assessing the rationality of one's actions or beliefs, the question we are asking is whether, in light of one's beliefs, their actions or other beliefs make sense? Take for example the following:

> *A* believes: If *X*, then *Y**;
> *X*;
> Therefore *Y*
> **Y* could be an action or a belief.

However, in reality, it could be the case that:

1. It is not the case that the claimed sufficient relationship between *X* and *Y* exists; and/or
2. It is not the case that *X*.

In either case *Y* does not follow as a matter of substantive truth, but *A* could be rational in both cases, provided *A* is not aware of 1 or 2. We could understand *A*'s contention that *Y*; while also contending that *A*'s belief that *Y* would be unreasonable.

Reasonable claims, beliefs, or actions are those that can be intersubjectively justified. Thus, to be reasonable in holding a belief we must be able to offer good reasons for our beliefs (upon which our actions and other beliefs are rationally based). This obviously begs the question as to what counts as a good reason. First, it must meet minimum standards of theoretic rationality; the reason is coherent in relation to, and consistent with, other reasonable beliefs, and it is sensitive to new information – that it is subject to change if new information demonstrates that it is not a good reason.

In addition, owing to the inter-subjective nature of the standard of reasonableness, a good reason must be a reason that *could be* accepted by others. Here, "could" is not intended as mere possibility. An agent *could* accept any reason. Rather, what is meant is that one could accept the reason in light of their prior reasonably held commitments and beliefs. There is a circle here, but it should be understood to be a virtuous and not a vicious circle. What counts as reasonable, and offering reasons for our actions and beliefs, should be thought of as an ever-evolving process. The circular reasoning invoked here is both self-reinforcing and self-critical. To be reasonable one must offer reasons that others could accept given the other's reasonable commitments.

Perhaps a more concrete example may help to explain the standard of reasonable deniability employed here. Imagine that Frank is a fan of his town's soccer club. He always wears the same shirt when he watches his club play. He believes that they will win if he puts on the shirt at just the right time before the game starts. Frank's actions are rational because one could make sense of his actions based upon his subjective beliefs about his shirt-wearing ritual. But Frank's actions are not reasonable. One need not accept Frank's underlying beliefs because they fail minimum conditions of theoretical rationality. In this particular instance his belief that his shirt-wearing ritual affects the game is irrational, and for that reason his actions are unreasonable.

A more distinctively moral example may be in order to help explain how one might be unreasonable owing to a failure to deliberate rationally. Such failures could include improper weighting of the options available, proper weighting but miscalculation, proper weighting and calculation but weakness of the will, or internal inconsistency. Imagine that an individual, Gertrude, is faced with a choice between saving her favorite car or saving a red-headed child.[76] If she chooses the car because she believes her car is simply more valuable than the child's life, then one could reasonably reject her claim because her assessment of the relative weight of the competing values cannot be justified.

What if Gertrude responds that she believes her evaluation to be correct? Is she being reasonable? Or, can you reject her position as unreasonable? One might contend that with regard to values it is impossible to make such determinations. Though I am not able to provide a determinative argument against this objection, there are a number of reasons that can be mustered to support my claim that Gertrude's weighting is improper, and that her position is unreasonable. Reasonableness is a matter of justification. The relevant question is whether her claim that she places a higher moral value on her car would not only explain her actions but could also justify them to those harmed? However, it makes the most sense to say that the claim simply makes her actions understandable. It does not justify her actions. In addition, as reasonableness is an inter-subjective standard of justification, to be reasonable Gertrude must take into account what others may or may not accept as a basis for assessing an object's moral value.

Alternatively, if she admits that the car is not as valuable as the child's life, but reaches a moral judgment that she ought to save the car, something in her calculations has gone awry. Not only is her action irrational, it is unreasonable. Gertrude may also appropriately weigh the alternatives, reach the correct moral decision as to what she ought to do, but fail to act accordingly. Lastly, she may offer a more substantive argument for her choice to save her car. Let us assume that she believes that human life is inherently valuable and ought to be respected and preserved; however, she hates red-heads and thinks that they all deserve to die. Thus, according to Gertrude, the red-headed child ought not be saved as a matter of morality. Her belief in the sanctity and value of human life is inconsistent with her belief that red-headed children deserve to die. Without further argument, Gertrude is unjustified in her belief that red-headed children deserve to die because the inconsistency renders her beliefs unreasonable.

It should be apparent that a standard of reasonable deniability has certain advantages. Under such a standard one is justified in rejecting an objection to one's position that does not require the same epistemic certainty required by a standard of wrongness *simpliciter*. For this reason the adoption of such a standard is likely to prove useful in the resolution of certain moral debates; for, if nothing else, it provides a framework for constructive dialogue providing a principled basis for assessing claims made within the discussion.

CONSTITUTIVE ELEMENTS OF A MORAL OBLIGATION OF HUMANITARIAN INTERVENTION

Before defending the existence of an all-things-considered moral obligation of humanitarian intervention, it is necessary to understand what a moral obligation of humanitarian intervention is. In other words, engaging in a critical assessment of the possible existence of a norm requires that one understand the defining features of the norm. We must know what the constitutive elements of the norm or rule are. Some are going to be shared by all norms of that type. For example, all claim rights share certain characteristics that make it appropriate to categorize them together as claim rights. These general characteristics serve as the basis for more detailed delineations that allow us to further individuate norms of that type. Again, looking to claim rights, the claim right to free speech is related to the claim right to freedom of assembly, but they are not the same thing. In which case, our understanding of the constitutive elements of each should reflect these distinguishing features.

In delineating the constitutive elements for a moral obligation of humanitarian intervention I have chosen to follow the convention of adopting the Hohfeldian typology.[77] Though Hohfeld developed the typology to understand legal rights, it is useful for understanding a wide array of legal and moral norms. For Hohfeld, understanding the constitutive elements of a norm is grounded in an understanding of the normative relationships defined and governed by the norm.[78] We are to understand the nature of the normative relationship (and by implication the norm) by identifying the content and scope of the normative relationship at issue. In addition, as moral obligations are supposed to play a role in our practical deliberations, to fully understand a moral obligation one must also understand its nature and strength.

According to Hohfeld, the content of a norm is constituted by the substance of the normative relationship that exists between those whose relationship is defined by the norm.[79] Conversely, the scope of a norm is constituted by those agents whose normative relationship is defined by the norm. In delineating the constitutive elements of a moral obligation of humanitarian intervention, though the question of scope and content will be discussed separately, they should be understood as two parts of a whole.

The first step in identifying the constitutive elements of a moral obligation of humanitarian intervention is the delineation of the content of the obligation that is grounded in a general understanding of the nature of obligations. A good place to start is with Cicero's discussion of obligations since his understanding, though vague, is particularly relevant to the task at hand.[80] For Cicero, understanding the content of a moral obligation involves understanding two aspects.[81] First, there is the conceptual question, what is an obligation? And second, the practical question, what is the function or role of an obligation?

The first question is about our understanding of the content of an obligation. In answering this question, Cicero claims that moral obligations fall into two categories – the intermediate and the absolute.[82] An intermediate obligation is a "plausible reason" for action.[83] An absolute obligation is that which is right, the right thing to do.[84] A moral obligation of humanitarian intervention has elements of both intermediate and absolute obligations. It is a special type of reason for action, but it is one far more demanding than just a plausible reason.

Though I will return to Cicero's account momentarily, its vagueness renders it an insufficient framework for a complete account of the content of a moral obligation of humanitarian intervention. Looking to Hohfeld for more clarity, as Hohfeld has demonstrated, obligations are complex, and in order to understand their content one must assess and understand the normative elements that comprise the norm in question.[85] Specifically, Hohfeld offers a detailed classification of the core elements of norms divided into jural correlatives and jural opposites.[86] For Hohfeld, the correlatives are duty and right, privilege and no right, power and liability, and immunity and disability.[87] The first two correlative relations are about the normative relations themselves and the second two are concerned with an agent's ability to change existing normative relations.

To understand the nature of a moral obligation in Hohfeldian terms, we must first ascertain whether a moral obligation is a privilege or a duty; and second what the nature of the jural correlative is. Despite the fact that Hohfeld seems to take the meaning of duty to be a given, one can discern from his discussion that a duty, as opposed to a privilege, is binding.[88] For Hohfeld, a privilege is a lack of a duty.[89] One who has a privilege is free to do, or to do otherwise, and the reasons for or against an action governed by a privilege are "ordinary" in the sense used by Cicero. A moral obligation is a demand on one's practical deliberations that deserves consideration distinct from that given to an ordinary reason. For Hohfeld, an obligation must be a duty and not merely a privilege.

The jural correlative of a duty is a right.[90] In Hohfeldian terms, the specific content of the moral obligation of humanitarian intervention consists of a moral duty to intervene militarily into the internal affairs of a sovereign state for humanitarian reasons, and a correlative right held by those who are suffering to demand such action on the part of the duty-bearer. The emphasis on the humanitarian and moral nature of the obligation means that the relationship is a moral as opposed to a practical or legal one, and that the relationship is based on distinctly humanitarian concerns. The former characteristic may be more readily understood; as for the distinctly humanitarian nature of the obligation, this means that the obligation to intervene is for moral reasons based simply on the suffering of individuals.

The delineation of the scope of the moral obligation of humanitarian intervention is a fairly simple matter, especially in light of the fact that the content has been determined. The scope of an obligation is constituted by the parties to the normative relationship governed by the obligation – who owes the obligation and to whom is it owed. The obligation to intervene is borne by states individually and the international community as a collection of duty-bearing states, and it is owed to the individuals or groups of individuals who are suffering due to the actions or inactions of their governments. Though perhaps obvious, the correlative right to demand intervention is held by those individuals who are suffering from some moral offense against their persons.

One might wonder why the duty is borne by sovereign states as opposed to individuals. This will be discussed in greater detail below, but an inherent limitation on an obligation is that one must be able to accomplish what the obligation demands for it to be the case that one is under the obligation. Humanitarian intervention can only be accomplished by a large-scale collective effort, an effort that individuals as individuals cannot accomplish, but of which states are capable.

To understand the constitutive elements of an obligation one might think that all that needs to be identified is the content and scope of the obligation, leading one to question the relevance of the identification of the strength of the obligation. However, as Cicero understood, there are two fundamental aspects of an obligation, the conceptual and the practical.[91] Understanding the former may take us a long way to understanding the constitutive elements of an obligation, but if we fail to account for the latter, we will have a less than complete understanding of the obligation itself.

The practical aspect of an obligation is concerned with the role an obligation ought to play in the practical deliberations of the agents to which it applies. Under the classic account of practical deliberation, we as rational creatures, when confronted with the question of what we ought to do in a particular circumstance, consider the relevant reasons for and against alternative courses of action. The goal of such deliberations is to determine "what ought to be done on the balance of reasons."[92] The metaphor of balancing reflects the idea that reasons have a weight, and that the weightier reason (or set of reasons) should determine how we ought to act. Under this classic account of practical deliberation, reasons are all first-order reasons, some weightier than others. Thus, the strength of a reason is a matter of comparative value or weight.

However, as Joseph Raz has argued, there are a number of phenomenological reasons for rejecting the idea that practical deliberation is concerned solely with the weighing and balancing of reasons of a single order.[93] Raz contends that there are both first and second-order reasons, and that the second-order reasons are often exclusionary in their effect.[94] Thus, according to Raz, there are two aspects of the strength of a reason, its nature and its weight. Here the Razian framework is used for a number of reasons. In addition to the phenomenological reasons Raz relies upon, the Razian framework more readily accommodates the Hohfeldian understanding of a moral obligation. Also, the framework governing the practical deliberations of states in the international arena is more easily understood if thought of in Razian terms.

To fully understand the Razian account of practical deliberation one must understand how conflicts of reasons are dealt with under the Razian account. Conflicts between reasons of different orders are resolved by a calculation different from the resolution of conflicts between reasons of the same order.[95] First-order reasons are reasons for or against action, and conflicts between them are resolved by balancing the respective weights of the reasons at issue.[96] Second-order reasons are reasons for or against the consideration of first-order reasons, and conflicts between second-order reasons are also resolved by assessing the balance of their relative weights.[97] The resolution of conflicts between first and second-order reasons is more complicated. The function of a second-order exclusionary reason is to preclude from consideration certain first-order reasons either for or against an action. Thus, as Raz notes, the conflict will almost always be resolved in favor of the second-order reason.[98]

A complete understanding of the strength of the moral obligation of humanitarian intervention would require an understanding of both its nature and weight as a reason. Despite this, in discussing the strength of the moral obligation of humanitarian intervention the focus here is on the nature of the obligation to the exclusion of its weight. First, because the resolution of conflicts between reasons requires the determination of the nature of the reasons involved. Are *all* of the relevant reasons involved merely first-order? Second-order? If all of the reasons are either first-order or second-order, the resolution of the conflict is a matter of determining the balance of reasons through an assessment of the relative weight of the reasons at issue. If, however, the reasons to the conflict are of different orders and a first-order reason is within the scope of the second-order reason's exclusionary effect, then that first-order reason will be precluded from consideration and its weight rendered irrelevant.[99] Consequently, one *must* determine the nature of the reasons involved before the weight of such reasons become relevant.

In addition, the identification of the constitutive elements of the moral obligation of humanitarian intervention only requires a discussion of the nature of the obligation to understand the role the obligation is to play in the practical deliberations of the agents to which the obligation applies. In identifying the constitutive elements, one is seeking to identify the existence conditions of the obligation; a conceptual matter. Practical deliberation is based on a particular logical structure. Under the Razian account, that structure involves reasons of different orders. From the perspective of practical rationality, understanding the existence conditions for determining what counts as an obligation requires that one understand where an obligation fits in the logical structure governing practical deliberation. The weight of a reason is a matter of substantive value, not logical structure. The nature of a reason, on the other hand, defines the role a reason plays in that logical structure. As such, determining the nature of an obligation is more relevant to the task at hand.

Lastly, unlike the weight of a reason, the nature of a reason can be understood in isolation from other reasons. The nature of an obligation does not depend on anything other than the role it is to play in our practical deliberations. Is it a first or second-order reason? The weight of a reason, on the other hand, is relative. It can only be understood in relation to other reasons involved in an actual choice situation. Consequently, a definitive identification of the weight of a reason is not possible as the weight of a reason will vary depending on the other considerations relevant to practical deliberations in a particular circumstance. Though there is no explicit discussion of the weight of the moral obligation of humanitarian intervention, much can be inferred from the discussion in the succeeding sections of this chapter.

At first glance it may seem that an obligation is merely a weighty first-order reason to act in accordance with the demands of the obligation. A moral obligation does have a first-order component, but it seems infelicitous, if we take the existence of such obligations seriously, to say that the first-order aspect completely explains the nature of a moral obligation. Consider the following example. Imagine that an individual (Albert) promises to help (Beatrice) move a large stone out of Beatrice's field. The day arrives for Albert to fulfill his promise. He recognizes that the promise gives him a first-order reason for helping Beatrice, but in his deliberations he weighs that reason against the fact that someone has just offered him two tickets to see his favorite cellist perform at the local park in a once-in-a-decade event. When combined with the many other reasons against helping Beatrice, Albert decides to go to the concert. He sees Beatrice the next day. She asks for a justification, and Albert provides an elaborate spreadsheet of his calculations – because that is the kind of guy Albert is. His calculations of the reasons for and against keeping his promise – assuming they are all first-order – confirm that his weighing of the first-order reasons leads to the conclusion that he ought, all things considered, to have gone to the concert and he refuses to apologize to Beatrice because he acted as he ought to have.

One should find that Albert's conduct and explanation leave something to be desired – and not just because of his use of a spreadsheet. Albert is correct in his conclusion that the promise includes a weighty first-order reason to fulfill the demands of the promise, but he fails to recognize that the resultant promissory obligation also has a second-order component. It precludes from consideration certain first-order reasons, such as those that may arise when one offers you a competing and pleasant alternative. A promissory obligation is a second-order exclusionary reason, as well as a first-order reason.

One alteration in our story may help one to understand this exclusionary component of moral obligations. Imagine that Albert had visited Beatrice to seek her release from the promise. Albert again presents Beatrice with the spreadsheet, and tries to get her to concede that a weighing of the first-order reasons indicates that Albert ought to go to the park and see his favorite cellist perform. To his surprise, she does see that the first-order reasons weigh in favor of Albert going to the performance, but she still thinks Albert ought to fulfill his promise because many of the reasons cited by Albert are simply not relevant in light of the promise made. The most likely explanation for the fact that Beatrice's response makes sense is that the promise gave Albert a second-order exclusionary reason to keep the promise.

As such, a moral obligation is both a first-order reason to act in accordance with the demands of the obligation, and a second-order reason to exclude from consideration certain first-order reasons against acting in accordance with the demands of the obligation. The strength of the second-order component of a moral obligation will depend upon its weight relative to other second-order reasons,[100] and the strength of the first-order component will depend upon the relative importance of the values served by or basis for the obligation.[101]

CONCLUSION

We can conclude from this discussion that there is conceptual space for a moral obligation of humanitarian intervention and that an obligation must have the following characteristics to count as a moral obligation of humanitarian intervention:

1. In order to accommodate the content, it must be a positive obligation to intervene that has its basis in reasons that are distinctively moral and humanitarian in nature;
2. To accommodate the scope, it must be borne by states individually and the international community as a collection of duty-bearing states, and it must be owed to individuals or groups of individuals; and
3. To accommodate the nature and strength, it must be both a second-order exclusionary reason to preclude from consideration first-order reasons against acting in accordance with the demands of the obligation, and a first-order reason to act in accordance with the demands of the obligation.

It is these same elements that serve as the existence conditions that must be accommodated by principles offered as moral justification for the existence of a moral obligation of humanitarian intervention.

Chapter 2

DEFENDING A MORAL OBLIGATION OF HUMANITARIAN INTERVENTION

INTRODUCTION

Chapter 1 focused on accomplishing two tasks; first, demonstrating that a moral obligation of humanitarian intervention is possible, and second, identifying the existence conditions for such an obligation. Building upon the groundwork laid in Chapter 1, the discussion in Chapter 2 is directed at accomplishing three distinct, but related tasks. First, the fact that an obligation is conceptually possible and that we can understand the conditions that must be met for it to exist does not justify its existence. A successful defense of a moral obligation of humanitarian intervention requires a justification. As such, the central ethical question to be addressed in Chapter 2 is whether there are any moral principle(s) capable of justifying a moral obligation of humanitarian intervention. The candidates to be considered are utilitarianism, rule-utilitarianism, Thomas Pogge's argument from a duty not to harm, and Henry Shue's account of basic rights.

Assuming the successful identification and defense of an account capable of accommodating the constitutive elements of a moral obligation of humanitarian intervention, the second task requires the identification and development of the conditions under which there would be an all-things-considered moral obligation of humanitarian intervention – the conditions under which no one could reasonably deny that there is a conclusive moral reason to act in furtherance of the obligation. Accomplishing this task involves an appeal to the skeptical objections and noninterventionist arguments from Chapter 1, and the identification of additional moral hazards associated with the use of force involved in a humanitarian intervention. Each of the objections rejected in Chapter 1 or moral hazards identified below are based on reasons that could provide a reasonable basis for rejecting the claim that there is an obligation to intervene in a particular case. For an obligation of humanitarian intervention to be an all-things-considered reason for action, it must be that under the specific circumstances no one could reasonably deny it. As such, the account must recognize and accommodate those reasons that could provide the basis for a reasonable rejection.

The last task undertaken in Chapter 2 is the first step in the transition from theory to practice. Looking at the Rwandan genocide and the choice of the international community not to intervene through the critical lens constituted by the conditions under which no one could reasonably deny that a moral obligation of humanitarian intervention exists, I argue that there was an all-things-considered moral obligation borne by the international community to intervene in Rwanda. If true, this implies that not only is such an obligation conceptually possible and morally justifiable, but there are actual circumstances under which the obligation should have been acted upon.

Before proceeding there are a number of preliminary matters to be addressed. First, to have an adequate understanding of the importance of the defense of an all-things-considered moral obligation of humanitarian intervention, it is essential to understand what an all-things-considered reason for action is. The role such reasons play in the practical deliberations of moral agents will be discussed in greater detail below, but for the moment a brief summary should suffice. In short, when faced with a choice of alternative courses of action we are confronted with reasons both for and against various actions. If we adopt the traditional instrumentalist view of practical deliberation, each reason's impact on our practical deliberations will depend on the nature of the reason as well as the relative weight/strength of the reason in comparison with other reasons relevant to the choice being made.

At this point in one's deliberations what one *ought* to do is not yet determined. What exists is merely a collection of relevant reasons that weigh in favor of or against an action. Practical deliberation is the process through which we reach a conclusive or all-things-considered reason for action. Conclusive reasons are the *outcome* of our practical deliberations. They are not matters for consideration; rather, conclusive reasons are directives to act. As such, defending a moral obligation of humanitarian intervention as an all-things-considered reason for action involves identifying the circumstances under which the moral requirement that the international community act is the outcome of (and not the input to) practical deliberation.

If we are ever to have an all-things-considered moral obligation to intervene, it will be under the conditions identified here. If successfully defended, the resultant account serves at least two important purposes. It would have implications for what states can be morally obligated to do in the international arena, and it would serve as the gateway for broadening the debate over humanitarian intervention.

CRITICAL ASSESSMENT OF ALTERNATIVE ACCOUNTS

Critically assessing the alternative justificatory accounts requires the development of a standard of evaluation and an explanation of how the evaluation of the various accounts will fare in relation to the standard. As to the former, the constitutive elements identified in Chapter 1 (the content, scope, and strength) serve the conditions that any candidate account must, at the very least, be able to accommodate.[1] As to the latter, whether an account can justify a moral obligation of any sort depends on the justifiability of the moral principle(s) upon which the account is based. To satisfy this threshold requirement, each of the candidate principles to be evaluated have widespread appeal, and are often relied upon to assess the morality of legal, political, and social institutions.

A Utilitarian Account

One might contend that there is a utilitarian justification for a moral obligation of humanitarian intervention. According to John Stuart Mill, an action is right if it tends to promote overall utility.[2] For Mill, as for other utilitarians, the utilitarian principle is determinative of what is morally required of an agent. At first glance, a utilitarian justification may seem promising. One could readily imagine circumstances under which utility would be promoted by intervention; thus, according to the utilitarian principle, one would be morally obligated to intervene.

There are, however, a number of reasons why utilitarianism fails to provide the necessary justification for a moral obligation of humanitarian intervention. First, though utilitarianism could provide a plausible basis for a moral obligation to intervene in particular cases in which utility would be promoted, it does not provide a basis for a moral obligation of *humanitarian* intervention. The humanitarian nature of the utilitarian obligation is only a contingent fact. The goal is the promotion of utility and reduction of suffering generally making no distinction between the suffering of those whose rights are being violated and the suffering that would be caused to the violators should an intervention be carried out. Protecting *individuals* from suffering is only relevant if, in a particular case, it promotes utility. One could imagine a situation in which a utilitarian obligation of intervention arises, and then alter the circumstances only slightly, and instead of intervening an agent would be morally obligated to allow the preventable suffering of individuals to continue if that would promote overall utility.

Second, the obligation of intervention justified by the utilitarian principle would fail to accommodate the scope of the moral obligation of humanitarian intervention. The moral obligation of humanitarian intervention is borne by certain agents (states and the international community) and is owed to individuals. Utilitarian obligations are not *owed* to anyone. The obligation is to promote utility. If an individual or group of individuals happens to benefit from the fulfillment of the obligation then so much the better for them, but those suffering do not have a basis for a demand against the bearer of the obligation that the obligation be fulfilled that is grounded in their individual suffering.

The failure of the utilitarian principle to accommodate the scope of a moral obligation of humanitarian intervention is most clearly understood when utility can be served equally by either of two actions. Imagine that an agent is faced with performing action *A* or action *B*. The actions are equivalent from the perspective of the utilitarian principle. Either produces the same amount of utility. *A* involves intervention to stop the suffering of individuals. *B* involves no intervention. The agent can choose *A* or *B* in fulfillment of the demands of the utilitarian principle, but the individual who would be helped by *A* does not have a moral basis to *demand* an intervention. At best, they have a basis for a request that intervention occur.

In addition, under a utilitarian account there is no principled reason for making a distinction between those suffering and those causing the suffering. Let us imagine that *B* (not intervening) produces more utility than *A* (intervening). Under a utilitarian account this would imply that we are morally obligated to act on *B*. What is troubling is that it is possible that one could imagine a version of *B* in which *B* produces greater utility because the intervention's use of force against those violating the rights of others causes too much suffering to the violators in service of the victims. In other words, as was noted above with regards to the ability of a utilitarian account to support a humanitarian obligation, if all that matters is utility then there is no principled basis for making a distinction between violator and victim.

Lastly, if an obligation of intervention is to count as a moral obligation of humanitarian intervention, it must act as a second-order exclusionary reason and a first-order reason to act. A utilitarian moral obligation of intervention is not a reason, first or second-order, to be entered into the deliberations of an agent, rather it is the *outcome* of such moral deliberations. For the utilitarian there are no prior existing obligations that count as reasons to be included as inputs into the practical deliberation of an agent. The only moral obligations to act are those that would promote the most utility. Certainly, none of the foregoing reasons for rejecting utilitarianism as a basis for a moral obligation of humanitarian intervention undermines the plausibility of a utilitarian justification for intervention, but they do demonstrate the inability of utilitarian theory to justify the relevant type of obligation.

A Rule Utilitarian Account

The utilitarian may, conceding the inability of direct utilitarianism to justify a moral obligation of humanitarian intervention, argue that the utilitarian principle is a secondary rule governing a multitude of primary rules intended to fulfill the demands of the secondary rule. Under this form of indirect utilitarianism, an individual's actions should be guided by the primary rules which are justified by the fact that if they are followed they have a tendency to promote utility.[3] This version of utilitarianism has come to be known as rule-utilitarianism.[4]

A moral obligation of intervention based on a rule-utilitarian justification would likely run as follows: utility would be promoted if, as a general rule, intervention were to occur whenever certain established circumstances arise. The rule-utilitarian justification, however, fails to justify a moral obligation with the necessary content for much the same reason that direct utilitarianism fails. Intervention may be demanded by the specific primary rule at issue, but the moral justification remains the promotion of utility. Humanitarian concerns related to the suffering of individuals are only ancillary concerns as the utilitarian demand is to promote utility.

A rule-utilitarian justification for a moral obligation of intervention arguably satisfies the third characteristic because primary rules can conflict. In such situations the conflicting rules act as second-order reasons precluding certain first-order reasons from consideration and they are first-order reasons to engage in a particular action. The utilitarian principle is the ultimate arbiter of such conflicts, which gives credence to the claim that rule-utilitarianism must, on at least some occasions, collapse into direct utilitarianism. Nonetheless, the rule-utilitarian obligation of intervention performs the appropriate role in the practical deliberations of an agent.

An example may help to elucidate this point. Imagine that each of the following primary rules tends, when followed, to promote utility:

1. One has an obligation to obey the law; and
2. One has an obligation to disobey arbitrarily discriminatory laws.

For the rule-utilitarian, when rule 1 is not in conflict with other primary rules it is determinative of what an agent ought to do. However, it may be the case that primary rules conflict, as rule 2 would conflict with rule 1 whenever arbitrarily discriminatory laws exist. In such circumstances neither rule can be determinative. It is in such cases of conflict that rule-utilitarian primary rules serve the appropriate role in an agent's practical deliberations. They are entered into the practical deliberations of agents as both second-order exclusionary reasons and first-order reasons for action. What an agent ought to do is determined by the degree to which either rule promotes utility – the strength of the rule from the utilitarian perspective.

A rule-utilitarian obligation of intervention would, however, not be able to accommodate the scope of a moral obligation of humanitarian intervention. Much like a moral obligation of intervention based on direct utilitarianism, the obligation justified by rule-utilitarianism would not give rise to a justified claim to intervention by those who would benefit from the intervention. The obligation is not owed to the beneficiaries of the obligation. It is not owed to anyone. The rule would be to intervene under certain circumstances, and the obligation to intervene would be based on the rule.

A rule-utilitarian could, however, respond that the rule requiring intervention should provide those who benefit from the intervention with a claim to the fulfillment of the moral obligation of intervention. The underlying justification would be that providing the beneficiaries of the rule with a *right* to call for an intervention would render the rule more effective, and thus better able to promote utility; thus providing a utilitarian reason for focusing on a rights-based justification for a moral obligation of humanitarian intervention.[5]

Thomas Pogge and the Right not to be Harmed

In seeking to justify the claim that the international community, and the developed world in particular, has a moral obligation to provide greater aid to the impoverished of the world, Thomas Pogge argues that we need only look to the uncontroversial obligation we each bear not to harm others.[6] The obligation, according to Pogge, is based on each individual's right not to be harmed.[7] Specifically, the violation of an individual's right not to be harmed gives rise to the rectificatory obligation borne by those who harmed or contributed to the harming of an individual to rectify the harm caused.

One could imagine a similar argument being made to justify a moral obligation of humanitarian intervention. If an agent harms or in some way contributes to the harm of an individual or group then that agent has a rectificatory obligation to alleviate the suffering and stop the harm. If, however, an agent does not contribute to the harm then they have no obligation to abate it.[8] In other words, if I am not harming you nor contributing to the harm you are suffering, then I have no obligation to help you. But if I am harming you or contributing to the harm you are suffering, then my actions create a special moral relationship under which I have an obligation to abate the harm you are suffering and compensate you for my violation of your right not to be harmed. If this can only be accomplished through an intervention, then fulfilling the obligation would require intervention.

But is a rectificatory moral obligation to intervene a moral obligation of humanitarian intervention? The rectificatory obligation would seem to be able to accommodate the second and third criteria. Regarding the second, scope-related, characteristic, there seems to be no principled reason as to why a rectificatory obligation could not arise between a state and an individual or group of individuals.

As to the role a rectificatory obligation would play in the practical deliberations of an agent, unlike a simple utilitarian obligation to intervene, a rectificatory obligation would be a reason for action to be considered in an agent's practical deliberations as opposed to an outcome of those deliberations. Thus, it is, at the very least, a first-order reason for action. Rectificatory obligations also act as second-order exclusionary reasons. Take, for example, the law of negligence in the United States. Much of tort law is built around the idea that we each have duties not to harm others. When one agent engages in negligent behavior and causes another to suffer an injury, under the law the negligent party has a rectificatory obligation to compensate the injured party for the harm suffered. The fact that the negligent party may have been planning on using the funds now dedicated to compensating the injured party for morally valuable projects is precluded from our consideration of whether the injured party should be compensated. This is not a judgment as to the justifiability of such rectificatory obligations. Rather, it is merely the identification of the role such obligations would play in our practical deliberations when and if they do arise.

Can a rectificatory obligation accommodate the required content of a moral obligation of humanitarian intervention? When it does arise, a rectificatory obligation would obligate the bearer of the obligation to act, and it would be based, at least in part, on the suffering of those to whom the obligation is owed. Thus, it would be both positive and based on moral concerns that are humanitarian in nature.

However, to understand a potential problem with this account, imagine that Kundu,[9] a small sovereign state, is engaged in a genocide against a particular ethnic minority within its borders. Kundu has few resources, exports very little to the outside world, and none of the aid it has received is being used to perpetrate the genocide. If the moral obligation of humanitarian intervention is to be based on a right not to be harmed and the rectificatory obligation that arises when that duty is violated, then, in this instance, there would be no moral obligation borne by the international community to intervene as very few outside of Kundu have contributed to or caused the harm being suffered. Ironically, the rectificatory obligation would be borne largely by the genocidaires.

This imagined circumstance may not be likely to occur, though one might argue that this is part of the Rwandan story; nonetheless, it is the very possibility of such an occurrence that is troubling and which leads to the intuition that something is lacking in a rectificatory justification for a moral obligation of humanitarian intervention. For an obligation to be a humanitarian obligation, it should be directly implied by the suffering of an individual and not mediated by the violation of a prior existing duty not to harm. A rectificatory obligation is an obligation to compensate for a past or present wrong that one created or to which one contributed, and not an obligation arising directly from the suffering of individuals. This is not to deny a role for rectificatory obligations. If one contributed or caused the harm being suffered, then one has an additional obligation tied to the special moral relationship that exists between violator and victim, but this is not the same thing as a distinctly *humanitarian* obligation.

Support for a Rights-based Account

Despite the fact that neither utilitarianism nor the principle of rectification are capable of justifying a moral obligation of humanitarian intervention, both lend support to human rights as a basis for such an obligation. As L. Wayne Sumner has argued, there are consequentialist reasons for a rule treating people as if they had rights.[10] Sumner argues that due to human fallibility and limited cognitive resources we are better able to promote welfare in the long run if we constrain our decision-making procedures by adhering to certain rules which prevent us from assessing the welfare-promoting qualities of each individual course of action.[11] As Sumner states,

> being also aware of our commitment to the goal of maximizing welfare, we have reason to fear that the temptation to make the attempt might be irresistible on each particular occasion. In order to defeat this temptation we will do well to pre-commit ourselves by announcing from the outset a requirement of acceptability for protocols whose function is to constrain acting on the basis of the cost/benefit test.[12]

One such rule should be the inclusion of rights, and specifically choice-protecting human rights.[13] As a consequence, if Sumner is correct, then there are consequentialist, if not entirely utilitarian, reasons for focusing our enquiry on the analysis of such a rights-based account.

Pogge, on the other hand, is more clearly focused on human rights as a basis for an obligation to act. However, Pogge's right not to harm and rectificatory principle as a basis fail to account for the distinctively humanitarian nature of the moral obligation of humanitarian intervention. Nonetheless, what the right not to be harmed and the principle of rectification demonstrate is the ability of a rights-based account to accommodate many of the structural characteristics of a moral obligation of humanitarian intervention.

THE BASIC RIGHT TO PHYSICAL SECURITY: EXPLICATION AND ANALYSIS

What would such a rights-based account look like? The explication and analysis that follows relies on Henry Shue's understanding of a "basic right,"[14] and specifically the basic right to physical security.[15] For Shue, a basic right is a right the existence of which is necessary for the enjoyment of all other rights.[16] So, if we have any rights at all, we must have basic rights. The right to physical security is a basic right because it is essential to the enjoyment of any other right. As to the specific characteristics of a basic right, according to Shue, any such right "provides (1) the rational basis for a justified demand (2) that the actual enjoyment of a substance be (3) socially guaranteed against standard threats."[17] Thus, the basic right to physical security would provide the right holder with the rational basis for a justified demand that their physical security be socially guaranteed against standard threats.

One might at this point ask, what distinguishes the right to physical security from the right not to be harmed? There must be a difference if the right to physical security is to support an obligation with the distinctively humanitarian nature that the right not to be harmed could not. The most striking difference between the two rights is related to the jural correlatives of each right. The jural correlative of the right not to be harmed is a duty to refrain from engaging in acts that harm or contribute to the harm of others.[18] This negative duty can give rise to a positive obligation to act, but only via the principle of rectification after the right has been violated. The jural correlative of the right to physical security includes both a (negative) duty not to harm and a positive correlative obligation to insure that the physical security of others is protected.[19] The positive obligation is not dependent on a mediating act or principle. It is a direct implication of the basic right to physical security.

In addition, this conceptual distinction gives rise to a practical difference. The right not to be harmed is more limited than the basic right to physical security. The latter's broader reach makes it likely that the basic right to physical security will give rise to a positive obligation to act in more cases. Returning to the fictitious example of the genocide in Kundu, the right not to be harmed would implicate only a limited number of duty-bearers; the primary ones being the genocidaires themselves. The basic right to physical security, on the other hand, would imply that the international community had an obligation to act to protect the physical security of those whose basic rights were being violated.

The discussion can now turn to determining whether the basic right to physical security is capable of accommodating the constitutive elements of a moral obligation of humanitarian intervention. To accommodate the scope of a moral obligation of humanitarian intervention, the underlying principle must support an obligation owed by states to distant others. Thus, the specific question that must be answered is whether the basic right to physical security held by distant others can serve as the rational basis for a justified demand that states (and the international community) act to fulfill the demands of the right? To demonstrate that states are able to bear such an obligation, it is at the very least necessary to explain how states *could* bear such obligations and demonstrate that a number of the more common objections fail to preclude this possibility.

As Shue notes, basic rights are "the morality of the depths."[20] They are the moral minimum to which each of us is entitled, and the very least that we are owed from all others. We can justifiably demand of each individual, with the capability to do so, that they act so as to socially guarantee the enjoyment of the substance of such rights against standard threats. This may appear to be a substantive claim in need of an argument. In the present analysis, however, the goal is to defend the ability of Shue's understanding of basic rights to accommodate the constitutive elements of a moral obligation of humanitarian intervention, and from that perspective this is a conceptual rather than substantive claim. For the moment, the substantive defense of Shue's account of basic rights will be set aside, but will be taken up again below.

The social guarantees to which an individual is entitled may be provided by the formation of social and political institutions. Such institutions would then, as part of their justification, be required to provide the requisite socially guaranteed protection. Individual obligations correlative to basic rights do not, however, end at a state's boundaries.

Basic rights are held by each individual and held against all others.[21] It is important to note that this should not be confused with the claim that basic rights and their correlative obligations are absolute, just that their demands and the role they ought to play in the practical deliberations of agents is not limited by political boundaries.

In many instances to demand that individuals as individuals fulfill such obligations to distant others would be unjustified for a number of reasons. Efforts by individuals would be inefficient and likely futile. The coordination of individual effort that would be demanded for such an endeavor to be successful would be unreasonable to expect, and likely be overly burdensome. What is needed is collective action on the part of a sufficient number of obligation bearers capable of providing the requisite socially guaranteed protection demanded by the right. There are a number of reasons for thinking that states (and the international community as a collection of duty-bearing states) are the appropriate institutions for the task.

First, assuming that the only way to fulfill the obligation to provide the social guarantees for the protection of the physical security of individuals is through military intervention; in the contemporary world, states have a monopoly on the military capabilities necessary to be successful. In addition, in the international arena states and the governments that control them mediate the relations between distant peoples. Therefore, if any one people, as individuals or as a collective, owe obligations to another, then states are already well positioned to carry out the task. As such, there are both practical reasons and reasons based on the structure of international relations in support of the proposition that states are the *de facto* bearers of the obligation to provide the necessary social guarantees. Lastly, to be most effective, the actions of states in their efforts at intervention will require coordination among the states themselves; providing an additional reason for states to act collectively – reasons for the international community to act as the bearers of the obligation.

There are a number of arguments intended to demonstrate that states are incapable of bearing obligations to distant others; none of which succeed. David Rodin offers a critical assessment of the various ways in which states could possibly be argued to be the bearers of rights or duties.[22] Rodin is primarily concerned with arguments seeking to justify a state's right of self-defense, and much of the skepticism about the ability of states to bear moral obligations to distant others can be found in the various arguments assessed by Rodin. For Rodin, there are two ways to explain the normative status of states in the international arena. According to Rodin, if a state is to bear obligations to distant others, the basis for the attribution must be found in either reductive or analogical reasoning.[23] Rodin, however, misses a third alternative capable of explaining how states could bear obligations to distant others.

Under the analogical argument, states have rights and responsibilities in the international arena because they are like individuals in domestic society in morally relevant ways. However, as Rodin points out in rejecting the analogical approach, such analogical arguments cannot support a state having rights or obligations as a state.[24] Rather, if a state is to have such rights and responsibilities it is going to have to be based on the rights and responsibilities of those who inhabit the state – such rights and responsibilities will need to *reduce* to an aggregation of the rights and responsibilities of the individuals who inhabit the state.[25] Rodin, however, demonstrates, at least for a state's right of self-defense, that a state's right to self-defense cannot be based on such a reductive strategy because the right of individual inhabitants to self-defense would not often imply a right on the part of states to use military force to pursue defense of the state.[26] Similarly, with regard to intervention, it is not likely that one could justifiably demand of an individual that s/he intervene to provide the social guarantees necessary for a distant person to be able to enjoy his/her physical security. So, if a state's obligations are to be based on the obligations of its inhabitants, one could not justify such an obligation under a reductive strategy.

Rodin's argument is based on the implicit assumption that the only alternative to an analogical strategy is a reductive strategy. This is, however, mistaken. There is an alternative not considered by Rodin – the obligation of states to intervene to provide distant others with the requisite social guarantees can be *derived* from the obligations individuals have to those distant others. This is different from the reductive strategy because it is based on the recognition that states as collectives are capable of accomplishing tasks that individuals are not. Thus, a state may actually have obligations beyond those which are held by individuals, but that are derived from the obligations borne directly by the individuals that make up the state.

Each individual has the obligation to provide every other individual with the social guarantees necessary for the latter to enjoy their physical security against standard threats. Fulfilling this obligation may on occasion require intervention. Owing to the practical limitations facing individuals, the coordination problems that would hinder the effectiveness of individual efforts to provide such social guarantees, and other pressing demands that might override the individuals' obligations; in cases where intervention is required, the demand that *individuals* intervene cannot be justified. As a collective, however, the inhabitants of a state would often be able to fulfill their obligations to distant others.

States are the institutions that represent their inhabitants in the international arena and mediate their inhabitants' interactions with distant others. A function of states is that they serve to coordinate the efforts of their inhabitants to solve coordination problems. As the institution which mediates the interaction between its inhabitants and distant others to which individuals owe an obligation, there is a derivative instrumental justification for states to be the bearers of the obligation to intervene.[27]

This derivative strategy depends on individuals having obligations to distant others. Henry Shue outlines two arguments critical of this proposition often made to demonstrate that individuals only have obligations to their compatriots. The first argument is based on the claim that one's obligations to others are based on being members of a community of sentiment – that one's obligations are based on the personal relationships that one shares with others.[28] The second argument is based on the claim that one's obligations to others are based on membership in a community of principle – that one's obligations are owed to those with whom one shares goals or a commitment to certain principles.[29]

One reason for rejecting these arguments is that, if correct, they would imply that we have no obligation not to harm others if they are outside of our community; a morally absurd proposition. Assuming, however, that there may exist special obligations based on one's membership in either a community of sentiment or a community of principle, what remains to be demonstrated, if the arguments are to be successful in supporting such "compatriot priority",[30] is that all moral obligations one owes to others are exhausted by the obligations that are reliant on membership in such communities. The fact that we, as individuals, may have additional moral obligations to those with whom we share our lives or to those with whom we share principled commitments, projects or goals, does not demonstrate that we cannot or do not have obligations to those outside of such communities.

There are also at least two practical or instrumental objections to attributing moral obligations to distant others to states. One such argument is based on what Shue calls the "comparative-advantage theory of government."[31] In this argument, it is acknowledged that individuals have obligations to distant others, but it is argued that the obligations, if they are to fall on any state, should fall on the state where those to whom the obligation is owed live. The underlying reason is instrumental in nature. It is claimed that those most familiar with the local conditions are best suited to fulfill the obligation, and for that reason each state should be the bearer of obligations to its own citizens.[32]

As David Luban has pointed out, this is an empirical claim that lacks support in the real world.[33] Nonetheless, even if this underlying claim were true, it does not imply that a state cannot have obligations to distant others, only that the state in which individuals reside is the primary holder of obligations owed to such individuals – a position defended by the ICISS in its development of the responsibility to protect principle. In addition, the circumstances under which an obligation of humanitarian intervention is likely to arise are instances in which the state is either an active participant in whatever is providing the threat to the physical security of individuals, or is ineffective in its efforts to fulfill its obligation to provide the requisite social guarantees. Under such circumstances, it would be unreasonable to rely on an argument that the government of that state is in a privileged position to know or do what is best.

Gerald Elfstrom presents a practical objection to the claim that states can bear obligations to distant others.[34] The specific concern raised by Elfstrom is that nationalism exists and that it may be a barrier to the development of the political will necessary for the populace to support a state in fulfilling its and its inhabitants moral obligations to distant others.[35] I have two responses to this concern. First, the fact that the individual inhabitants of a state refuse to recognize their moral obligations casts a shadow over the moral character of those people, and does not in any way undermine the existence of such obligations.

But I take the heart of Elfstrom's concern to be a more complicated matter. His concern is with the practical resolution of a real-world moral tragedy – in his case, global distributive justice and global poverty. Thus, if we are serious about solving the problem and not merely pointing out the relevant moral characteristics of the problem, then we will have to acknowledge such practical barriers and identify potential solutions. Though certainly not a fully developed resolution to this dilemma, nationalism and the national identity that it is based upon can be used to motivate individuals to support the fulfillment of their moral obligations to distant others. If such obligations are framed, not as an imposition of outsiders on the populace of a state, but rather as a matter of national interest or national pride, then nationalism may serve as a motivational tool. This does not mean that the humanitarian nature of the situation is rendered clandestine, but rather that the humanitarian aspects become the focus. It is a point of pride for a state and its inhabitants to live up to its and their moral obligations. It is a virtue to be pursued, not a burden to be avoided.

From the previous discussion we can conclude that there is good reason to believe that the basic right to physical security would imply an obligation that would accommodate the scope of a moral obligation of humanitarian intervention. However, throughout the discussion of the ability of a rights-based account to accommodate the scope of a moral obligation of humanitarian intervention, a particular content of the obligation has been assumed. Thus, the next question to be addressed is whether the basic right to physical security implies an obligation that accommodates the content of a moral obligation of humanitarian intervention. Answering this question requires that we first identify, with greater specificity, what a basic right to physical security is a right to.

Simply put, the content of an individual's basic right to physical security would include a justified demand to have one's physical security socially guaranteed against standard threats. The keys to explicating the content of the moral obligations implied by the basic right to physical security lie in determining what counts as a standard threat to physical security and what duties or obligations are correlative to basic rights. It is important, in understanding what counts as a standard threat, to understand why we ought to distinguish a standard threat from a possible threat. This is a matter of the breadth of the content of the right. Specifically, what is it a right to, and from which threats do individuals have a justified demand for socially guaranteed protection? As Shue points out, the socially guaranteed protection cannot be against *all* threats to the substance of the right because such a demand would be too burdensome, and, though not logically impossible, it would cast doubt on the right itself since the demand is supposed to be justified.[36]

But what exactly is a standard threat? If a right is the basis for a justified demand on the actions of others, the threats from which individuals are entitled to socially guaranteed protection must be those from which such protection can be "justifiably demand[ed] of others."[37] Shue identified a number of considerations that should matter in assessing whether the demanded protection from a threat would be justified. Standard threats to the substance of a right and those from which protection should be socially guaranteed are those that are "most common," "serious," "typical," "eradicable," and "remediable."[38]

Though instructive, this list of properties intended to delineate a standard threat is in need of refinement. From the five properties listed by Shue, one can derive three specific conditions for what counts as a standard threat. First, the claims that to be a standard threat a threat must be eradicable and/or remediable are specific instances of a more general principle that the threats which one is justified in demanding protection from are threats from which protection can be effectively provided. A threat from which protection cannot be provided cannot count as a standard threat as the demand could not be justified since the effort expended would be futile.

Second, a standard threat for Shue must also be typical and/or common. Shue cannot mean that one does not have a right to socially guaranteed protection against threats to the substance of a right that rarely occur. For it is often those rare occurrences that are the most glaring examples of a failure to provide the necessary social protection for the substance of a right. Instead, if we look again to the underlying claim that for a right to be effective the demanded protection must be justified, requiring that the threat be common or typical would serve an epistemic role. One could not justifiably demand that the substance of one's rights be protected against an unknown threat. Thus, the threat must be known or, at least knowable. What the known or knowable threats to the substance of a right are will depend, to a great extent, on the substance of the right itself.

Shue also contends that the threat must be serious. It is not clear why seriousness is not contained in the prior properties of a standard threat. It would seem that any known or knowable and remediable threat to a basic right is serious. The seriousness of a threat may, however, refer to the probability of a threat being actualized; referring to a threat that is an actual as opposed to a speculative threat to the substance of the right. It would be one that is either intended to prevent the enjoyment of the substance of a right or has a high probability of preventing such enjoyment.

In addition, Shue contends that what may count as such a threat is likely to change as times change.[39] For example, a few centuries ago smallpox may not have counted as a standard threat to health as it was *not remediable* by the medical techniques of the time. It would be unreasonable to *require* social guarantees against threats that cannot be protected against. However, as medicine and the understanding of such diseases advanced, a cure for smallpox became a reality, and arguably the threat of smallpox since it could be remediated became a standard threat.

There is one additional and important aspect of a standard threat that Shue fails to recognize. If standard threats to the substance of a basic right are those from which one is justified in demanding socially guaranteed protection, the threat from which one is entitled to protection cannot be morally justified. If the threat in question is a morally justified threat, then it is morally permissible. This would give the agent engaging in the threat a moral entitlement to engage in the underlying behavior. It would, at the very least, be paradoxical to say that a basic right gives the right holder a rational basis for a justified demand of socially guaranteed protection against a threat when the threatening moral agent has a moral entitlement to engage in the threat.

Thus a standard threat to the substance of a right is one against which protection can be provided, it must be known or knowable, the relationship between the threat and the substance of the right must be direct and either intended to prevent the enjoyment of the substance of a right or with a high probability of preventing such enjoyment, and the threat must not be morally justified. Though a more precise explication of a standard threat would, under ideal conditions be preferable, the understanding provided is sufficient for the purposes of this discussion.

Understanding what counts as a standard threat only provides one with an understanding of one aspect of the content of a moral obligation implied by a basic right. One is to be protected against standard threats, but in what way? As Shue argues, a basic right implies a moral obligation that the *substance* of the right be socially guaranteed – a right holder must be able to enjoy the substance of the right as a matter of entitlement, rather than as a matter of luck or beneficence.[40] Thus, for a basic right to be fulfilled one must actually have the substance of the right provided and protected by social and political institutions.

Determining whether an obligation of intervention would be implied by the basic right to physical security requires that we first understand what counts as a standard threat to physical security. Harm to an individual inflicted by other human agents would seem to be an obvious candidate. Such harm is certainly a threat from which socially guaranteed protection could be provided. It is the type of threat that is known or knowable. By its very nature, such harm would be a direct threat to the physical security of right holders. However, it is the case that in many instances harm or the threat of harm to the physical security of a right holder may be justified. Thus, we must distinguish between justified and unjustified threats of harm.

For the purposes of the present project, a complete discussion of the difference between justified and unjustified threats to physical security would be needlessly lengthy and complicated. An action is justified if it is based upon a particular type of reason, namely one that renders the action in question morally permissible. It is important to understand that the present reference to reasons is not concerned with the reasons people take themselves to have, or reasons that provide an explanation for an agent's action – subjective reasons. Rather, the reference is to a conception of objective reasons – reasons as relations between facts in the world and agents.[41] Reasons that justify an action or attitude are based on the normative relationship between the agents involved. For a reason to justify an agent harming or threatening harm to another's physical security, it must be based on the fact that the agent's harming or threatening harm to another's physical security is necessary to protect something of sufficient moral value. In other words: to be justified in harming or posing a threat of harm to a holder of the basic right to physical security, it is necessary that (1) the harm or threat of harm to the physical security of others is necessary to protect something of sufficient moral value; and (2) only as much harm as is necessary to serve (1) is permitted. A harm or threat of harm to the physical security of a holder of the basic right to physical security would be unjustified if it failed to meet either of the two identified conditions. Such an unjustified harm or threat of harm would be a candidate for a standard threat to physical security. These two conditions are not likely to exhaust the necessary and sufficient conditions for harm or a threat of harm to be justified, but they should suffice for present purposes.[42]

As to the content of the obligations implied by the basic right to physical security, at least two relevant questions remain. First, is the basic right to physical security capable of implying an obligation to intervene? Second, would that obligation be distinctively humanitarian? Addressing the latter question first, an obligation that is distinctively humanitarian is, at the very least, one that is based on the suffering or circumstances of individual moral agents, and is one in which the requisite normative relationship between obligor(s) and obligee(s) is basic and does not depend on the fulfillment of additional moral conditions. Lastly, to be distinctively humanitarian, the obligation cannot be directed at the promotion of some alternate moral good. Rather, it is an obligation to the individual as an individual and not for some other purpose.

Basic rights are held by individual moral agents, the obligations implied by basic rights are directly implied by those rights without the need for any additional mediating principles, and the obligations implied by basic rights are directed simply at the fulfillment of the demands of the right and are not directed at the promotion of any alternate moral good. Obligations implied by the basic right to physical security meet all three conditions, and as a consequence, are distinctively humanitarian.

Returning to the first question raised above, is the basic right to physical security capable of implying an obligation to intervene? Under the appropriate circumstances, if providing the socially guaranteed protection demanded by the right to physical security required intervention, then there would exist an obligation to intervene. This, however, begs the question, "What are the appropriate circumstances?" Identifying the "appropriate circumstances" will depend on the identification of a standard threat to physical security which requires intervention for physical security to be socially guaranteed. I will not propose such a standard threat now; rather, I will assess whether the genocide in Rwanda would count.

Whether the basic right to physical security is capable of implying an obligation to intervene of the requisite nature (first-order reason to intervene and second-order exclusionary reason) remains to be determined. The key to understanding the nature of an obligation implied by a basic right is to be found in the fact that a basic right serves as a rational basis for a justified demand that the substance of the right be socially guaranteed against standard threats. It should be readily apparent that if a moral obligation to intervene is implied by the basic right to physical security, it would, at the very least, be a first-order reason to intervene. But, is such an obligation a second-order exclusionary reason?

There are a number of reasons for accepting the conclusion that the obligation to intervene implied by the basic right to physical security is a second-order exclusionary reason. First, Joseph Raz has proposed a phenomenological test for assessing whether we *treat* a particular reason as a second-order exclusionary reason.[43] According to Raz, we treat a reason as a second-order exclusionary reason if the following phenomenological story can be told about our practical deliberations involving the reason at issue: for any reason (X), if the balance of first-order reasons directs that we perform action (A) but our all-things-considered practical judgment is either not (A) or that we ought to perform some other action that is not (A), (X) is taken to be a second-order exclusionary reason if it is the reason that explains why we ought not act on our first-order evaluation. In other words, (X) is not merely being balanced in our first-order evaluation, rather (X) affects the first-order balancing by excluding reasons that would otherwise be relevant.

An (oft-cited) example may help to elucidate the test. Imagine that there is a stop sign in the middle of the desert. You are traveling late at night and the chance that you are going to be caught if you fail to heed the stop sign is practically nonexistent. The stop sign places you under (at the very least) a legal obligation to stop. Thus, you have a first-order reason to stop, but you have a number of countervailing first-order reasons to continue on without stopping. We can assume that your first-order reasons for not stopping (it is late, you are late and in a hurry, there is no one else around, etc.) outweigh your first-order reasons for stopping. You, however, choose to stop. In your explanation, you say that the fact that you had a legal obligation to stop rendered certain reasons irrelevant to your consideration of how you ought to act. If you choose not to stop, we may understand why – you are acting on your first-order balance of reasons – but, provided the law was not contra-dicted by a countervailing moral consideration, we would be justified in criticizing you for failing to adhere to the obligation. In this instance, we are treating the obligation to stop as a second-order exclusionary reason.

It is likely that an obligation of humanitarian intervention based on the basic right to physical security would pass this phenomenological test. This, however, is merely a descriptive account explaining the phenomenology associated with a second-order exclusionary reason. It is a *post facto* explanation rather than a way to understand how we should treat an obligation to intervene when we are engaging in practical deliberation. It may be relevant that this is how we do treat such moral demands, but it cannot be determinative of how we ought to treat them. There are, however, a number of additional reasons for accepting the claim that obligations are second-order exclusionary reasons.

The first consideration is an argument that our considered moral judgments about the nature of obligations reveal that they are to be treated as second-order exclusionary reasons. Let us begin with the following question: If one has an obligation to X, why should that be thought of as a second-order exclusionary reason?

> Scenario 1: Let's assume that the obligation to X is an ordinary first-order reason for action, a first-order reason to X. This would mean that whether or not one ought to X is a matter of weighing. If the countervailing reasons against X-ing outweigh the obligation to X, then one ought not to X.

One problem with thinking about obligations as first-order reasons for action is that the countervailing reasons against X-ing may be entirely practical. Recall the example of Albert and Beatrice. What if Albert decided he was not going to fulfill his promise, not because there was some more pleasant experience for him to engage in, but simply because he would be inconvenienced? It would at the very least be odd to say that a moral obligation to do something (help Beatrice) can be defeated by purely practical reasons, short of practical impossibility, against the performance of the action. There is something different about a reason based in a moral obligation. It is not like other first-order reasons.

One might concede this point, but argue that moral obligations are nothing more than *very weighty* first-order reasons. This proposition does not stand up to much critical scrutiny. Imagine that the obligation to X is an obligation of reciprocity to help a neighbor finish a project. There is little left to be done, but the neighbor is expecting and relying upon your help. It is not clear why we should think of this obligation as exceptionally weighty, unless we believe that there is something distinct about obligations. Yet, it would be wrong to fail to fulfill the obligation for reasons of a purely practical nature, even if those practical considerations appear to be as weighty, if not more so.

> Scenario 2: Let us assume instead that the obligation to X is a second-order exclusionary reason precluding certain first-order reasons against X-ing from consideration in the practical deliberations of states, and a first-order reason to X.

In this case, the obligation to X is weighed against other second-order reasons and it is only those first-order reasons that are not precluded by the exclusionary effect of the obligation that are weighed at the first order.

Let us return to the example of the reciprocal obligation to help your neighbor. If your neighbor claims that you are under an obligation, then s/he is claiming that at least some of the purely practical reasons for failing to fulfill the obligation are precluded from consideration. Pursuant to this understanding of the nature of obligations, one could see why a weak first-order obligation could still have the effect one thinks it ought to have. Admittedly, if the obligation to X is a significant moral obligation, whether it is a first-order reason and/or a second-order reason may be irrelevant when factored in to our practical deliberations.

Returning to Cicero's discussion of obligations, we find an early assessment of the role obligations are supposed to play in our practical deliberations.[44] Specifically, they are reasons for acting in accordance with the demands of an obligation even in the face of interests that command otherwise.[45] If we look to more contemporary accounts of legal, conventional, and moral obligations, the claim to their status as obligations is supposed to grant them a second-order exclusionary role in our practical deliberations. Take, for example, the obligations of judges in a legal system. Provided the case being decided by a judge is one to which a law applies, judges in a legal system are under an obligation to apply the law.[46] What this means, according to Raz, is that a judge "regards himself as justified in acting on some reasons to the exclusion of others."[47]

Simply stated, our considered moral judgment reveals that one aspect of obligations is that they likely include second-order exclusionary, as opposed to merely first-order, reasons. As such, those who would still claim that obligations are merely weighty first-order reasons bear the burden of demonstrating that obligations are, in fact, first-order reasons. Nonetheless, it is reasonable to conclude, for purposes of this discussion, that one aspect of an obligation is that it operates as a second-order exclusionary reason. As such, if the basic right to physical security does, under the appropriate circumstances, imply a moral *obligation* of intervention, then that obligation is a second-order exclusionary reason precluding certain first-order reasons against intervention from consideration.

One might be skeptical about this claim about the nature of all obligations. Even assuming the skepticism is warranted, this does not imply that the obligation of humanitarian intervention is not a second-order exclusionary reason. There are at least two arguments that can be pressed in response. First, if it can be demonstrated that all obligations correlative to rights are second-order exclusionary reasons, then the obligation of humanitarian intervention implied by the basic right to physical security would be such an obligation. Alternatively, one could provide an argument that directly addresses the obligation of humanitarian intervention implied by the basic right to physical security.

In either case, we need to look to the role rights play in our practical deliberations. It is fundamental to our understanding of the claim that one has a right that we believe the holders of the right have an *entitlement* to the substance of the right. If I claim that I have a right that Y do X, then I am claiming that I am entitled to Y X-ing and that Y is under an obligation to X. When claiming such a right, I am not claiming that Y's obligation to me is merely a reason for Y to X, I am claiming that Y must X unless some other moral reason for action outweighs Y's obligation to me to X. I am claiming that the obligation Y owes to me precludes her from even considering certain reasons in her practical deliberations over whether she ought to fulfill her obligation to me – that certain reasons against X-ing are simply irrelevant.

Assuming that I am correct in my claim that I have a right to X held against Y, then if Y were to fail to X and offered no other reasons for the failure other than practical reasons short of practical impossibility, then Y simply does not understand what it means to be the bearer of an obligation that is correlative to a right. If, on the other hand, Y's failure was due to the fact that Y (believed that she) had a competing moral obligation that outweighed her right-based obligation to me, her failure would be justified if she properly weighted and weighed the competing moral claim.

If, however, one is not convinced of the claim that all obligations correlative to rights are second-order exclusionary reasons, this argument can still succeed if it can be demonstrated that there are good reasons for believing that the obligation of intervention implied by the basic right to physical security is such a reason. If we assume that human rights exist, which we must if we are to determine what role human rights ought to play in the practical deliberations of other agents, they cannot simply be ordinary reasons for action. If they were simply ordinary reasons for action, one would be able to deny another's rights if a sufficiently weighty countervailing first-order reason were to arise. By their very nature, human rights act as constraints on the practical deliberations of those who bear the correlative obligations. But how? A human right precludes others from considering certain reasons for action. Specifically, it precludes others from considering certain reasons against the fulfillment of the obligation correlative to the basic right.

Second-order exclusionary reasons are not, however, limitless. The strength of such reasons is limited by other second-order reasons, and the breadth of a second-order reason is limited by the extent of the first-order reasons they preclude.[48] What this means is that another countervailing second-order reason might outweigh the second-order reason in question, or that certain first-order reasons against the action that the obligation in question supports are outside the reach of the exclusionary aspect of the obligation. The relevance of these limitations will become more apparent when I assess whether the basic right to physical security would have implied an all-things-considered moral obligation of humanitarian intervention in Rwanda.

To this point the argument has been conditional. *If* one accepts the existence of the basic right to physical security, or human rights at all, then there may exist circumstances under which it would be unreasonable to deny that a moral obligation of humanitarian intervention exists. I have yet, however, to offer an argument for the existence of the basic right to physical security. There are, however, good reasons for our acceptance of the claim that such a right does exist.

First, we act and speak as if the basic right to physical security exists. Though not determinative of the question of whether the basic right to physical security in fact exists, it evinces a widely held belief in the existence of such a right. In the domestic realm our legal, political, and social institutions are concerned, at least in large part, with the promotion and protection of individuals' rights to their physical security. Upon reflection it seems to be a fundamental moral and political proposition that a community that is unable to, or chooses not, to protect its inhabitants' physical security is one that is failing in a morally significant way.

In fact, our political rhetoric is not so much concerned with whether such a right exists, but how best to serve that right, and a condemnation of those that fail to do so. In H. L. A. Hart's terminology, we have taken the "internal point of view" on the existence of the basic right to physical security.[49] We are committed to the protection and promotion of physical security through the formation and maintenance of social and political institutions, we engage in a critical dialogue with others that is built around such commitment, and we criticize any who (or accept criticism ourselves if we) fail to fulfill the demands of the basic right to physical security.

We can also look to the international political arena for evidence in support of the belief that such a right exists. The creation of treaties and conventions dedicated to the promotion and protection of human rights evinces a belief in, if not a commitment to, the existence of the basic right to physical security.[50] Here too the political rhetoric surrounding basic rights to subsistence and security takes as its starting point the existence of such rights. It is from this basic premise that critical discussions and criticism proceed.

One may recognize that there is widespread consensus as to the existence of the basic right to physical security, that there is not only rhetoric but action in accordance with the belief that the basic right to physical security exists, but deny that the right in fact exists. The denial is likely to take either of two forms. One might claim that the basic right to physical security does not exist in the form proposed by Shue. An example of such a denial would be Pogge's claim that the substance of such rights are rights to noninterference. In the case of physical security, this would mean that the obligations of others are exhausted by the requirement that they not interfere with the physical security of others. An alternative form of denial may come from those who deny that the rhetoric surrounding rights is based on anything real.

As to the former, I have already addressed why I believe the claim that correlative to rights are only negative obligations ought to be rejected. Thus, if one believes (as Pogge does) that there are human rights, then I believe that one is committed to the acceptance of the existence of certain basic rights, including the basic right to physical security. The alternate form of denial can be further disaggregated. One may be claiming that there is a moral minimum to which we are each entitled, but the moral minimum should not be thought of in terms of rights and correlative duties – denying the existence of a basic right to physical security, but not the existence of morality. On the other hand, one may simply be pressing an extreme skepticism about morality; that morality does not exist apart from our conventions about what it is.

If one is a committed skeptic, then there is little that can be offered except the following. First, our conventions seem to indicate that basic rights are a part of our morality. Second, if one believes that lives can get better or worse, it must be the case that one way in which a life can get worse is by having one's physical security threatened when the prevention of and protection from such threats is possible. One would likely desire the protection from such threats for oneself. In addition to the fact that consistency would demand the same for others, such protection is likely to be best accomplished through social and political institutions that provide such protection for all. The more people who are outside the protection afforded by such institutions, the greater the threat those outside pose to those inside.

As to the first form of denial, the same considerations that lead many of us to believe that there is a basic right to physical security should lead others to its functional equivalent. If there is a basic moral minimum, a line below which no one should be allowed to fall provided we are capable of fulfilling the obligation or preventing the fall, one's physical security would surely be a part of that moral minimum.

CHARITY OR JUSTICE

There remains at least one substantial objection to the role a moral obligation of humanitarian intervention is argued to have on an agent's practical deliberations. Thus far, it has been assumed that all moral obligations are univocal in at least one sense – all other things being equal, they are nondiscretionary demands on one's practical deliberations. Looking to the distinction between complete and incomplete obligations, it is often argued that only the former are nondiscretionary. Many contend that obligations to distant others are, by their very nature, incomplete obligations admitting of a wide range of discretion. As such, they are incapable of making the requisite nondiscretionary demand on an agent's practical deliberations. Since the moral obligation of humanitarian intervention is an obligation to distant others, under this view it would be incomplete, and would be incapable of making nondiscretionary demands on an agent's practical deliberations.

This objection depends on an obligation's source being determinative of its nature and strength, and determinative of the role it ought to play in the practical deliberations of an agent.[51] The underlying argument would be:

Premise 1: Only complete obligations make nondiscretionary demands on an agent's practical deliberations.

Premise 2: Only matters of justice, special relationships, or promises can give rise to complete obligations.

Premise 3: Only negative obligations can count as matters of justice.[52]

Premise 4: The moral obligation of humanitarian intervention is based neither on a promise nor a special relationship, and is a positive obligation.

Conclusion: The moral obligation of humanitarian intervention cannot be complete, and therefore does not make nondiscretionary demands on the practical deliberations of agents.

For the sake of argument, I will concede the truth of Premise 1 and assume that the moral obligation of humanitarian intervention is based on neither a promise nor a special relationship.

Let us begin with Premise 3. This sets a standard that defines the boundary of justice. It is argued that the moral obligation of humanitarian intervention falls outside that boundary and for that reason cannot be a matter of justice; consequently, the moral obligation of humanitarian intervention cannot make the requisite nondiscretionary demands on an agent's practical deliberations. There are two possible bases for the claim that only negative obligations can count as matters of justice. First, as many libertarians claim, to require more of an agent would be a violation of an individual's rights of self-ownership.[53] Second, as Onora O'Neill points out, for many liberals the argument is based on the claim that positive obligations require a conception of the "good for man" or the "good life" that is based on broad, if not universal consensus to which we do not have epistemic access, and thus cannot serve as a reasonable basis for action.[54] Consequently, we cannot require that an agent act on them.

With regard to Premise 2, its basis can be found, at least in part, in the discussion of the underlying basis for Premise 3. Obligations of justice must be complete because they are determinate with regards to the scope and content of the obligation.[55] Negative obligations (such as obligations of noninterference) are argued to be inherently complete as they require that *each* of us refrain from doing certain things to every other one of us. O'Neill, however, points out that this does not make them complete in the abstract, but only in their actual application, and the determinacy of such obligations will admit of degrees.[56]

In addition, and accepting for the sake of argument the claim that obligations of justice are inherently complete, Premise 2 is implicitly based on the claim that obligations to aid that are not based on a promise or special relationship are inherently and irreparably *incomplete*. There are two potential bases to support such a claim. First, as was discussed above, one might argue that, owing to the plurality of conceptions of the good life and lack of epistemic access as to which is correct, the content and scope is inherently indeterminate. Second, even if we can identify a widely shared conception of the good life, it may be argued that we are neither able to determine how to promote the good life for any given individual nor are we able to determine upon whom such an obligation should fall.

There are two distinct but related responses to this objection; either one could serve as the basis for a separate reply, but should also be understood jointly. In the first response, accepting for the sake of argument the truth of Premise 2; the moral obligation of humanitarian intervention should be considered to be a matter of justice, and thus capable of being complete. As to the second response, accepting the truth of Premise 3; positive obligations (to aid, of charity, of beneficence) can be completed and the source-based distinction between complete and incomplete obligations should be rejected.

Justice, I take it, is the moral minimum to which we are each entitled. With this conception of justice in mind, if the moral minimum to which we are each entitled implies, either directly or indirectly, a positive obligation then the claim that being a negative obligation is a necessary condition for being a matter of justice fails and certain positive obligations may then make nondiscretionary demands on our practical deliberations.

If we understand an entitlement to *X* to mean that one has a claim on others to have *X* provided, then this would mean that if *X* was part of the moral minimum to which we are entitled, then *X* must be provided as a matter of justice. If we are entitled to anything at all we are entitled to our physical security.[57] As a consequence, the physical security of each individual must be provided as a matter of justice. In some cases fulfilling this obligation may require intervention. Thus, the moral obligation of humanitarian intervention implied by the basic right to physical security as a matter of justice may directly imply a positive obligation to intervene.

Relying on the explication previously introduced, there are at least two objections that might be levied against this argument. First, it could be claimed that the obligation to provide physical security cannot be a matter of justice because it is a positive obligation to act. Positive obligations require a particular conception of the good life to which we do not have epistemic access, and thus cannot serve as the basis for a justified demand on others. The objection is based on the proposition that there are no epistemically unproblematic conceptions of the good life, and to require one to aid another based on a particular conception of the good life cannot be demanded of another and thus cannot be an action to which one could be entitled. If it can be shown that a particular obligation to aid is not epistemically problematic then it would seem that this objection would fail.

The obligation under consideration is an obligation to aid in only the most minimal sense. Specifically, it is an obligation to protect individuals from an unjustified threat to their physical security. Does this require having an epistemically problematic conception of the good life? Even those obligations that merely demand noninterference are intended to protect individual conceptions of the good life. If that is the case then there is something implicitly valuable about people being able to act upon their own conception of the good life. If their physical security is threatened, they will be unable to do so. This does not involve an epistemically problematic conception of the good life; rather the protection of an agent's physical security is a necessary condition for any conception of the good life.[58] Thus, our presumption should be that action to protect the physical security of others is fundamental unless it is demonstrated in a particular instance that this is not the case.

The alternative objection would challenge the claim that an entitlement of justice to *X* is to have *X* provided.[59] Rather, it would be argued that an entitlement to *X* as a matter of justice simply means that others refrain from interfering with your pursuit of *X*. This objection cannot be based on concerns of incompleteness, as such problems will or can be resolved. This line of objection is based on a substantive claim about the nature and limits of the demands of justice; requiring more than noninterference would unjustifiably infringe upon the rights to liberty of those upon whom the obligation would fall.[60]

This objection is based on the proposition that rights to liberty are virtually absolute, meaning that only under the most exceptional circumstances can they be infringed upon. As Nozick claims with regard to the right of self-ownership, "It will be as if an *absolute* side constraint prohibits their being sacrificed for any purpose."[61] If, however, rights to liberty are not so demanding, one could claim that an obligation to act is a matter of justice either because it outweighs the right to liberty, or because it is outside the normative reach of the entitlement implied by the right to liberty.

Any conception of rights to liberty as absolute should be rejected for the following reasons. First, if all such rights are absolute, then we have no means by which we can resolve conflicts of different types of rights, for example it would be impossible to resolve a conflict between one person's right to liberty of action with another's right to dispose of their property as they see fit. In addition, a conception of rights as absolute gives rise to the morally absurd proposition that we are forbidden from forcing a person to part with a portion of their property even if doing so would serve to protect a significant number of lives. It may be the case that it would be an unjustified demand on your right to liberty if I were to claim that you had to sacrifice your life for mine, but this is not what is being claimed. Rather, the claim is that you must sacrifice resources to support a military effort to stop others from taking my life.[62]

Another reason for rejecting the conception of rights underlying this objection is that those making the objection are focused on only one half of the binary relationship that defines the normative implications of the demands of justice. The demands of justice imply negative obligations, but those obligations are based on the entitlement to noninterference held by individuals. In many cases an individual's right to bodily security – an entitlement of justice to not have their bodily security interfered with – is violated. In such cases it is not enough to look only to the fact that the obligations directly correlative to the right are negative. The right of noninterference gives rise to an obligation on all others to insure that the right be fulfilled – it is still an entitlement to not be interfered with. Fulfillment of this entitlement will in some cases require intervention because the right to noninterference when violated requires positive action to stop the violation and to insure that violations of the right cease.

To argue otherwise would lead to the unreasonable proposition that one only has a claim of assistance against those who are violating his/her rights. An example may help to understand why this would lead to an absurdity. Imagine that we are committed to the idea that everyone has a right not to have their physical security interfered with, and we come across an individual being beaten and we could, without risk of harm, stop the assault. However, when the individual asks us to call for help, we say that there is no moral requirement that we do so. In fact, we say, their demand should be made to their assailants, since they, not we, are the ones violating their right.

There is one additional objection that must be noted. One may, in the end, deny that a basic right to physical security is a matter of justice. In that case, those obligations that it implies cannot be matters of justice and if the source of an obligation determines whether consideration is discretionary or not, then such obligations would not need to be considered in our practical deliberations. This objection, if correct, would imply that there are no matters of justice, for if there are any, the basic right to physical security must be one, as it is necessary to the enjoyment of all others. As Henry Shue notes, the function of the basic right to physical security, as well as other basic rights, is "to provide some minimal protection against utter helplessness to those too weak to protect themselves."[63] If those making this objection persist, all that can be offered in response are the arguments already made and my concurrence with Shue's belief that "few, if any would be prepared to defend in principle the contention that anyone lacks a basic right to physical security."[64]

Turning now to the second response, arguing in the alternative, I will accept the truth of Premise 3, but argue that one ought to reject Premise 2. The underlying claim that supports the objection being considered is that the *source* of the obligation determines the nature and strength of the obligation. Matters of justice are complete and matters of charity are incomplete. This distinction is too blunt, and misconceives the relationship between completeness and justice. When the requirement of completeness and its relationship to justice is properly understood, it entails that under certain circumstances the moral obligation of humanitarian intervention implied by the basic right to physical security is complete.

I do not deny that there is an important distinction between complete and incomplete obligations. What needs to be discerned, however, is the basis for such a distinction. How are we to determine whether an obligation is complete or incomplete? To be complete one must be able to identify with sufficient specificity the scope of the obligation and its content. Completeness, however, does not depend on the identification of the nature and strength of the obligation; rather the completeness of an obligation is relevant to our determination of the obligation's nature and strength.

A complete obligation is one that admits of little or no discretion. This begs the question, discretion as to what? A complete obligation admits of little to no discretion in our consideration of the obligation in our practical deliberations. If we know the scope and content of the obligation with sufficient specificity, and the obligation is one that places moral demands on us then we *must* consider those moral demands in our practical deliberations. Those who contend that the source of an obligation is determinative of an obligation's completeness must explain how the source of an obligation can preclude us from determining to whom the obligation is owed, who bears the obligation, and what it is an obligation to do.

One might object that a complete obligation is an all-things-considered moral ought, and that only matters of justice can satisfy such a condition.[65] What that would mean is that only those obligations that outweigh and override all other obligations in our practical deliberations are complete. If that is what is meant by a complete obligation, then I will concede that the moral obligation of humanitarian intervention is not complete, but then neither are most moral obligations that are often taken to be complete, no matter their source. Such an obligation would have to be absolute and indefeasible. Such obligations may exist, but they are not going to be the type of obligation that we typically think of as being complete. The obligation not to lie, not to kill, and not to harm are all obligations in which the scope and content of the obligation is determinate, and thus one is required to consider such obligations in their practical deliberations. But none of these obligations are complete if completeness requires that they always override or outweigh all other obligations and/or other reasons for action.

There is no principled reason to think that only matters of justice could fulfill such a role unless obligations of justice are the only ones for which the scope and content of the obligation can be identified with sufficient specificity. One might contend that as a matter of fact, most if not all obligations of justice are complete in just the sense being described, and most if not all obligations of charity are incomplete in just the sense described, and that this gives us good reason for the distinction. Assuming this is an accurate portrayal of the facts about obligations of justice and obligations of charity, it does not provide a principled reason for distinguishing complete from incomplete obligations based on their source. At best, it provides us with a heuristic reason for presuming that obligations of justice are complete and obligations of charity incomplete.

Another objection that may be raised against the possibility of obligations of charity being complete is that the content of an obligation of charity is going to vary from person to person as there is no universal conception of the good life, and we have no way of knowing what is good for each agent we encounter. Thus, the *content* of the obligation lacks sufficient specificity. In addition, the scope of an obligation of charity cannot be identified with sufficient specificity. In any particular case it would be unclear to whom the obligation is owed, or from whom help could be justifiably demanded. On the other hand, if the obligation is owed by each of us to everyone who is in need, the obligation becomes too burdensome and our lives and life goals are sacrificed for the good of others; which, in the end, due to the plurality of subjective conceptions of the good life may actually do more harm than good.[66]

If we think that obligations should only be thought of in isolation from the everyday circumstances in which they arise, then it may be the case that positive obligations to act are incapable of being complete. However, it would seem that if our concern is with the effect an obligation should have on our practical deliberations about what we ought to do, then we must consider the circumstances under which an obligation arises. To assess the nature of an obligation in isolation from other relevant considerations, especially moral ones, would undermine the understanding that we are seeking to attain.

As such, if there is a single instance in which an obligation of charity when viewed in light of the surrounding circumstances would identify with sufficient specificity the scope and content of the obligation then it is possible for an obligation of charity to be complete. Demonstrating that such an obligation exists implies that it is not the source of the obligation that determines whether an obligation is complete; rather, an obligation is complete if under the surrounding circumstances the scope and content of the obligation can be identified with sufficient specificity.

One example of such an obligation alluded to earlier is Ernest Weinrib's argument for a duty of easy rescue.[67] Weinrib argues that under certain conditions one is morally obligated to aid an individual who is in need of rescue. In response to the complaint that a moral duty of rescue would be incomplete owing to the fact that, in isolation, one cannot identify with sufficient specificity the scope and content of the obligation, Weinrib assesses the obligation not in isolation, but in a particular circumstance. Specifically, Weinrib argues that in an emergency situation in which a single individual is at risk of serious harm and another individual could help and is the only one capable of helping, the circumstances surrounding the emergency situation will identify with sufficient specificity the content and scope of the obligation. The obligation that in isolation was incomplete is rendered complete when viewed in light of the relevant surrounding circumstances.

Obligations of charity will be amenable to such circumstantial reconstruction to varying degrees. As a consequence, even if the possibility of such an obligation does exist, it merely allows for the possibility that the moral obligation of humanitarian intervention could be such an obligation. It remains to be determined whether there is a conceivable circumstance in which the basic right to physical security would imply an obligation to intervene in which the content and scope of such an obligation is identified with sufficient specificity. This question will be set aside for the moment and will be revisited in the assessment of the Rwandan genocide.

In addition to the possibility that the surrounding circumstances will help complete the obligation, Onora O'Neill offers an interesting but underdeveloped resolution to the problem of incompleteness. O'Neill argues that the problem of incompleteness can be resolved through the institutionalization of the obligation.[68] In short, by institutionalizing the obligation we would match those in need of aid with those who are capable of providing it; thus resolving at least one aspect of the problem of incompleteness – the scope of the obligation. O'Neill fails to address, however, the contention that the content of obligations from charity cannot be identified with sufficient specificity.

There are two significant challenges that could be made to the claim that the institutionalization of an obligation of charity would identify with sufficient specificity the content of the obligation. First, in order to institutionalize an obligation and match those in need of aid with those capable of providing it, one must know the content of the obligation in advance, as that is what is being institutionalized. However, according to the objection under discussion, the content is indeterminate. Institutionalization does not resolve this indeterminacy.

Someone might contend that since the institutionalization of the obligation is conventional, we can choose whatever content of the obligation we want. This would, however, miss the point of the objection. From the perspective of conventional systems, what we can institutionalize is limited only by practical concerns. What we want from the institutionalization of a moral obligation requires more. The question is not what can we institutionalize, but what are we justified in institutionalizing. Thus, from O'Neill's argument we can take away the following lesson. Once we have identified, with sufficient specificity, the content of a moral obligation of charity, we can, through the institutionalization of the obligation, identify with sufficient specificity, the scope of the obligation by matching those in need with those capable of providing the aid needed.

The argument begs the question of whether the content of the moral obligation of humanitarian intervention can be justified independently. To the extent that the discussion to this point is accurate, it can be. From a rights-based perspective, if we are to have any rights at all we must have basic rights. The most fundamental basic right is a right to our physical security for without physical security one is incapable of enjoying his/her other rights as rights. In addition, if there is anything that is common among conceptions of the good life, it must be physical security. For without the certainty that physical security provides, the possibility of a good life (by any measure) is greatly diminished.

We have been considering the objection that the moral obligation of humanitarian intervention implied by the basic right to physical security, since it is not an obligation of justice and only obligations of justice can be rendered complete, admits of a wide range of discretion in our practical deliberations. The concern at the heart of the objection is that obligations to act admit of a wide range of discretion, either because they are not complete or, assuming the source-dependent argument is correct, because they cannot be matters of justice. However, there are good reasons for believing that the basic right to physical security and the obligations it implies are matters of justice; or in the alternative, that the source-dependent objection is false and an obligation to act can be rendered complete either by the circumstances under which the obligation arose, or through the institutionalization of the obligation.

ADDITIONAL CONSIDERATIONS

The moral obligation of humanitarian intervention is not an all-things-considered moral obligation to act. To say that it makes a nondiscretionary demand on our practical deliberations, or in this case on the practical deliberations of states, does not mean that whenever it arises we ought to act on it. Therefore, in order to understand when the international community is morally obligated, all things considered, to engage in humanitarian intervention, we must understand what other moral conditions must be met and what other moral considerations must be accounted for in our practical deliberations – that set of conditions under which no one could reasonably deny that a moral obligation of humanitarian intervention exists.

These additional conditions are identified by looking back to some of the previously discussed objections to the permissibility of humanitarian intervention. Though none implies the impermissibility of intervention, each is based on relevant considerations that should be accounted for in our assessment of whether, in any particular case, it would be reasonable to reject the demand that the international community fulfill the moral obligation of humanitarian intervention. The identification of these additional conditions will serve two purposes. First, if we are to understand under what conditions the moral obligation of humanitarian intervention should be considered to be an all-things-considered moral ought, then as a matter of practical deliberation it would need to outweigh or preclude other relevant countervailing moral considerations. The additional conditions to be identified below are the most likely countervailing moral considerations. Second, as noted previously, the project being pursued is, at least in part, a justificatory one. Successfully accounting for the underlying concerns of those who object, on theoretical grounds, to the moral permissibility of humanitarian intervention likely renders continued objection on their part unreasonable.

Looking first to the skeptical objections, these objections come in various forms and from various quarters. Though the skepticism to which each is committed ranges from an outright denial of the possibility of normative theory at the international level to a claim that the obligations of international morality placed on states are drastically weaker versions of their domestic counterparts, the tie that binds the various forms of skepticism together is the priority they assign to the interest of the state. Essentially, the skeptic claims that humanitarian intervention is morally impermissible or practically irrelevant because the only effective obligations a state can have are to itself or to its own inhabitants. It can never have an effective external obligation – an obligation to distant others.

However, as was discussed above, the mere fact that governments have internal obligations does not preclude states from having external obligations. The strongest justification for the skeptic's claim is that a state is to serve the interests of its inhabitants and that acting to aid distant others sacrifices fulfillment of the internal obligations a state has to its own inhabitants to the weaker external obligations it may have to distant others. What we learn from these skeptical objections is that in many cases external obligations will require a state to sacrifice some of the resources instrumental to the fulfillment of its internal obligations. In some cases, the sacrifice required will be too great, and the moral obligation to intervene will be outweighed by the relevant internal obligations at issue.

Thus, an additional condition on an all-things-considered moral obligation of humanitarian intervention is that if the internal sacrifice on the part of the interveners is too much, it would be reasonable to reject the moral obligation to intervene. Obviously, this leaves open the question as to what counts as too much. However, this is not a question that can be answered in the abstract, but will require the careful consideration of the relevant aspects of a particular circumstance. Needless to say, the internal sacrifice must be of sufficient moral significance to outweigh the obligations to distant others implied by the basic right to physical security.

The relevant aspect of the communitarian objection to the moral permissibility of a moral obligation of humanitarian intervention is the claim that cosmopolitan theories, like the one pressed here, fail to properly acknowledge or account for the moral value of community. The value of community comes from its necessary relationship to human flourishing and to the pursuit of moral and political self-determination of a people. The value is such that it ought to be protected against the outside imposition of political systems or substantive moral values.

What we learn from this objection is that, as a general proposition, communities have value, and that value ought to be considered in our practical deliberations when considering our moral obligations in the international arena. This, however, does not preclude the possibility that under the appropriate circumstances an all-things-considered moral obligation of humanitarian intervention exists. The value of a community as a relevant countervailing consideration against the moral obligation of humanitarian intervention will depend on the existence of only a single community in the state in question, on whether a community of the relevant sort exists, and on the degree to which the community in question fulfills the functions which justify our ascription of value to a community.

The mere fact of community and the fact that intervention will interfere with or undermine the community will not automatically outweigh the moral obligation of humanitarian intervention implied by the basic right to physical security. One could, however, reasonably reject an all-things-considered moral obligation of humanitarian intervention if a community of moral significance is being threatened and the rights violations at issue do not warrant the harm caused to such a community.

The next condition is derived from our understanding of the moral value implicit in the instrumental argument against humanitarian intervention. The instrumental argument is that the state system, and the respect for state sovereignty upon which it relies and demands, is instrumental to the provision and maintenance of international peace and security. It is argued that humanitarian intervention undermines this instrumental relationship between the protection of state sovereignty and international peace and security; and, as a consequence, renders humanitarian intervention morally impermissible.

The instrumental nature of this argument is the key to understanding its limitations. Let us begin with the assumption that international peace and security is worth protecting – hardly a controversial assumption. First, since the claim is that states ought to refrain from intervening into the internal affairs of other states to insure that international peace and security is maintained, if in any particular instance international peace and security is actually served by intervention or if intervention would not upset international peace and security then the concern over international peace and security is not a reasonable basis for an objection to intervention. Second, since the justification for the prohibition on intervention depends on the instrumental value between nonintervention and international peace and security, the demandingness of the prohibition against intervention will depend on the degree to which adherence to it tends to serve the goal of international peace and security. Thus, the demandingness of the prohibition is not absolute but conditional on the instrumental relationship upon which its justification is based.

Lastly, the instrumental argument assumes, but fails to demonstrate, that international peace and security – the peace and security between states – is the only relevant moral value to be considered. When properly understood, international peace and security is an instrumental value. The value attributed to international peace and security is justified by its instrumental relationship to the provision and protection of the rights of individuals and the communities to which they belong. It is certainly possible that in some cases maintaining international peace and security will stand as an obstacle to the protection and/or promotion of the values upon which the value of international peace and security is based. In such cases international peace and security lacks the moral force which would in turn justify the prohibition against intervention.

Assuming the value of state sovereignty to the state system and the instrumental value of the state system to international peace and security, it would be reasonable for one to presume that, all other things being equal, states ought to refrain from intervening militarily into the internal affairs of other states. This presumption could be rebutted if it could be shown that the maintenance of international peace and security is an obstacle to the fulfillment of the values that the maintenance of international peace and security is supposed to serve, that international peace and security is outweighed by some other relevant moral consideration, or that in any particular instance international peace and security is either not implicated or is actually being served by intervention. However, one could reasonably reject a moral obligation of humanitarian intervention in any case in which the presumption is not rebutted.

There are a number of other concerns that may be raised against the moral obligation of humanitarian intervention which have yet to be discussed. In her discussion of NATO's intervention in Kosovo, Samantha Powers identifies as the most salient the concerns over *perversity*, *futility*, and *perfidy*.[69] None, however, is an absolute objection to the permissibility of intervention, nor are they objections to the possibility of an obligation of intervention. Rather, they are cautionary tales, warning of the moral hazards that may result from certain practical or epistemic problems associated with humanitarian intervention; as such, it would be reasonable to reject claims that the international community ought to act to fulfill the moral obligation of humanitarian intervention if intervention is likely to lead to the realization of any of these hazards.

There are at least two distinct ways in which the concern over futility is related to the possibility of an all-things-considered moral obligation of humanitarian intervention. First, futility is a concern related to any claimed obligation. If one's actions would be futile, it would be reasonable for one to reject the claim that one had an obligation to engage in such actions. In the common parlance of moral philosophy, the concern over futility is related loosely to the proposition that ought implies can. Thus, it would be reasonable for one to reject a moral obligation of humanitarian intervention if the intervention was likely to fail in fulfilling its humanitarian goals.

The concern over futility also relates to an all-things-considered moral obligation of humanitarian intervention in a more specific way. The criticism is that by their very nature humanitarian concerns can never be served by military action as military action is anathema to such concerns.[70] However, in many instances one could not at the same time maintain that one is committed to the humanitarian values upon which the basic right to physical security relies, and claim that military intervention is inherently contradictory with that right. Military intervention may be the only way to protect and/or respect the right. So understood, the argument from futility would not provide the basis for a reasonable rejection of a moral obligation of humanitarian intervention.

Rather, what is likely meant by those who claim that military action cannot serve humanitarian purposes is that the risk that more harm will be caused by military action than will be prevented is too great. This concern is what Powers calls the concern over perversity.[71] Those who raise the concern over perversity claim that we are not able to predict with certainty the short or long-term consequences of an intervention. The risk of worsening the situation by military intervention and causing more harm than good is too great; therefore, we should refrain from intervening.

The concern over perversity does not provide the basis for an absolute prohibition on intervention, but it highlights an epistemic uncertainty of moral significance that faces those deciding whether to act on a moral obligation of humanitarian intervention. What are the likely consequences of the intervention? In addition, the concern over perversity is a relevant consideration in one's assessment of how the intervention ought to be prosecuted and what must be done afterwards. However, the question of whether an intervention should occur is distinct from the question of how it ought to be prosecuted. Nonetheless, it would be reasonable for one to reject a moral obligation of humanitarian intervention if it is likely that the intervention will worsen the situation.

The concern over perfidy is based upon the possibility that an oppressed group may either exaggerate the nature of the oppression and violence it is being subjected to, or that it may actually use violence to provoke retaliation and a humanitarian crisis in an effort to draw the international community into an internal conflict by creating the need for a humanitarian intervention.[72] At a more general level, the concern over perfidy is based upon the possibility that the more we engage in humanitarian intervention and the more acceptable it becomes, the more such abuses will occur.

Like any slippery slope argument, it is only as good as the reasons underlying each slip in the slide. This is not to say that such concerns are unwarranted. But we need to understand the basis for the supposed slide. It is not just that more interventions will occur, but that those who are provoking the retaliation which in turn leads to the intervention are being rewarded. Again, this is not a concern over the justifiability of a moral obligation of humanitarian intervention; rather it is a concern over how the intervention is prosecuted, and what is done after the military campaign in support of the humanitarian cause has been completed.

It is not clear why this should stand as an objection to intervention on behalf of the innocents whose rights are being violated. The obligation requires that those whose rights are being violated be provided the necessary social guarantees against standard threats to their security. If that means they need to be protected from both sides, then so be it. Nonetheless, the nature of the methodological approach being employed here requires the acceptance of all reasonable concerns. To account for this concern, provocateurs should not be rewarded by a humanitarian intervention, as doing so may encourage others to employ a similar violent strategy. As such, one could reasonably reject a moral obligation of humanitarian intervention if, as conducted, the intervention would encourage others to engage in provocative actions in an effort to entice a humanitarian intervention by the international community.

CONCLUSION: STATEMENT AND APPLICATION OF PRINCIPLE – AN ALL-THINGS-CONSIDERED MORAL OBLIGATION TO INTERVENE IN RWANDA

From this discussion one can infer that the following make up that set of conditions under which no one could reasonably deny that a moral obligation of humanitarian intervention exists:

1. The circumstances must be a violation of the basic right to physical security thus giving rise to the moral obligation of humanitarian intervention;
2. Fulfillment of the moral obligation of humanitarian intervention does not require the obligation bearing states to make substantial internal sacrifices;
3. Intervention would not irreparably harm the existence of a community of moral significance;
4. Intervention would not unjustifiably compromise international peace and security;
5. Those bearing the obligation are capable of effectively fulfilling the obligation of humanitarian intervention;
6. Intervention would not worsen the situation that the intervention is intended to resolve; and
7. Intervention would not undermine the presumption against intervention or reward provocateurs that use violence in their efforts to cause the circumstances that trigger humanitarian intervention.

It is important to note that the conditions are conjunctive. If all but one are met, one would still have a reasonable basis upon which to reject an all-things-considered moral obligation of humanitarian intervention.

A brief overview of the importance of the conditions delineated may be useful. Condition 1 determines whether a moral obligation of humanitarian intervention exists and must be considered in a state's practical deliberations. To borrow from traditional just war theory, it serves as the basis for the claim that humanitarian intervention would be based on a just cause. It should also be noted that for the moral obligation of humanitarian intervention to exist, it must, much like our understanding of the *jus ad bellum* condition by the same name, be a last resort.

Conditions 2–6 can also be thought of in terms that may be familiar to those acquainted with traditional just war theory. Conditions 2, 3, and 4 can be thought of an explicit statement of what constitutes a proportionate response. Conditions 5 and 6 are about the probability that the intervention will be successful. Lastly, Condition 7 is an additional condition that is distinctive, and tied directly to a concern peculiar to humanitarian intervention, and is more similar to the conditions that one might find in a discussion of *jus in bello* as opposed to *jus ad bellum*.

One might note that the conditions fail to emphasize either right authority or right intention; two additional and important conditions found in traditional just war theory. As to the former, the discussion in Chapter 4 regarding the institutionalization of the norm developed in Chapter 3 addresses this condition. As to the latter, it is implicit in the concept of an all-things-considered moral obligation of *humanitarian* intervention that the determinative motive for the intervention must be based in the goal of protecting the basic right of physical security.

1. The circumstances must be a violation of the basic right to physical security thus giving rise to the moral obligation of humanitarian intervention

In Rwanda during the genocide of 1994, if you were a Tutsi or moderate Hutu with Tutsi sympathies you were constantly under the threat of violence against your person, including the threat of death. If anything is a standard threat to physical security, the threat of unprovoked and unjustified violence against one's person is such a threat. The basic right to physical security provides the rational basis for a justified demand that one's physical security be socially guaranteed against such threats. Provision of such socially guaranteed protection would have required that the Hutu extremists conducting the genocide be stopped. Since the government was supporting the genocide, outside intervention would have been necessary to the provision of such socially guaranteed protections. The first condition is met.

2. Fulfillment of the moral obligation of humanitarian intervention does not require the obligation bearing state to make unreasonable internal sacrifices

Some might argue that had intervention been pursued the commitment of resources necessary to effectively accomplish the goals of the intervention would have caused an unjustified sacrifice of the internal obligations of states. To stand as a reason upon which a reasonable rejection could be based, it must have been the case that the sacrifice required would have an unjustifiable impact on the ability of the duty-bearing states to fulfill their internal obligations.

According to Lt-Gen. Romeo Dallaire, the leader of the United Nation's Peace Keeping force in Rwanda at the time of the genocide's commencement, a force of 5,000 well-armed soldiers with the necessary logistical and military support could have stopped the genocide and provided the necessary conditions for the resumption of the Arusha Accords, which would have provided Rwandans with the necessary socially guaranteed protection of their physical security. Various African nations had volunteered to man the intervention. All that was needed from the international community was logistical support and military supplies. The claim that this would have required substantial and unjustifiably large internal sacrifices by states is simply false, and for this reason such a claim would fail as the basis for a reasonable rejection of an all-things-considered moral obligation of humanitarian intervention in Rwanda.

3. It must be the case that the intervention would not irreparably harm a community of moral significance

The first question to be addressed with regard to this condition is whether Rwanda, during the genocide, counted as a community of moral significance; if it did not then one need not assess this condition further as it was not deserving of protection. To be a community of moral significance, and thus deserving of protection against intervention, we must be able to identify the community in question and it must fulfill and protect the rights of its inhabitants. It is clear that in the case of Rwanda during the genocide there was no such community, and the community that would have been protected by nonintervention was comprised of the Hutu extremists engaged in the systematic violation of the rights of Rwanda's Tutsi population.

In addition, the intervention would have served to re-establish the implementation of the Arusha Accords which would have promoted and protected a community of moral significance. Thus, the claim that intervention in Rwanda would have irreparably harmed a community of moral significance would fail as the basis for a reasonable rejection of an all-things-considered moral obligation of humanitarian intervention in Rwanda.

4. It must be the case that international security is not unjustifiably compromised by the fulfillment of the moral obligation of humanitarian intervention

Prior to the genocide the Rwanda Patriotic Front and the Rwandan government had entered into a peace and power-sharing agreement, the Arusha Accords, which was intended to bring peace, not only to Rwanda, but to the region as a whole. The renewal of violence by the Rwandan government under the control of the Hutu extremists undermined the Arusha Accords and international peace and security. Military intervention and the re-establishment of the Arusha Accords would have increased international security, not undermined it. In addition, as a matter of historical fact, the genocide created millions of refugees who poured into neighboring countries further destabilizing the region. Thus, the claim that intervention would have undermined international peace and security is belied by the facts; and as a consequence, fails as the basis for a reasonable rejection of an all-things-considered moral obligation of humanitarian intervention in Rwanda.

5. It must be the case that those bearing the obligation are capable of effectively fulfilling the obligation of humanitarian intervention

The obligation to provide the socially guaranteed protection of physical security against standard threats was borne directly by individuals. It would be reasonable for one to reject the claim that individuals *qua* individuals were under an obligation to conduct an intervention as their effort would likely be futile. However, states are the instruments by which individuals are capable of coordinating their efforts and fulfilling such obligations. States individually, or the international community as a collection of duty-bearing states, could have provided the logistical, political, and military support necessary for the intervention to be successful. As a consequence, the claim that the effort would have been futile would fail as the basis for a reasonable rejection of an all-things-considered moral obligation of humanitarian intervention in Rwanda.

6. *It must be the case that intervention would not worsen the situation that the intervention was intended to resolve*

One might claim that when intervention was finally attempted through Operation Turquoise, the French forces actually made the situation worse, and so it would be reasonable to conclude that intervention would have made the situation worse no matter when it was attempted or by whom. Such an assertion is belied by the facts. The French had waited until the Rwanda Patriotic Front had essentially stopped the genocide, and then the French operated under the assumption that both Tutsis and Hutus had engaged in mass killings despite the fact that French government officials knew otherwise. If Operation Turquoise teaches us anything, it is the need to act quickly in the case of genocide and that the international community must have a real commitment to the intervention and its humanitarian goals.

7. *It must be the case that the intervention would not undermine the presumption against intervention or reward provocateurs who use violence in their efforts to cause the circumstances that trigger humanitarian intervention*

The Rwandan genocide began amidst an effort for peace, and was the result of unprovoked violence against innocent civilians by the genocidaires. This does not even fit the case of perfidy. In addition, according to Dallaire, the Rwanda Patriotic Front refrained from military action until it was absolutely clear that the international community was going to do nothing. The presumption against intervention was clearly rebutted in this case and the facts of the situation would have highlighted the fact that only in extreme cases would military intervention be used. Thus a charge of perfidy would fail as the basis for a reasonable rejection of an all-things-considered moral obligation of humanitarian intervention in Rwanda.

Conclusion: An All-things-considered Moral Obligation of Humanitarian Intervention

In conclusion, there existed an all-things-considered moral obligation to intervene in Rwanda in 1994 to prevent the genocide from occurring or to stop it once it had begun. Each of the relevant conditions has been met, and as a consequence there is little basis for a reasonable rejection of the claim that such an obligation existed. I believe that I have demonstrated that it would be unreasonable for one to reject that a moral obligation of humanitarian intervention existed as an all-things-considered obligation in the case of Rwanda. But, admittedly, I have not accounted, nor do I think I have the mental capacity to account, for the multitude of arguments that have not been considered. Nonetheless, even if such an argument exists, I remain convinced that our better considered moral judgment, based on the arguments I have presented and critiqued, should lead us to the conclusion that an all-things-considered moral obligation of humanitarian intervention is possible, and that it did exist in the case of Rwanda.

Chapter 3

THE NORMATIVE FRAMEWORK OF INTERNATIONAL RELATIONS

Article 2
The Organization [the United Nations] and its Members in pursuit of the Purposes stated in Article I, shall act in accordance with the following Principles:
1. The Organization is based on the principle of the sovereign equality of all its Members . . .
4. All Members shall refrain in their international relations from the threat or use of force against the territorial integrity or political independence of any State, or in any other manner inconsistent with the Purposes of the United Nations.[1]

INTRODUCTION

In Chapter 2 it was argued that the international community, as a collection of duty-bearing states, bore an all-things-considered moral obligation of humanitarian intervention to prevent or stop the genocide in Rwanda. However, as we are all now painfully aware, intervention did not occur. Assuming that there was a conclusive moral reason to intervene in Rwanda, what went wrong? One reason for the failure was not a matter of morality *per se*; rather the prevailing view at the time was that the principles and institutions governing the practical deliberations of states precluded states from considering moral reasons for action that would require interference in the internal affairs of another sovereign state. As such, the moral obligation of humanitarian intervention would have been precluded from the practical deliberations of the international community.

The fact that a system of conventional rules exists tells us nothing about whether the system is justified. As such, the next issue to be

89

addressed is whether the principles and institutions that governed the practical deliberations of states (and the international community) during the Rwandan genocide can be justified? If not, what rules ought to govern the international community's practical deliberations when the international community is faced with a grave humanitarian crisis? Chapter 3 is focused on answering these questions and setting the stage for a discussion of the institutionalization of the moral obligation of humanitarian intervention to be taken up in Chapter 4.

With regard to the first question, the answer begins with a discussion of some of the most commonly cited arguments in support of the claim that states ought *not* to consider interventionist moral demands in their practical deliberations. I conclude that none of these arguments is capable of justifying a principle of practical deliberation with such a preclusive effect. In response to the second question, I argue that a rebuttable presumption of nonintervention should guide the practical deliberations of the international community.

It is important to note the significance of the analysis in Chapter 3 to the larger discussion and the transition from theory to practice. The role of the political philosopher is complicated by the inherently interdisciplinary nature of the field of study; moving between the philosophical and the practical, using our analytic skills to critically assess the theoretical underpinnings of claims made or positions taken in politics, ethics, law, and international relations. To have success in this endeavor, it is essential to be able to converse in the conceptual language of one discipline, then another, and back again.[2]

In addition, my focus on the right of nonintervention as it relates to the practical deliberations of states is based in part on the desire to have an impact on the way states act in the international arena. To have such a desired effect, one must begin with the practical deliberations of the agents with which one is concerned. With that goal in mind, I find Onora O'Neill's discussion of the challenges faced when seeking to affect the practical/ethical reasoning of other agents to be insightful. O'Neill claims that "[w]hat is needed is a theory of obligation which is not only universal and critical but accessible to the relevant agents and agencies."[3]

It is the notion of accessibility that is of particular relevance to this discussion. The critical assessment of the normative framework of international relations must be accessible to those whose decisions are governed by it. Taking O'Neill's concerns to heart, there is a need for a common grounding from which the critical analysis can proceed; and the discussion in this chapter is intended, in part, to bridge the gaps between a number of related but distinct disciplines. For that reason, the methodology employed in the critical analysis that follows begins with the identification of arguments pressed by those seeking to defend the right of nonintervention, and then proceeds to a critical assessment of those arguments on the terms presented.

THE NORMATIVE FRAMEWORK OF INTERNATIONAL RELATIONS, STATE SOVEREIGNTY AND THE RIGHT OF NONINTERVENTION

To begin, one must have an understanding of what is meant by the normative framework of international relations. The normative framework of international relations (also referred to as the "normative framework") is constituted by the principles that govern the practical deliberations of states. Two aspects of the normative framework must be discussed – the scope of the framework and the content of its governing principles. There are many who argue that the scope of the normative framework is constituted and exhausted by sovereign states. In his discussion of the role of human rights in international relations, David P. Forsythe has noted that "it has been widely believed that the state, not the individual is the basic unit."[4] As to international law Michael Byers notes, "States are usually considered to be the only holders of full legal personality. In principle, all States have the same degree of legal personality, and in that sense all States are formally equal."[5] Finally, but less approvingly, Charles R. Beitz has pointed out that the presumption that states are the only relevant actors in international relations is taken to be necessary in contemporary international political theory.[6] Though this view may be changing, it remains a high hurdle for anyone seeking to press an argument that requires international legal and political institutions to be primarily concerned with the interests of individual human beings. As to the content of the normative framework, "the core principle has been said to be state sovereignty and noninterference in the domestic affairs of states" – a right of nonintervention possessed by all sovereign states held against all other sovereign states and the international community.[7]

The conflict between the normative framework of international relations and the moral obligation to intervene in Rwanda should be apparent. A moral obligation to intervene in Rwanda (or anywhere else) would be based on the basic right to physical security held by, and correlative duties borne by, individuals. Since, traditionally, the scope of the normative framework extends only to sovereign states, the concerns of individuals *as individuals* were considered to be beyond the scope of the normative framework. Thus, violations of the Rwandan Tutsis' individual rights were not, in and of themselves, relevant reasons for states to consider in their practical deliberations.

More readily apparent is the conflict between the right of nonintervention and the moral obligation of humanitarian intervention. Under the normative framework, the only generally accepted exceptions to the right of nonintervention are threats to international order – international peace and security.[8] If the internal actions of a state pose a threat to international order, intervention may be permissible to protect international order. Violations of the basic right to physical security sufficient to trigger the moral obligation of humanitarian intervention would not necessarily pose a threat to international order. Thus, when the basic right to physical security is being violated but international order is not threatened, intervention would not be justified.

Though the normative framework is changing, many hold fast to the basic principles that led the international community to choose not to intervene in Rwanda.[9] To determine what went wrong in Rwanda in 1994 and to insure that it does not happen again, one needs to understand the nature of the normative framework operative in 1994. In particular, one must understand the notion of state sovereignty relevant to international relations, the right of nonintervention, and the various relationships that are thought to connect the two.

Under the normative framework of international relations, the possession of sovereignty by a state is presumed to entail that the state in question possesses certain rights and privileges in relation to other states individually and the international community as a collection of sovereign states. One such right, and the one most central to this discussion, is the right of nonintervention. But how could the possession of sovereignty grant a political organization an entitlement to oppress, exploit, and even kill its own inhabitants without the fear of interference from other states? To answer this question, one must understand what it means for a state to have sovereignty.

The discussion here begins with the classic account provided by Thomas Hobbes as it serves as the starting point for much of the contemporary discussion of sovereignty and the role it plays in the state system.[10] The sovereign comes into existence and is granted its normative standing through the creation of a social contract.[11] For Hobbes, the standing of the sovereign is based on the condition that the "commonwealth" created provide internal peace and security from outside interference.[12] These are the necessary and sufficient conditions for the political organization in question to be sovereign. As Hobbes states,

> The only way to erect such a Common Power, as may be able to defend them from the invasion of Forraigners, and the injuries of one another and thereby to secure them in such sorts as that by their owne industrie, and by the fruites of the Earth, they may nourish themselves and live contentedly; is, to conferre all their power and strength upon one Man, or upon one Assembly of men, that may reduce all their Wills, by plurality of voices into one Will . . .[13]

Sovereignty, for Hobbes, is comprised of the powers and rights possessed by the sovereign.[14]

A more contemporary assessment of the classical account is provided by Robert Keohane. According to Keohane, "[t]he classic unitary conception of sovereignty is the doctrine that sovereign states exercise both internal supremacy over all other authorities within a given territory, and external independence of outside authorities."[15] Keohane fails, however, to mark an important distinction in how we ought to understand the role of sovereignty in the normative framework of international relations.

On this point, Christopher Morris has recognized that, at least in discussions over the nature of sovereignty, "[i]t is common to distinguish internal and external aspects of sovereignty".[16] However, for many scholars of international relations and international law, the conceptual distinction between internal and external sovereignty is not simply rhetorical; it is essential. The two types of sovereignty can be individuated based upon the different relationships that define them. Understanding this difference helps to explain why many have thought that external sovereignty is relevant to the normative framework of international relations, but internal sovereignty is not. I hasten to note that this is not a position that I endorse; though it does provide insight into why the normative framework of international relations resulted in the international community's choice not to intervene in Rwanda.

As Morris notes, "[i]nternal sovereignty pertains to the governance of the realm; external sovereignty, to independence of other states."[17] In other words, internal sovereignty is related to the internal affairs of a political organization; and the relevant parties to the constitutive relationship are the governmental institutions of states and those they govern.[18] Under the classical account of sovereignty, a state has internal sovereignty if it is the supreme political authority within a particular territory.[19] So what exactly does that mean? In short, a state's claimed authority must be the source of all other political authority within a given territory and the state must claim a monopoly on the legitimate use of force within that territory.[20] As internal sovereignty is a matter of internal political relations, and the understanding of the normative framework of international relations under discussion is concerned with external political relations, internal sovereignty is largely irrelevant to our understanding of the relationship between sovereignty and the normative framework of international relations.

External sovereignty, on the other hand, is concerned with the relations between states; it is "an attribute which political bodies possess in relation to other such bodies."[21] The normative framework of international relations is built around this conception of sovereignty. To understand external sovereignty and the role it plays in the normative framework of international relations, it is important to understand the difference between external sovereignty as a descriptive matter and external sovereignty as an attribution of normative status. The two notions may, as Hobbes seemed to think, be inexorably tied together in that having sovereignty in the descriptive sense makes a political organization sovereign which, in turn, serves as the basis for the possession of the rights and duties of which the normative notion of sovereignty is comprised.[22] For reasons discussed below, such an account is untenable.

To possess external sovereignty in the descriptive sense is a matter of meeting certain factual conditions. A state possesses external sovereignty if it stands in the requisite relationship to other similar political organizations – that a state is politically independent of other states.[23] On the other hand, under the normative use of the term, sovereignty is intended to signify a complex web of rights and duties possessed by political organizations with external sovereignty; most important to this discussion is the right of nonintervention. The normative status ascribed to states that possess external sovereignty is a conventional matter institutionalized in international relations and international law. Without an argument connecting the two, the normative status associated with the ascription of sovereignty is distinct from the satisfaction of the factual conditions necessary for the possession of sovereignty. An independent justification for the rights attributed to sovereign states is needed.

Of particular importance to this discussion is the fact that the normative framework of international relations is based on the relationship between external sovereignty and the right of nonintervention. However, before we can assess the nature of this relationship, we must understand the right of nonintervention. Rights are typically constituted by claims (legal, conventional, or moral) held by one entity against another which are a source of duties borne by the latter and owed to the former. They are, in Hohfeldian terms, jural correlatives.[24] As discussed above, the explication of a right, duty, or obligation will include the identification of the content, strength, and scope of the norm at issue.[25]

Beginning with the scope, if we are to understand the right as an operative principle of the normative framework, since it is a fundamental principle governing the normative framework of international relations it should be consistent with the scope of the normative framework itself. Since, under the normative framework of international relations, the only relevant actors are presumed to be sovereign states, the right of nonintervention is held by sovereign states, and the correlative duty to refrain from intervening is borne by states, both individually and collectively.

As to the content of the right of nonintervention and its correlative duty, the right of nonintervention is presumed to give a right-holding state a claim to be free from outside interference, and that it should be allowed to govern its internal affairs as it sees fit. The claimed liberty, though absolute with regard to the internal affairs of a state, does admit of certain limitations with regard to actions affecting other states. Under the right of nonintervention, actions of a state are limited much like the actions of an individual under Mill's harm principle.[26] Under Mill's harm principle, individuals have a great deal of discretion over how to exercise their rights; including that they may act in ways that harm themselves provided they are not harming others. As such, the rights of others are an implicit limitation on an individual's rights. I cannot exercise my right in a way that harms yours. Analogously, as to its internal affairs, under the right of nonintervention a sovereign state has a protected liberty to engage in any action that does not harm another state or pose a threat to international order.

As to the correlative duty, states as bearers of the duty are under an obligation to refrain from engaging in actions that interfere with the protected liberty of the right holder. The duty, however, does not require the bearer of the duty to refrain from interfering when the actions engaged in by the right holder go beyond the protected sphere of liberty governed by the right of nonintervention. Thus, the duty demands that the duty bearer not intervene in the internal affairs of another state provided that the right-holding state's actions are not going to harm the duty bearer, or pose a threat to international order.

Finally, regarding the strength of the right, other than the maintenance of international order, the right of nonintervention is presumed to be the weightiest second-order exclusionary reason to be considered in the practical deliberations of states in the international arena.[27] What this means is that provided international order is not at stake, the duty to refrain from intervening correlative to the right of nonintervention is presumed to be a conclusive reason for states not to interfere in the internal affairs of another state. It is both a first-order reason for noninterference and a second-order reason to exclude from consideration reasons for action the fulfillment of which would require intervention, and it is the latter aspect of the right that requires justification.

To sum up, the right of nonintervention is a right held by sovereign states to govern their internal affairs as they see fit free from outside interference, and it gives rise to a correlative duty borne by all other sovereign states and the international community as a collection of duty-bearing states not to consider reasons for action that would require the violation of another state's sovereignty. This is a fairly crude understanding of the nature of the right of nonintervention; however, it should suffice for this discussion.

Returning to the discussion of the relationship between the right of nonintervention and the possession of external sovereignty, under the normative framework of international relations, the right of nonintervention is argued to be either implied by or derived from the possession of external sovereignty. If the right of nonintervention is to be implied simply by the possession of external sovereignty, the general argument must run as follows:

> If a state has the ability to protect and maintain its political independence then it has a claim held against other states to remain politically independent without the threat of intervention.

As a matter of conceptual implication, this cannot be correct. The ability to do something does not imply a right as a protected liberty to engage in that action. It would make no more sense to say that a state has a right to be politically independent because it has the ability to remain so, than it would be to say that I have the right to torture puppies because I have the ability to do so.

One might contend that in assessing this argument the focus has been on the wrong notion of sovereignty. The objection might run as follows:

> Of course, the possession of state sovereignty does not imply the right of nonintervention. The possession of state sovereignty is a descriptive fact, and cannot, without more, imply a normative principle. However, as was noted previously, in addition to the descriptive notion, sovereignty often refers to the normative status one state has in relation to other states, and one important aspect of a sovereign state's normative status is that sovereign states have the right of nonintervention. Thus, the right of nonintervention is not only implied by the possession of state sovereignty under this normative understanding, it is constitutive of sovereignty.

Hobbes's understanding of the relationship between being a sovereign and its possession of the rights and duties associated with the normative understanding of sovereignty is captured by the argument underlying this response. Nonetheless, the response would fail as it begs the very question that needs to be answered – whether the right of nonintervention, as an aspect of sovereignty under this normative connotation, can be justified.

An alternative version of this justification is discussed by Mark W. Janis. According to Janis, the relationship between the right of nonintervention and external sovereignty arose out of the Peace of Westphalia.[28] Under this account, the relationship is the result of a set of legal accords *designed* to provide peace and security and is based upon the idea that respect for the external sovereignty of each state would be the best means of providing peace and security.[29] Hans Morgenthau argues that the right of nonintervention was actually a result of the French revolution and the claim by the French that under international relations other states were obligated to refrain from interfering in the internal affairs of France.[30] Under either account it is claimed that the right of nonintervention is related to external sovereignty through conventional rules designed to resolve a political/moral crisis, and not by some sort of inherent or necessary implication.

One might contend that an implication based on a conventional set of rules should be sufficient; that the set of rules taken together justify the constitutive rules that make up the system. However, conventional systems and the rules of which they are comprised are open to our adjustment or elimination should they prove to be unjustified; morally or practically. Such systems require justification with regard to the purposes they are intended to serve and the rules of which they are comprised. Consequently, the existence of a conventional system cannot provide the justification for the principles that are constitutive of the system itself. What is needed is, at the very least, a convincing moral argument justifying the system.

This lack of necessary implication should not be taken as a denial of the moral significance of the right of nonintervention. Rather, the lack of direct implication merely refocuses the discussion. The right of nonintervention is a normative principle that needs to be justified, and as it is not necessarily implied by the possession of external sovereignty, it needs an independent justification through arguments that explain why the possession of external sovereignty *should* entail a right of nonintervention.

At this point, one might contend that the descriptive project with which the discussion is at present concerned has been abandoned – the explication of the right of nonintervention as an operative principle of the normative framework of international relations. The claim would be that the contention that the right of nonintervention is not implied by state sovereignty is more a matter of conceptual criticism than simply a description of the relationship that is presumed to exist. Such an objection, however, would miss the point. A failure to recognize the lack of implication between the possession of state sovereignty and the right of nonintervention, and a failure to acknowledge the conventional relationship between state sovereignty and the right of nonintervention would render the descriptive account a mere strawman argument. In providing this alternative view of the relationship, the proper focus of analysis has been identified – the justificatory arguments for the right of nonintervention as a conventional rule of the normative framework of international relations.

JUSTIFYING THE RIGHT OF NONINTERVENTION

The arguments offered as justifications for the right of nonintervention fall into three basic categories: arguments from autonomy, arguments from the principle of anti-paternalism, and instrumental arguments. In order to avoid confusion, it is important to note that the term 'instrumental' is being used to refer to arguments that are based on the contention that a right of nonintervention is instrumental to the provision and protection of international peace and security. This distinction is important because many of the arguments to be discussed might be considered instrumental arguments of one sort or another.

Arguments from Autonomy

Justifications for the right of nonintervention based on autonomy come in at least three forms, two of which are based on the domestic analogy. Beitz, though not a proponent of arguments based on the domestic analogy , succinctly captures the underlying analogy, "like persons in domestic society, states in international society are to be treated as autonomous sources of ends, morally immune from external interference, and morally free to arrange their internal affairs as their government sees fit."[31]

One version of the analogical form of the argument is grounded in the proposition that international relations is like a Hobbesian state of nature. For Hobbes the state of nature is a war of all against all.[32] Under such circumstances it would be irrational for any single individual to conform his/her behavior to the demands of morality unless one could be assured that others would do so as well. Consequently, since no individual agent can be certain that others would respect such demands, morality is not relevant to the determination of how an individual ought to act in the state of nature.[33] Since in the state of nature no one has reason to abide by a moral code that would require him or her to act against his/her own best interest, the natural law that exists in the state of nature is for each individual to act prudentially.[34] Men join together to form societies as a matter of self-interest, and morality is created when the reigns of authority and power of enforcement are granted to a sovereign through the formation of a social contract.[35] If, however, no contract is created and no sovereign granted the power to enforce the demands of morality, the only guiding principle for individual action would remain prudence.

As to the justification for the right of nonintervention, there is no sovereign in the international arena to enforce the demands morality might place on states; as such, sovereign states are like individuals in a Hobbesian state of nature, and as Hobbes states, "every common-wealth, (not every man) has an absolute liberty, to do what it shall judge (that is to say, what that man, or assembly that representeth it, shall judge) most conducing to their benefit."[36] As a consequence, just like individuals in a Hobbesian state of nature, the only principles guiding a state's actions are self-interest and prudence. To act otherwise would be irrational.

It is hard to see how such an account could imply a right of nonintervention. In a circumstance in which a state could benefit by intervening in the internal affairs of another state it would entail the opposite – that as a matter of self-interest or prudence, a state would be obligated to intervene. In fact, under such an account, if self-interest demanded it, a state would be obligated to engage in an aggressive war. I will not consider this argument further as it is incapable of justifying a right of nonintervention.

An alternative, and more promising, form of the argument from autonomy is based upon John Stuart Mill's understanding of the nature and value of autonomy to individuals.[37] This argument again invokes the domestic analogy.[38] The central feature of this account is the recognition that the value of individual autonomy is so important that it ought not to be interfered with. As Mill states, "In the part [of an individual's conduct] which merely concerns himself, his independence is, of right absolute. Over himself, over his own body and mind, the individual is sovereign."[39] The argument proceeds by claiming that the value of sovereignty to a state is analogous to the value of autonomy to an individual; thus, by analogy, sovereignty ought not to be interfered with.[40]

The third and final form of the argument from autonomy is not analogical. Michael Walzer argues that the right of nonintervention can be justified by appeal to Mill's arguments regarding self-determination.[41] Walzer, however, explicitly recognizes that acts by a state or a government that "shock the conscience" may, as an exception to the right of nonintervention, justify intervention.[42] Walzer's conclusion that we are (at the very least) permitted to intervene when events internal to another state shock the conscience of mankind seems correct, but his arguments and methodology are lacking and his standard unnecessarily demanding and too vague to be useful.

In short, a standard that relies on what actually "shocks the conscience" is too reliant on intuitions and subjective evaluation to serve any useful purpose. If what Walzer means is that intervention is permitted when actions internal to another state *should* "shock the conscience of mankind," then an argument is needed to explain why one act *should* shock the conscience while another *should not*. It is not enough to look to the international community's reaction after a genocide; because, as a matter of historical fact, at the time of the perpetration of a genocide the consciences of a sufficient number of people were not shocked.

In addition, Walzer's argument for the permissibility of humanitarian intervention is built around the claim that a stringent right of nonintervention is justified and that the occasions that "shock the conscience" are exceptions to the rule. One could accept Walzer's argument for the right of nonintervention, but reject his claim that it admits of any exceptions. Lastly, Walzer's standard is disturbingly *post hoc*, as if the only way we can be sufficiently certain that a horrific event that ought to be prevented is going to occur is to wait for its actual occurrence. For these reasons, I am focusing on the underlying argument, but thought it only fair to recognize that Walzer shares the intuition that humanitarian intervention is, under certain circumstances, at least permissible.

Returning to Walzer's argument, in defense of the right of nonintervention, to be self-determined,

> The members of a political community must seek their own freedom, just as the individual must cultivate his own virtue. They cannot be set free, as he cannot be made virtuous, by any external force. Indeed political freedom depends upon the existence of individual virtue, and this the armies of another state are most unlikely to produce . . .[43]

For Walzer, the importance of self-determination in political matters gives rise to the duty borne by states to refrain from interfering in the internal affairs of another state. As Walzer goes on to state the value of self-determination gives rise to the

> right of a people "to become free by their own efforts" if they can, and nonintervention is the principle guaranteeing that their success will not be impeded or their failure prevented by the intrusions of an alien power.[44]

To respect the liberty of the individual inhabitants of a state, the inhabitants of that state must be allowed to "seek their own freedom" free from the interference of other states.

Anti-paternalism as a Justification for the Right of Nonintervention

A second form of justificatory argument for the right of nonintervention is based upon various arguments against paternalism in international relations.[45] Much like Mill's contention that paternalism with regards to individual liberty cannot be justified,[46] Walzer notes, "[a]s with individuals, so with sovereign states: there are things that we cannot do to them, even for their own ostensible good."[47] One of these "things we cannot do to them" is to intervene in their internal affairs. First and foremost this argument depends upon the successful defense of the principle of anti-paternalism as a governing norm of international relations.

There are a number of arguments based on the principle of anti-paternalism to be considered. One argument is analogical and is based on Mill's arguments against paternalism in the lives of individuals. An alternative account relying on the principle of anti-paternalism is based on the contention that the principle of anti-paternalism in international affairs is justified because it is a value-neutral principle that recognizes that there are competing conceptions of the good, and that each sovereign state should be left to choose its own conception of the good from amongst such competing conceptions. It is important to note that the notions "the good" and "conceptions of the good" are being used in a loose sense referring simply to the moral system that people accept to guide their behavior. This is not meant to preclude a conception of the good that is rights-based.

Regarding the first form of the argument, its proponents are S. I. Benn, R. S. Peters,[48] and R. J. Vincent.[49] The argument they press in support of the principle of anti-paternalism as a justification for the right of nonintervention is similar to Mill's argument for the rejection of the principle of paternalism as it relates to individual agents. As Benn and Peters claim, "The duty of noninterference rests on the assumption that the claims of a state's members will generally be better served if they are left to work out their own salvation."[50] This is analogous to Mill's argument from anti-paternalism justifying the claim that a state should not interfere with the self-regarding actions of an individual.[51] The specific justifications offered by Mill fall into two categories. First, Mill claims that individuals are in an epistemically privileged position when it comes to knowing what is in their best interest. Second, Mill claims that the harm caused by interference with individual liberty, even if intended to benefit the individual, will outweigh any potential benefits.[52]

According to Beitz, similar to Mill, Benn and Peters contend

> that intervention in a state's internal affairs cannot be justified on paternalistic grounds because the intervening state is unlikely to be impartial and because, in any event, a state is more likely to know its own best interests than any other state.[53]

Like Mill's reasons for rejecting paternalism in the lives of individuals, Benn and Peters's reasons are contingent, and the success of the argument depends on the truth of its underlying factual claims. Is it actually the case that states are in a privileged epistemic position with regards to their best interests?

The other version of the argument from anti-paternalism takes two distinct forms. One is offered by William E. Hall, and the other by Jovan Babic. Hall seeks to justify the application of the principle of anti-paternalism to international relations by first noting that there are competing conceptions of the good; and that with regard to individuals the principle of anti-paternalism is generally recognized as a neutral position that allows individuals to pursue their own conceptions of the good.[54] Hall then invokes the domestic analogy, claiming that states in international relations are analogous to individuals in domestic society.[55] Therefore, if the principle of anti-paternalism is a principle governing the treatment of individuals in domestic society, it is, by analogy, a principle that ought to govern the way states treat one another in international relations.

Babic's argument, on the other hand, does not rely on the domestic analogy. Rather, Babic's argument is rooted in respect for individual human rights.[56] Babic contends that states ought to refrain from interfering in the internal affairs of other states, even if such interference is intended to serve the interests of the latter state's inhabitants, because the former's "value system" or "definition of 'good'" is but one amongst a number of different competing conceptions.[57] Respect for individual human rights requires that states show tolerance for the conceptions of the good chosen by individuals in other states even if such choices appear to be morally or practically wrong.[58]

Instrumental Justification for the Right of Nonintervention

The final justificatory argument to be addressed is based on the claim that the right of nonintervention is instrumental to achieving the goal of international order. As Janis has pointed out, the pre-Westphalian interactions between states were violent and anarchic:

> The conflicting allegiances of Europe had contributed to the terrible toll of confusion, death, and destruction from 1618 to 1648. In the mid-seventeenth century many Europeans sought a simpler, and it was hoped, safer set of loyalties.[59]

Many have argued that the respect for the sovereignty of states expressed by the right of nonintervention converted the chaos of the pre-Westphalian world into "international order."[60]

Looking to the Charter of the United Nations for some guidance regarding the meaning of international order, one of the "Purposes of the United Nations" is to "maintain international peace and security."[61] Michael Taylor's account of social order at the domestic level provides some insight into the Hobbesian account of the role of sovereignty in the international arena.[62] For Taylor, domestic social order "refers to an absence, more or less complete, of violence, a state of affairs in which people are relatively safe from physical attack."[63] It is the desire for social order that grounds our understanding of the Hobbesian social contract.[64] The analogous desire upon which the instrumental argument would be based in the international arena is the desire by states for international peace and security ("international order").

As such, to understand this argument it is essential that one understand what is meant by international peace and security. The relevant notion of peace should be consistent with the presumed scope of the normative framework of international relations that the only relevant actors are sovereign states. As such, threats to international peace are threats to the peace between states. Similarly, international security refers to the security of a state from aggression or intervention by other states. A state is secure if other states refrain or are prevented from engaging in either aggressive action toward the state or intervention into the internal affairs of the state. If states refrained from acting on reasons the fulfillment of which would require intervention, then international peace and security would, at the very least, be more likely.

In recent times, other concerns related to humanitarian crises as a basis for military action have arisen. These contemporary concerns are based in the potential that any justification for intervention into the internal affairs of another state may be used as a pretext for less salutary purposes. As Stanley Hoffmann has pointed out:

> in a world of states, sovereignty [and the right of nonintervention] protects one against outsiders trying to topple the government or to set up a puppet regime or to impose their views of what is good and right – hence the particularly strong attachment of countries recently liberated from colonial rule to the principle of nonintervention.[65]

The right of nonintervention is also argued to prevent the possibility of a state using a humanitarian or other proffered moral justification as a pretext for an aggressive war.

CRITICALLY ASSESSING THE JUSTIFICATORY ARGUMENTS

The next step in the critical evaluation of the normative framework of international relations and the right of nonintervention in particular is determining whether any of the arguments discussed above are capable of justifying a principle of nonintervention that precludes moral interventionist reasons for action from the practical deliberations of states and the international community. First to be addressed are the various

Millian analogical arguments from autonomy and anti-paternalism. Next will be the argument from self-determination offered by Walzer, and the arguments from anti-paternalism offered by Hall and Babic. Lastly, the instrumental argument is critically assessed, and though it fails to justify a principle with the sort of preclusive effect that the right of nonintervention has often been thought to have, it is the most promising argument for framing the way we *ought* to think about what sort of principle would be justified.

The Millian Analogical Arguments

For an analogical argument to succeed it must be the case that the grounding proposition or argument is sufficiently similar to the proposition or argument being justified by the analogy. As the analogical arguments being discussed rely on the domestic analogy, it must be the case that individuals in domestic society are sufficiently similar to states in international relations, and that the relationship between the relevant parties and the identified properties and principles are sufficiently similar as well.

To use a simple analogy to explain, one might claim that a referee is to a soccer match what a judge is to a courtroom. Whether this analogy is a good one will depend on what the analogy is intended to convey about either the referee's role in a soccer match or a judge's role in a trial. One might be seeking to defend or explain the idea of judicial discretion. In which case, the judge like the referee has varying degrees of discretion at different times during a trial as well as in different trial settings. If, on the other hand, one is trying to defend the claim that much like the rules governing the referee in the soccer match, the rules governing the judge are entirely conventional and do not rely on morality for their justification; the analogy is less clear and the proposition being defended by the analogy in much greater need of an independent defense. In short, the strength of an analogical argument is going to depend both on the specific aspect of the relationship that is being defended by the analogy and the similarity between the relevant aspects of the claimed analogous pairs.

The grounding proposition of the analogical arguments is that individuals are the paramount, if not the only, relevant moral agents in the domestic sphere. Thus, for the analogy to hold, states in the international arena must be the paramount, if not the only, relevant moral agents in the international arena. One can assume that, *as a matter of convention*, states are the only relevant moral agents in international relations. However, as was noted above, one cannot rely on the conventions one is seeking to justify to justify the conventions themselves. In addition, the claim that states are the only relevant moral agents in international relations is contradicted by actual practice. As Charles Beitz has pointed out, there are a multitude of nongovernmental organizations and secondary associations that are given moral consideration when a state is determining what it ought to do.[66]

What is needed is an argument demonstrating that states ought to be considered paramount in the international arena. Such an argument would have to demonstrate that individual moral agents, when juxtaposed with states, are not of paramount moral concern. If we make the assumption that a state's moral legitimacy is determined by the degree to which the state serves the interests of its inhabitants, then, in the domestic case, the moral value of the state cannot be greater than the moral value of the individuals it is intended to serve as its worth depends on the degree to which it serves the interests of its inhabitants. As a consequence, to support the analogy, one would have to explain why the value of the individual inhabitants of a state, which are normatively prior to the value of the state in the domestic arena, are trumped by the value of the state in the international arena without relying on the claim that states are paramount in international relations.

If states aren't the only relevant moral agents in the international arena, there are further problematic implications for the analogical arguments. Common to both Millian analogical arguments is the claim that an individual's right to noninterference is limited by the rights of other relevant moral agents to be free from harm or interference.[67] It is accepted that the rights of states in international relations are limited by the rights of other states. However, if states are not the only relevant moral agents, then when a state's actions pose a threat of harm to the rights of other relevant moral agents, including individuals, states cannot claim that their actions are protected by a right of nonintervention. In the cases that would give rise to an obligation of humanitarian intervention, individuals are being harmed or are being threatened with harm and thus the state cannot claim a right of nonintervention; at least not under this argument.

As to the principle of anti-paternalism in particular, according to Mill, with regard to the individual in domestic society, the principle is justified by the fact that an individual knows what is in his/her own interest better than anyone else could, and/or that any interference with the individual's autonomy is likely to produce a greater harm than it prevents.[68] Even if we assume that this is true in the individual case, it would seem to have very little empirical support when it comes to states that are violating or allowing the violation of their citizens' basic rights. In addition, in such cases, the advent of mass communication, globalization, and growing intercultural exchange makes the claim that a state *always* knows, better than outsiders, what is in the best interests of its inhabitants an unlikely proposition.[69] Lastly, in any case where it is clear that the state is acting against the better interests of its inhabitants, for example failing to respect the basic right to physical security, the justification fails. The contingent nature of the justification is incompatible with a *right* of nonintervention.

As to the analogical argument from autonomy, we can assume for the sake of argument that Mill is correct in his claim that the value of autonomy to individual agents is inherent. We can also assume that Mill is correct in his claim that there are actions in which an individual engages that only affect the individual him/herself. Since individual autonomy is inherently valuable, interference with an individual's exercise of his/her autonomy in such self-regarding cases would be an unjustified infringement. For the analogy to hold, it is not enough to demonstrate that the relationship that exists between sovereignty and the state and autonomy and an individual are sufficiently similar; it must also be the case that the value of sovereignty is sufficiently similar to the value of individual autonomy. Since sovereignty is conventional, the system of which it is a part can claim whatever it likes about the relationship between sovereignty and states. As such, I will assume that as a matter of convention the first proposition is true.

However, even if we assume that the value of sovereignty to a state is analogous with the value of autonomy to an individual human agent, this fails to entail a right of nonintervention. The analogy employed tells us little about what might be implied by state sovereignty or what its value is. The argument points out nothing more than that the relationship that exists between sovereignty and states is analogous to the relationship that exists between autonomy and individual human agents; it must also be the case that the value of sovereignty is similar enough to the value of autonomy such that it ought not be interfered with.

For Mill, autonomy is a set of capacities possessed by an individual.[70] Specifically, it is the set of capacities that give human agents the ability to rationally direct their lives. It is the possession and exercise of such capacities which make the individual's choice of action of paramount, if not inherent, value.[71] Similarly, the possession of sovereignty by a state is a matter of the state possessing certain capacities, viz. the ability to maintain its political independence. However, the ability to maintain political independence fails, without more, to render a sovereign state's choice of action of paramount, nevertheless inherent, value. The ability of a state to maintain its political independence is valuable to the extent that it serves the interests of its inhabitants – the moral agents the state is intended to serve. As a consequence, sovereignty is only instrumentally valuable. The value of sovereignty is neither paramount nor inherent; rather it is dependent on the degree to which respecting a state's sovereignty serves the interests of the individuals and groups inhabiting the state. Consequently, the analogical arguments from autonomy fail.

Criticism of Walzer's Argument from Self-determination

For Walzer, the right of a political community to self-determination is based on the right held by each individual to create a political community of their own choosing.[72] Thus, according to Walzer, the right of nonintervention is necessary to respect the right of political communities to self-determination, which is itself justified by its instrumental role in respecting each individual's right to political self-determination. As such, since the right of a political community to self-determination is derived from the right held by each individual to political self-determination, a political community's right to self-determination cannot simply entail a principle or norm that renders irrelevant the other rights held by individuals unless it can be demonstrated that the right of individuals to political self-determination outweighs the basic right to physical security.

Additionally, Walzer's claim that the right of a political community to self-determination implies a right of nonintervention is undermined by a potential internal conflict. For Walzer, a political community's right to self-determination is based upon each individual's right to political self-determination. As such, the role a political community's right to self-determination should play in the practical deliberations of states depends upon the degree to which respecting that right would serve the underlying individual rights. Basic rights are those that are necessary to the enjoyment of any other rights. In this case, respect for the basic right to physical security is necessary to an individual's enjoyment of his/her right to political self-determination.

However, if Walzer is correct, the right to political self-determination justifies a right of nonintervention that permits states to violate the basic rights of their citizens. But, if the right to political self-determination depends on respect for the basic right to physical security, then the violation of the basic right to physical security undermines the right to political self-determination. It is normatively incoherent to claim that the right to political self-determination allows for the violation of the basic right to physical security because the basic right to physical security has normative priority over the right to political self-determination. In short, since the effect of the right of nonintervention is the preclusion of moral considerations related to the respect or disrespect for basic rights, it would be normatively problematic to defend a right of nonintervention based on Walzer's understanding of the right to political self-determination.

Lastly, the right of a political community to collective self-determination fails to justify a preclusive principle of nonintervention for much the same reason that the value of state sovereignty fails. The principle of noninterference with individual liberty is derived from the value of individual self-determination which is, according to Walzer, essential to the development of individual virtue.[73] Similarly, the principle of nonintervention is argued to be derived from the value of the political self-determination of communities which is essential to the political development of a community.

The value of the development of individual virtue is arguably inherent. The value of the development of a political community is, on the other hand, instrumental and is dependent on the degree to which the political community actually developed serves the goals and purposes from which its value is derived. Consequently, a preclusive principle of nonintervention is not justified; rather we are left with a reason for not intervening. In cases where refraining from intervention would further the goals intended to be served by self-determination, that reason would be weighty. In cases where respecting a political community's right to self-determination would undermine the very goals that justify the right, the reasons in support of nonintervention would be weaker and more susceptible to being outweighed by countervailing reasons.

Criticism of Hall's and Babic's Arguments from Anti-paternalism

Like many of the arguments discussed above, Hall's argument is analogical, but what distinguishes Hall's argument from the Millian analogical arguments discussed previously is that Hall argues that the value of the principle of anti-paternalism is derived from its value-neutrality.[74] This is a standard commitment of most liberal pluralists. Value-neutrality is argued to be necessary at the domestic level because it allows individuals to develop their own conceptions of the good. By analogy, according to Hall, anti-paternalism should also govern the interactions of states in the international arena since there are competing conceptions of the political good from which states might choose. Hall's argument fails because it is simply not the case that all conceptions of the good, or political good for that matter, are equally valuable and deserving of respect.

To support a preclusive principle of noninterference at the individual level it would have to be the case that we are not capable of making judgments about competing conceptions of the good that individuals adopt. Due to epistemic uncertainty over which is correct, there may be a wide range of conceptions of the good that ought to be tolerated. However, this does not imply that *all* conceptions of the good are deserving of such toleration. If a conception of the good involves the violation of others' basic rights then such conceptions ought not to be tolerated.

For example, it might be the case, as it was during the Rwandan genocide, that one group's conception of the good is built, in part, around the denial of the humanity of another group. As has been the case in other instances of ethnic cleansing, genocide or mass atrocity crimes perpetrated against a religious, ethnic or cultural group, the persecution begins with definition of the persecuted group as "the other". In Rwanda, the Hutu extremists also believed that it was their duty to eradicate these "cockroaches" – the Tutsis – from Rwanda. The conception of the good that informed the choices of the interahamwe and other extremist Hutus is not one that deserves toleration. In any case, the grounding proposition that the value of the principle of anti-paternalism to individuals in domestic society is its absolute value-neutrality fails.

Analogizing this proposition to the international arena only magnifies its flaws. First, even if we assume that individuals can have conceptions or definitions of the good, the idea that states *qua* states can have *a* conception of the good borders on the absurd. There may exist a consensus amongst the inhabitants of a state over a conception of the good; but if the underlying principle of this argument is respect for the pluralistic nature of the good, then a consensus should in no way define a state's conception of the good as there are those who subscribe to competing conceptions equally deserving of respect. More importantly, in the cases that we are concerned with here, the basic right to physical security is being violated, and conceptions of the good that involve such violations do not deserve toleration. Lastly, if the value of anti-paternalism is its value neutrality; though this makes some sense when discussing individual conceptions of the good, it makes no sense when discussing collective conceptions that include a minority. Under such circumstances, anti-paternalism actually privileges one conception over the other.

Turning to Jovan Babic's argument that respect for individual human rights justifies a principle of anti-paternalism in international relations; we begin by assuming that there is a plurality of conceptions of the good, and that one ought to be tolerant of a wide range of such conceptions. This does not imply, however, that judgments about others' conceptions of the good cannot be made. Tolerance is only a virtue if we are being tolerant of reasonable differences – differences based on reasonable disagreement. If we are concerned with human rights, conceptions of the good that involve the denial of basic rights are conceptions that are unreasonable and ought not to be tolerated. When we tolerate atrocity, injustice, or the violation of basic rights, tolerance is apathy in the face of evil.

In addition, under Babic's argument, the applicability of the principle of anti-paternalism to international relations relies upon the truth of the following claim: that there exists a conception of the good to which the individuals of a state are committed.[75] In the circumstances we are contemplating here, cases in which there would be a moral demand for humanitarian intervention, it is possible that a majority of the individuals in the state in question may have arrived at a consensus on a conception of the good. However, it would be absurd under such circumstances to claim that there is a single conception of the good to which the individuals of the state are committed. In the end, Babic fails to support the claim that a principle of anti-paternalism is appropriate for the relations between states.

In either case, a right of nonintervention is not justified by the principle of anti-paternalism. Rather, the principle that is justified by anti-paternalism is one that recognizes that there are numerous conceptions of the good deserving of toleration, and to the extent that a conception is reasonable and does not involve a commitment to the violation of the basic right to physical security, it should be respected.

Criticism of the Instrumental Argument

We are left to consider the possibility of an instrumental justification for the right of nonintervention. Under this form of argument, the right of nonintervention is implied by the instrumental relationship between state sovereignty and the provision and maintenance of international peace and security. The success of the instrumental justification for the right of nonintervention depends on the truth of two propositions. First, it must be the case that, without nonintervention, international peace and security could not be provided or maintained – that nonintervention is necessary for international peace and security. Second, it must also be the case that international peace and security is either the only relevant value in international relations, or that it is the paramount value to be considered.

First, it would seem to be reasonable to assume that if states were to adhere to a right of nonintervention, such restraint would make international peace and security more likely. This does not imply, however, that nonintervention is necessary for international peace and security. There may, in fact, be instances under which adherence to the right of nonintervention undermines international peace and security, or in which violation of the right would not affect international peace and security. In either of these cases, the preclusive nature of the right is not justified because the means-ends relationship upon which the justification depends does not exist.

Some might contend that it is incoherent to claim that intervention for any reason can either promote or not affect international peace and security. The underlying claim would be that, as a matter of simple quantification, before the intervention there was less violence than after the intervention, and thus more peace and security before the intervention and less after the intervention has begun. First, this is a counterfactual claim that an intervention would pose a greater threat to international peace and security than does the internal violence giving rise to the moral obligation to intervene. This is a dubious claim at best, and it may be the case – as it likely would have been in Rwanda – that intervention actually promotes international peace and security even if understood from this quantitative perspective.

In addition to the possibility that in some cases intervention may actually promote or not impact international peace and security, the understanding of peace and security the objection relies upon is mistaken. The quantity of violence or lack thereof may be one relevant aspect of international peace and security, but there must also be a qualitative aspect that is at least as important as well as an assessment of the amount of violence and instability over time. The justness and durability of the peace should matter. Humanitarian intervention could improve international peace and security, or at least not diminish it, in this qualitative respect.

In fact, this is one area in which developing international norms seem to recognize the fact that internal strife can result in threats to regional and international order. For example, despite the fact that Operation Turquoise was too little too late and more than misguided, the rationale for the intervention was that the effects of the genocide in Rwanda were spilling over into neighboring territories. In short, the genocide had resulted in a threat to regional stability. It would be hard to argue that earlier intervention would have worsened this situation. In addition, if Dallaire is correct, earlier intervention would have avoided not only the deaths of hundreds of thousands of Rwandans, it would have avoided much of the refugee crisis that destabilized the region.

Second, even if we assume that a principle of nonintervention is necessary for international peace and security, it does not follow that the *right* of nonintervention is justified. Since what needs to be justified is a principle with a preclusive effect on the practical deliberations of states and the international community, for the right of nonintervention to be justified by the instrumental argument it must be the case that international peace and security is either the only relevant goal to be served in international relations or it must be the weightiest goal to be served. If it is not the only relevant goal, then it could be possible that a more fundamental or weightier goal is served by violating international peace and security. In which case, that moral goal should not be precluded from the practical deliberations of states or the international community.

International peace and security is neither the only relevant goal nor the weightiest. International peace and security is pursued for its extrinsic value – it is valuable because it is a means to the promotion of or respect for other more fundamental values. If we look to the underlying motivation for the international community to pursue international peace and security, it is not for the sake of international peace and security itself. Rather, the peace and security between states is pursued so that individuals and communities can flourish.[76] As such, it cannot be the only relevant goal to be pursued in international relations.

In addition, since the value of international peace and security is derived from its instrumental value, it cannot be the paramount or weightiest goal of international relations. For this to be the case the instrumental relationship between international peace and security and the values it is intended to serve would have to justify the elimination of considerations of those more fundamental values when such considerations conflicted with international peace and security.

Admittedly, it is being assumed that the proposition that international peace and security is extrinsically valuable is relatively uncontroversial, and the critical analysis is based upon this assumption. One might, however, object to this assumption. It could be claimed that though international peace and security may have extrinsic value, its value is not solely instrumental – there is value in international peace and security for its own sake. Even if this were true, it would still have to be demonstrated that international peace and security was of paramount value when it conflicted with other values.

RECONSTRUCTING THE NORMATIVE FRAMEWORK: LESSONS LEARNED

The discussion in this section is built around the assumption that for various reasons the practical deliberations of states need to be governed by rules.[77] However, the one rule that is no longer justifiable is a right of nonintervention. Nonetheless, many of the arguments offered as justifications for a right of nonintervention are grounded in relevant moral considerations which should be accounted for by any rule that is to govern the practical deliberations of states. In the discussion that follows, the most relevant considerations gleaned from the critical analysis of the justificatory arguments are explicated. It is then argued that a *presumption* of nonintervention can accommodate such concerns. Finally, I argue that a presumption of nonintervention should be adopted to govern the determination by the international community of whether, in any particular instance, humanitarian military intervention should be pursued.

One might wonder how this is any different from Walzer's exception to the legalist paradigm; that intervention is permissible if it "shocks the conscience of mankind."[78] In the discussion of Walzer's argument from self-determination, it was argued that his methodology, if not his conclusion, is problematic. Notwithstanding these aforementioned concerns, a *presumption* of nonintervention is distinct from Walzer's rule. First, for Walzer, humanitarian intervention is only permissible as an exception to the rule. It is a circumstance that requires us to violate the rule. Under a presumption, the possibility of the permissibility of a humanitarian intervention is within the purview of the rule.

Second, the "shock the conscience" standard is *post facto*. If we are only permitted to intervene in those instances in which the conscience of mankind is shocked, we are only permitted to intervene if the atrocities have reached such a horrific level that the "conscience of mankind" has been shocked. Under a presumption of nonintervention, one need not wait until the massacres have reached such levels of barbarity. In fact, under a presumption of nonintervention, much of the bloodshed required for Walzer's exception could be avoided as we are required to provide protection against such violations.

On the other hand, one might be concerned that the critical assessment of the justifications for a right of nonintervention could be taken to imply that, with regards to humanitarian intervention, the practical deliberations of states ought to be unencumbered by any rules that are not themselves directly related to such humanitarian concerns. Such an understanding would be based on a false choice: that either the normative framework of international relations is to be governed by a right of nonintervention; or that the normative framework is to be governed by no rules at all. A presumption of nonintervention represents an alternative proposition. It is a moderate principle that recognizes the values to be served by nonintervention, but also allows for other moral reasons for action to receive their proper consideration in the practical deliberations of states.

The rejection of the right of nonintervention as the governing principle of the normative framework is not a rejection of the goals and values to be served by such a rule. In fact, perhaps the most valuable lesson we learn from the critical analysis that led to the rejection of the right of nonintervention, apart from the fact that the rule is not justified, is that respect for state sovereignty is not devoid of value. But the value of state sovereignty is limited as opposed to absolute, and instrumental as opposed to inherent; two characteristics of the value of state sovereignty that lend support to the adoption of a presumption of nonintervention.

As to the specific arguments addressed and lessons learned from the critical discussion of the justificatory arguments in support of a right of nonintervention; beginning with the analogical arguments (the arguments from autonomy and anti-paternalism), we learn that the values and principles relevant to the international arena are not analogous to the domestic. Simply extrapolating from the domestic to the international – claiming that states in the international arena are analogous to individuals in domestic society – fails to account for the fact that there are relevant and significant differences between the grounding relationship and the relationship intended to be defended by the analogy. The moral agents and relationships at the international level are fundamentally different and more complex than those that exist at the domestic level. Any principle which is expected to govern the practical deliberations of states in the international arena should recognize and accommodate the complexity of the agents and relationships that exist at the international level.

Even if we assume the validity of the analogical arguments, the value of respecting state sovereignty is limited, at least in the same way that respecting the autonomy of individuals and individual choice is limited. If respect for an individual's exercise of her liberty was absolute, we would never be justified in interfering with her exercise of her liberty. However, even Mill concedes that when the exercise of one's liberty unjustifiably infringes upon the rights and interests of other relevant moral agents, interference to prevent the unjustified infringement is permissible. Similarly, in those instances where the exercise of state sovereignty involves harm or a threat of harm to another moral agent, whether or not to interfere should not be precluded as a possible course of action. The principle we adopt to guide the practical deliberations of the international community when considering intervention should reflect this limitation on sovereignty.

Turning to Walzer's argument from self-determination, Walzer argues that respecting sovereignty is essential for promoting the political self-determination of the community. It is reasonable to assume, all other things being equal, that the political self-determination of a community is valuable; and that respecting sovereignty will aid in the ability of a political community to be self-determining. However, even by Walzer's own argument, the value of communal political self-determination is extrinsic. Specifically, political self-determination to a community is valuable to the extent that it serves individual political self-determination.

Thus, in relation to political self-determination, the value of respecting state sovereignty is extrinsic. Under this argument, it is an indirect means to respecting individual political self-determination. As a consequence, the value of respecting state sovereignty is dependent, at least in part, on the degree to which such respect would, in fact, serve the goal of individual political self-determination. In most cases respecting state sovereignty will promote both the collective self-determination of communities and individual political self-determination. The principle governing the normative framework should reflect this instrumental relationship between political self-determination and state sovereignty.

Looking next to the arguments from anti-paternalism of Hall and Babic; focusing first on the underlying epistemic claim, it is reasonable to assume that there is epistemic uncertainty over which conception or definition of the good is correct, and that it is morally valuable to allow agents to exercise their autonomy in choosing a conception of the good. As such, respecting state sovereignty is likely to render the ability to make such choices more secure. When choice is being exercised in a reasonable manner, intervention should be considered an unjustified imposition of one conception of the good for another, an act of unjustified moral imperialism by the interveners. In other words, the value of neutrality that is promoted and served by the principle of anti-paternalism is appropriate when the conception of the good chosen is a reasonable one.

However, it is not always the case that neutrality is the best policy in moral matters. Nor is moral imperialism inherently wrong. In some cases, the value of avoiding moral imperialism and allowing an individual or a group of individuals to exercise their autonomy in choosing their conception of the good will pale in comparison to the harm that would be caused by not intervening – the unjustified violation of the basic right to physical security being just one example. Our principle should allow individuals to choose their conception of the good from amongst the plurality of reasonable conceptions of the good, but it should not leave the international community impotent in the face of grievous harms.

We are left to consider the critical discussion of the instrumental argument. First, however, it should be noted that there is something particularly paradoxical about the instrumental argument. For various reasons, the instrumental argument is likely the most compelling of the justificatory arguments; in large part because the instrumental argument explicitly recognizes that respecting the sovereignty of a state is a means to respecting more fundamental values. Specifically, the instrumental argument is based on the proposition that respect for the sovereignty of a state is instrumental to a variety of intuitively valuable goals of international relations. The paradox arises because it is the instrumental nature of the justification that renders it incapable of supporting a right of nonintervention with a preclusive effect on the practical deliberations of states. Under the instrumental argument the most that can be claimed – and one of the lessons we learn – is that the sovereignty of a state should be respected to the extent that such respect would actually fulfill the goals upon which the instrumental justification relies.

The goal to which the instrumental justification is directed is international order. Thus, the value of respecting state sovereignty is dependent on the degree to which respecting state sovereignty would serve the goals of international peace and security, which may in turn be dependent on the degree to which the fulfillment of such goals furthers the promotion of more fundamental values, such as human flourishing. Nonetheless, in most cases international peace and security is going to be a worthwhile, even if not the weightiest, goal to be pursued; and respecting the sovereignty of states will in most cases be instrumentally valuable to the achievement of that goal. Thus, the principle governing the normative framework of international relations should account for the fact that respect for the sovereignty of states will often be instrumental to the achievement of international peace and security.

Lastly, there were a number of other concerns that arose in the discussion in Chapter 2 regarding the defense of a moral obligation of humanitarian intervention. Specifically, the concerns over perfidy, pretext, and futility are all relevant considerations that should be accounted for by the principle governing the practical deliberations of states when considering whether to intervene.

REASONS IN SUPPORT OF A PRESUMPTION OF NONINTERVENTION

Before proceeding to the defense of a presumption of nonintervention, there is at least one particularly relevant challenge that must be addressed. Throughout, it has been argued that one of the foundational rules presumed to govern international relations, the right of nonintervention, cannot be justified. It would be reasonable to conclude that the arguments presented not only support the rejection of a right of nonintervention, but that these same arguments lend support to a presumption of *intervention* in cases in which the moral obligation of humanitarian intervention arises as a reason for action.

At a very general level, the considerations weighing in favor of the adoption of *a* rule are ones that have been discussed at length and would support the justification of a wide range of rules; as such, the statement here will be brief. Simply put, without a rule (or set of rules) of some sort, the relations between states are likely to be chaotic and unstable. The direct impact of this instability will be on international order itself, but to the extent that international order is instrumentally valuable to other more fundamental goals, the lack of international order would undermine our ability to achieve these more fundamental goals. For example, it is reasonable to assume, all other things being equal, that international order is instrumentally valuable to human flourishing. As such, if international order is undermined, the promotion of human flourishing is likely to be undermined. If such reasons are compelling, then we need a rule of some sort to provide structure to the interactions between states.

In addition to avoiding the negative implications that could arise if the international arena were not governed by any rules, the adoption of a rule (or set of rules) will have a number of positive effects. A rule governing the behavior of states may not lead to peace, but it will likely increase the predictability of state behavior and provide a basis for reasonable expectations on the part of others in the global community. In turn, such predictability and stability are likely to promote other valuable ends. Especially in a world of increasing globalization, if individuals and communities know what to expect from the international arena with a reasonable degree of certainty, then they can set goals for themselves and engage in efforts at achieving those goals without the constant fear that the actions of another state will unexpectedly interfere with their plans.

Neither the need for a rule nor the advantages of having the international arena governed by a rule as opposed to having no rule at all, identify what that rule should be. However, what rule is adopted is as important as the adoption of a rule. If the wrong rule is adopted, the stability and predictability that is afforded by the rule may be oppressive and exploitive, if not patently unjust. Why a presumption of nonintervention? Why not a presumption of intervention? Why a presumption at all?

Before offering reasons in support of the claim that a rebuttable presumption of nonintervention should be adopted, it is necessary that one have an understanding of the role the presumption would play in the practical deliberations of states. A presumption is a rule or principle that governs our deliberations about a particular practical or theoretical matter. The role played by a presumption is one of burden-shifting. A presumption privileges a particular belief or action above other alternative or opposing options. The starting point for our practical deliberations, if we are deliberating about a matter governed by a presumption, is in favor of the presumed action. It is not an open question.

However, since presumptions are not determinative of the outcome of the deliberations to which they apply, presumptions can be defeated; they are rebuttable. For a presumption to be rebutted, it must be demonstrated that it is outweighed by countervailing considerations. The presumption being discussed here, a presumption of nonintervention, would privilege the option of nonintervention; however, the presumption could be rebutted if it could be demonstrated with sufficient certainty that an injustice is occurring, that the injustice demands and could be rectified by intervention (of some sort), *and* intervention is necessary to fulfilling the demands of justice.

The question of why, if there is to be a rule at all, the rule should be a presumption is conceptually prior to the determination of which way the presumption should go; as such it is necessary to defend the adoption of a presumption first. A presumption, by its very nature, does not preclude the consideration of reasons that weigh against the action or choice favored by the presumption and allows for the possibility that the presumption will be rebutted. As a consequence, it provides a common framework for deliberation and a degree of stability and pre-dictability while also recognizing that there are relevant countervailing considerations that ought to be accounted for in the practical delibera-tions of states. Since it allows for such countervailing considerations to rebut the presumption, it does not succumb to the same criticisms that are raised against rules that are exclusionary in nature, such as the right of nonintervention.

But should the presumption be for or against intervention? There are a number of relevant considerations that lend support to the propo-sition that a presumption of nonintervention ought to be adopted. Specifically, there are certain general principles of morality that can only be accommodated by a presumption of nonintervention. The pre-sumption of nonintervention is also able to accommodate the lessons learned from the previous critical discussion and lessons learned, and is able to protect against the moral hazards identified in the defense of the moral obligation of humanitarian intervention in Chapter 2.

The argument in defense of a presumption of nonintervention begins with the assumption that it is a general principle of morality that one needs to justify one's interference with the actions of, or harm that one's actions may cause to, another. In the case of humanitarian intervention, or intervention of any sort employing military means, the act of intervention is likely to interfere with the activities of other moral agents. At the very least it is, by definition, being conducted against the wishes of the sovereign government. More importantly, since humani-tarian intervention employs, at the very least, the threat of physical violence to achieve its goals, it can be presumed to involve harm to the interests of others. As such, the act of intervening needs to be justified. A presumption in favor of intervention places the burden, not on those interfering with the actions of others or causing harm, but on those who may be harmed or whose actions are being interfered with. On the other hand, a presumption of nonintervention would place the burden on the intervener to demonstrate the justifiability of the interference or the harm being caused. Thus, the presumption of nonintervention is consistent with the moral requirement that such interference be justified.

One might, at this point, argue that either humanitarian interven-tion is justified by the circumstances that have given rise to the demand for intervention, or it is not; and whether a justification exists is not going to depend on who bears the burden of persuasion. Such criticisms fail to account for the practical reality of the situation relevant to the discussion. First, this is a matter of how states should interact with one another in the global arena, and the question is one of justification *to* another party, not simply whether a justification exists. Second, the question at the heart of the issue is epistemological and not ontological in nature. The matter of justification is in most cases going to be debated. The question is not whether a justification exists, but in the midst of such debate what should the *status quo* be, and who should have to argue against it. If the rule is to provide structure to the interactions between states and guide the behavior of states in their interactions as members of the international community, it cannot simply be to act when one believes that one is justified in doing so. That is the very issue the resolution of which the rule is intended to govern.

Another principle of morality, and one that can be found in traditional just war theory as well, is that military force should not be considered as a first option. It should be a last resort.[79] Such a constraint on the use of military force allows for the possibility of diplomatic efforts to resolve the problem without violent conflict and the damage it inevitably causes. The ICISS report defending the responsibility to protect places a heavy emphasis on this requirement. In fact, the first responsibility borne by the international community is a responsibility to prevent.[80] A presumption of nonintervention respects this principle in a way that a presumption of intervention cannot. Under a presumption of intervention we are privileging the option of conflict, thus undermining the last resort constraint and the diplomatic alternatives for which it allows.

One might object that the circumstances under consideration – the violation of basic rights – is such a pressing moral demand that the international community cannot wait for diplomatic efforts to run their course, and that the reasons which support the last resort condition are either outweighed or not even relevant. In most cases, however, this is what is at issue – whether the circumstances warrant intervention. As a consequence, we cannot simply assume that the conditions are such that intervention is warranted. Second, if it is patently obvious that the basic rights of individuals are being violated, then, all other things being equal, the presumption against intervention will be easily rebutted. Thus, a presumption of nonintervention will, in questionable cases, allow for the possibility of a diplomatic resolution and avoid unnecessary violence, but in those cases in which the violation of the basic right to physical security is obvious the presumption will not stand in the way of quick action.

Turning now to the ability of a presumption of nonintervention to accommodate the lessons learned from the critical discussion of the arguments offered as justifications for the right of nonintervention, one of the most important lessons learned is that the principle we adopt should acknowledge that the value of respecting state sovereignty is not absolute. A presumption of nonintervention accomplishes this by privileging respect for state sovereignty, while also recognizing the limitations on the value of respecting state sovereignty. It is not enough, however, to merely recognize the fact that the value of state sovereignty is limited. The rule we adopt should also recognize that state sovereignty has instrumental value. Much of the discussion to follow will explain how a presumption of nonintervention can accommodate this concern.

The principle adopted to govern the normative framework of international relations, and specifically the question of intervention, should also be compatible with the complexity of international relations. This means that the rule adopted should provide the structure necessary to guide the behavior of states, but also be flexible enough to accommodate the varied demands on the actions of states; including the demands of morality in the international arena. With regard to humanitarian intervention, the rule adopted must provide the basis for reasonable expectations of behavior while recognizing that in certain circumstances the demands of morality will require intervention. A presumption of nonintervention accomplishes both of these tasks. States can expect to be free from intervention if they abide by certain basic moral demands – basic rights. Yet, if they violate the basic rights of the individuals inhabiting the state, the state becomes the possible subject of intervention. The state is the "possible" subject of intervention because the inclusion of a reason for action in an agent's practical deliberations does not mean that the reason will be conclusive.

Another lesson that we learn from the critical discussion of the justificatory arguments is that there are good instrumental reasons for adopting a presumption of nonintervention. The right of nonintervention arguably serves many important values and valuable states of affairs – political self-determination, international order, and reasonable pluralism. In most cases, respect for state sovereignty will promote international order, self-determination, and reasonable pluralism; and will not conflict with the moral demands of basic rights. Thus, as a general rule, it would make sense to presume that state sovereignty should be respected in order to promote those values and valuable states of affairs.

In those cases in which the violation of the basic right to physical security demands the violation of state sovereignty, the presumption places the burden of proof on those seeking to challenge the presumption. It is presumed that the proper course of action is nonintervention unless those advancing the interventionist cause can demonstrate that there are sufficient countervailing considerations which show either that the values associated with state sovereignty or the goal of international order are outweighed or not relevant to the particular case at issue.

In addition to the specific lessons learned from the critical discussion of the justificatory arguments, there are numerous epistemological problems with acting on reasons related to matters internal to another state. As was discussed previously, despite their disagreement over nonintervention, Michael Walzer and David Luban seem to agree that "the lack of fit between government and people should be 'radically apparent' to justify intervening, because intervention based on misperceptions is horribly wrong."[81] Here, the "lack of fit" justifying intervention would be based on the state's complicity with or inability to stop the violation of its inhabitants' basic rights. Thus, to deal with the concern shared by Walzer and Luban, before intervening we must have knowledge sufficient to justify the claim that the circumstances giving rise to the moral demand for intervention are violations of the basic right to physical security and not merely a case of moral imperialism, perfidy, or pretext. A presumption that places the burden of proof on those in favor of intervention would protect against such epistemically based moral hazards.

There is at least one additional moral hazard associated with intervention that must be addressed. Jovan Babic argues that if we were to abandon a stringent normative principle against intervention and allow for the permissibility of intervention in the internal affairs of another state in cases where the basic right to physical security would demand such action, there would be an inevitable slide to the acceptability of intervention as a tool to pursue state interests in foreign affairs.[82] In short, any compromise in the right of nonintervention would eventually result in a system of rules that failed to include any limitation on intervention; thus, sacrificing the international order provided by a system of international legal and political institutions grounded in a commitment to state sovereignty and the right of nonintervention.

Slippery-slope arguments are only as good as each step in the slide from the intuitively morally acceptable to the intuitively morally troubling. Here, the argument is that the move away from the right of non-intervention should not result in ad hoc assessments of the propriety and desirability of humanitarian intervention. Rather, the presumption of nonintervention would allow for the intuitively acceptable proposition that the demands of basic rights should be accounted for in the practical deliberations of states without allowing the unfettered slide to a general acceptance of intervention as a tool of foreign relations.

There is one final point that should be stressed relevant to the defense and understanding of the presumption of nonintervention. As with any presumption, the bases for the presumption determine the conditions relevant to assessing whether the presumption has been outweighed. There is at least one alternative defense of a presumption of nonintervention that ought to be considered. Specifically, Jeff McMahan contends that Walzer's argument for a principle of nonintervention based on the collective right of self-determination supports a *presumption* of nonintervention rather than a strict rule against intervention.[83] In support of this proposition, McMahan offers two distinct interpretations of Walzer's arguments. Under one interpretation, the presumption of nonintervention is based on the proposition that to be morally justified humanitarian intervention must respect the collective right to self-determination.[84] The other is based on Walzer's claim that the success of an intervention will depend, at least in part, on the attitude the potential beneficiaries have towards the intervention.[85]

The fact that there are alternative arguments for a presumption of nonintervention is not necessarily a problem for the argument I have presented. If the alternative arguments lead to a presumption with the same conceptual extension and practical impact as the presumption I have defended, then one would have more evidence of the correctness of the understanding of the presumption of nonintervention defended here. With regards to the first argument alluded to above, this is not the case. A presumption based on the requirement that the collective right to self-determination be respected is different to a presumption based on the instrumental nature of the principle of nonintervention, and the difference between these presumptions is not limited to the categorical difference in their underlying bases. McMahan's defense of a presumption of nonintervention based on the collective right to self-determination would be far more restrictive than the instrumental presumption defended here.

Under McMahan's argument, to be justified a humanitarian intervention must be respectful of the collective right of self-determination. McMahan recognizes that in cases of grave humanitarian crises wherein the state is participating in or permitting one group within society to violate the basic rights of another group within society, that even though the violators and victims are all of the same nationality they may be two distinct political communities; consequently, respect for the collective right to self-determination does not prohibit intervention.[86] In addition, the right held by the violators does not include a moral permission to violate the rights (individual or collective) of the victims. As such, humanitarian intervention to stop such violations would not necessarily be violative of the collective right held by either of the communities (violators or victims) involved.

Nonetheless, to be justified, any humanitarian intervention must be respectful of the collective right held by the intended beneficiaries of the intervention. One way to respect the collective right to self-determination is to act on the expressed wishes of that community since the expression of the community's desires is an exercise of the right itself. In the case of humanitarian intervention, McMahan argues that consent to the intervention by the potential beneficiaries is just such an exercise of the right. Consequently, humanitarian intervention conducted with the consent of the potential beneficiaries is respectful of the collective right to self-determination and, for that reason, not unjustified.

The reason this "requirement of consent" gives rise to a presumption is tied to the fact that in many instances of grave humanitarian crises the victims are unable to express their views on intervention. McMahan concludes that when clear expressions of consent are lacking we should presume that the victims would prefer that no intervention occur. The practical difference this argument would have for how we understand the presumption of nonintervention can be understood by imagining a set of circumstances where it is clear that the presumption against intervention I have defended has been rebutted, but the international community is unable to ascertain the specific view the potential beneficiaries have on the intervention; we are to presume that they don't want intervention unless we can piece together circumstantial evidence to the contrary. Thus, under McMahan's argument intervention is rendered less likely.

Since the ultimate goal of this project is practical in nature, the fact that the different arguments have different practical implications implies a need to choose between the two accounts. There are a number of reasons for rejecting this version of McMahan's argument. A number of critiques will be set aside to focus on what I find to be the most significant problems with McMahan's argument from the collective right of self-determination.

For McMahan's understanding of the presumption to be correct, what must be defended is the proposition that in the face of uncertainty as to the victim community's view of the intervention, we ought to privilege the belief that there is a lack of consent over the belief that a community and the individuals suffering the violations of their basic rights would welcome an intervention. In the argument presented by McMahan, the justification for the presumption is the relationship between consent and the collective right to self-determination; that consent is sufficient to satisfy the requirement that the collective right to self-determination be satisfied. This argument would be stronger if the relationship between consent and the collective right of self-determination was a necessary one; that consent was necessary to respect the collective right to self-determination. There may, however, be a number of ways to respect that right that do not depend on consent. For example, the means used in the intervention and post-intervention reconstruction by the international community may be carried out in a way that is respectful of the collective right to self-determination. One might establish safe areas where those who are seeking to flee the violence could find protection; this would allow those who do not want the aid of the international community to remain independent.

One might concede that the relationship between consent and the collective right of self-determination is merely a relationship of sufficiency, but contend that action based on consent is the best way to respect the collective right of self-determination. This, however, assumes that denying an intervention to protect the basic rights of individuals within the victims' community is within the scope of moral discretion provided by the right. If the collective right is grounded in the rights held by the individuals that make up the community, there is a problem in claiming that the community can sacrifice the basic rights of the individuals that make up the community. In most instances it may be the case that consent by the community is an appropriate expression of the self-determination of the community. However, in cases of grave humanitarian crisis where the basic rights of individuals are being violated, the fact that the ostensive community to which they belong is unwilling or unable to do what is necessary to protect their basic rights significantly impacts the legitimacy of the community's claim to hold the right of self-determination for the collective. The community's collective right of self-determination should not be interpreted to include the moral permission to sacrifice individuals.

The last critical point is a critique of the basis for presuming a lack of consent. If anything, lack of consent by beneficiaries in the case of grave humanitarian crises should be considered an open question. In addition, a representative's claim that those whose basic rights are being violated don't want help should be viewed with skepticism and not privileged unless there are good reasons to trust the claim; and even then I am not convinced that this renders a humanitarian intervention unjustified because it violates some sanctified notion of a collective right to self-determination.

The second argument offered by McMahan in support of the presumption of nonintervention is one to which I am sympathetic, and relies upon the instrumental value of the victim community's consent to the likely success of a humanitarian intervention.[87] In short, the argument is based on Walzer's conjecture that the success of an intervention is less likely when the intended beneficiaries have withheld their consent because they would prefer that the international community not intervene. Walzer further contends that when outside forces seek to interfere with the internal affairs of a political community, the members of the political community – even those whose rights are being violated – will come together to repel the interveners. Consequently, without the consent of the potential beneficiaries of the intervention, the intervention itself is likely to prove futile.

Though both arguments pressed by McMahan are grounded in the importance of the consent (or dissent) of the intended beneficiaries of the proposed intervention, the value of consent in the present argument is not based on consent as an exercise of the collective right of self-determination. Rather, the consent of the intended beneficiaries is an indicator of the support the intervening forces are likely to have from the population they are trying to help, and the *support* is instrumentally valuable to the success of the intervention. Thus, the focus of any instrumental analysis related to consent should, in the end, be grounded in the degree to which the consent, dissent, or silence is an indication of support.

However, before addressing the relationship between the consent of the intended beneficiaries and any proposed humanitarian intervention, it is necessary to have an understanding of the relationship between the support of the victim community and the success of a humanitarian intervention. Is support by the victim community necessary for a successful intervention, or does it merely make success more likely? The claim that support is necessary is an unlikely proposition for a number of reasons. First, for the proposition to be true, it would have to be the case that there are not any circumstances under which an intervention would succeed without the support of the intended beneficiaries of the community. As this is a contingent factual claim, as opposed to a conceptual implication, it would be nearly impossible to demonstrate the truth of this proposition.

In addition, the support at issue is about the attitude the intended beneficiaries of the intervention have towards the intervention. Attitudes are not static. They may change for a variety of reasons. For example, the attitude may be based on misinformation, and the nature of the attitude may be dependent on its underlying basis. Consequently, even if we begin with the assumption that a victim community has a negative view of a humanitarian intervention, that attitude may change because of information provided ahead of the intervention; or, if the basis for the attitude is that certain forces are not welcome or certain means not preferred, it may be possible to construct an intervention that accommodates the attitude. In either case, consent from the outset is not necessary for the success of the intervention.

Second, the fact that the consent of the victim community is not a necessary condition for the success of a humanitarian intervention does not undermine its claim to be instrumentally valuable. If the consent of the victim community renders the success of the proposed humanitarian intervention more likely, then, other things being equal, it is better to have the consent of the victim community than not. Assuming the truth of the proposition that consent/support is instrumentally valuable to the success of an intervention – a reasonable assumption – it does not support a general presumption of nonintervention in those instances in which the consent of the victim community cannot be ascertained. Nor does it lead to the conclusion that one should presume that the victim community has not consented, nor that the victim community's attitude to the proposed intervention is a negative one.

If anything, since the support of the victim community is but one amongst many relevant interests involved in the assessment of the likely success of a humanitarian intervention, the lack of information regarding the victim community's attitude should be treated as neither supporting nor undermining the likely success of a humanitarian intervention. However, and consistent with McMahan's underlying proposition, if the international community is able to ascertain the view of the victim community, this should weigh in the more general determination of whether the intervention will be futile or produce perverse results. As such, McMahan's instrumental argument can be read to be consistent with the presumption of nonintervention proposed here.

CONCLUSION: RECONSTRUCTION OF THE NORMATIVE FRAMEWORK

What exactly would the normative framework look like if it was governed by a presumption as opposed to a right of nonintervention? As discussed at length above, under the right of nonintervention, certain moral reasons for action, including the moral obligation of humanitarian intervention, are precluded from consideration if they are related to matters internal to another state and would require interference with the internal matters of another state. If justified, this would lead to a fairly simple structure for the deliberative process involved. The right would act as a filter, precluding the international community from considering certain moral reasons for action. However, there does not seem to be a viable justification for a principle with such a preclusive effect.

Under the presumption, on the other hand, even though nonintervention is privileged, no morally relevant reasons are precluded from consideration. As a consequence, when engaging in practical deliberations in which interventionist moral reasons for action have been raised, states engaged in such reasoning will be faced with a greater number of considerations, and, as a result, required to engage in a more complex deliberative process.

It should be no surprise that the structural differences between a normative framework governed by a presumption of nonintervention as compared with a right of nonintervention results in significant practical differences in the outcomes of such deliberations. The most obvious is that if interventionist reasons for action are not precluded from consideration at the outset, there is a possibility that under the appropriate circumstances what ought to be done, all things considered, is intervention. Under the right of nonintervention, on the other hand, the actions of states would (or should) never be based on moral reasons that demand intervention into matters internal to another state.

In the discussion that follows in the final section of Chapter 4, the practical difference the adoption of a presumption of nonintervention would have made in Rwanda will be discussed in greater detail. Simply put, if the normative framework was governed by the right of nonintervention, or even if those who had power to do anything believed that it was so governed, this would explain the international community's refusal to intervene. However, under a reconstructed normative framework of international relations governed by a presumption of nonintervention, the international community would have had an all-things-considered obligation to intervene in Rwanda.

Intervening in the internal affairs of another state is not an act that should be taken lightly. However, the normative weight that is given to state sovereignty and international order is often misplaced. I do not deny the value of either, but I do question the degree to which views that sanctify their value are justified. I have defended the existence of a moral obligation of humanitarian intervention in Rwanda, and argued that the obligation was owed to the individual victims of the Rwandan genocide, and that the obligation was borne by states individually and the international community as a collection of duty-bearing states.

And now it has been demonstrated that the normative framework, accepted by many at the time of the Rwandan genocide, precluded such moral reasons for action from consideration in the practical deliberations of states, and that the right of nonintervention which governed the practical deliberations of states was unjustified. In its stead, the normative framework of international relations ought to be governed by a presumption of nonintervention.

What remains is an explicit discussion of the institutionalization of the presumption; however, before engaging in that discussion, a more detailed explication of the presumption is in order. This requires the explicit identification of the considerations relevant to the question at hand, which is a matter of identifying the conditions under which the presumption would be rebutted. It is important to note that questions of rebuttal will, in wider practice, be a matter of degree; however, and as will be discussed below, when applied to Rwanda rebuttal of the presumption cannot be reasonably disputed.

The first set of considerations is based upon the valuable states of affairs that are served by the presumption. First, nonintervention is instrumental to both individual and communal political self-determination. Thus, one relevant consideration in determining whether the presumption is rebutted is whether those advocating intervention can demonstrate that political self-determination is not being infringed upon, or that the infringement is justified. This begs a difficult question that cannot be fully addressed here; what sorts of actions fall within the ambit of what might be considered morally valuable political self-determination? Are all acts with political ends to be considered valuable as a matter of political self-determination, or should our understanding be more limited? At the very least, those actions that fail to respect the basic rights of others cannot be considered morally defensible as a matter of political self-determination. In which case, interfering with such acts is not interference with political self-determination; nor is it an unjustified infringement on the political self-determination of the perpetrators of the human rights violations.

Another instrumental goal to be served by the presumption of non-intervention is the protection of reasonable pluralism, and protection against unjustified moral imperialism. Specifically, intervention should not result in the imposition of one conception of the good for another reasonable conception of the good. Determining whether this consideration in support of the presumption has been rebutted is a more complex consideration than it may at first appear. The advocates of intervention must demonstrate either that the bases for intervention are principles or conceptions of the good to which those whose actions are to be interfered with are also committed, *or* that the actions that are claimed to give rise to the demand for intervention are not based on a reasonable conception of the good.

One additional way in which a conception of the good can fail to be reasonable is in its application. Those against whom intervention is being sought may be committed to a reasonable conception of the good, and they may believe that their actions are in accordance with the reasonable conception of the good to which they are committed; however, if the connection between the conception of the good and the actions they take in accordance with that conception is not reasonable then the application is unreasonable. For example, as is the case in many cases of mass violence against an ethnic, religious, or cultural minority, the larger group may be committed to human rights but deny that the members of the persecuted group are human.

If the intervention being contemplated in such an instance is based on the very conception of the good that the targeted individuals are committed to, then intervention would not be an imposition of another conception of the good, but would actually be in accordance with the conception of the good to which the targets of intervention are committed. One final comment with regards to this consideration, the advocates of intervention must also demonstrate that intervention is not going to cause more harm than the conception of the good under attack.

The final instrumental goal to be served by the presumption of non-intervention is the maintenance of international peace and security. First, there is the question of whether intervention in any particular instance is likely to undermine international peace and security. On this point, the consideration can be met if it can be demonstrated that intervention will either have no discernible effect on international peace and security, or that international peace and security will actually be served. However, and as was discussed above, international peace and security is itself of instrumental value. It is only valuable to the extent that maintaining international peace and security serves other more fundamental goals. Thus, consideration of the effect of intervention on international peace and security in the determination of whether the presumption has been rebutted is not simply a matter of assessing whether or not international peace and security will be undermined by intervention. If the advocate of intervention can demonstrate that the goals to be served by international peace and security will be better served by intervention, even if intervention undermines international peace and security, then this consideration in favor of the presumption will have been rebutted.

One might be concerned that the complexity of assessing the presumption with regard to the goal of international peace and security identifies an inherent flaw. Specifically, the complexity of this consideration, especially if deliberation reaches this level of analysis, is likely to prove problematic. First, it may prove problematic because there may be disagreement over the goals to be served by international peace and security, and even if there is agreement over the goals to be served, there may be differing ideas about whether intervention serves such goals better. I do not find this to be a determinative problem for the presumption. If anything, it demonstrates that the presumption has some teeth to it; it is not a strawman and is not likely to be blown over by the slightest consideration in favor of intervention. In addition, there are likely to be gray areas in which we should not expect there to be a clear and decisive answer. Any principle that claims that there are always easy answers to moral questions is one of which we should be wary.

The second set of considerations are those based upon concerns one may have over any rule that weakens the prohibition on intervention in international relations. First, one may be concerned about the possibility of perfidy, that one group is engaging in actions against the state and provoking retaliation by the state with the specific goal of enticing the international community to intervene to fight its battle for it. In addition, there is a concern over the generation of perverse results; that the intervention will lead to greater harm and a larger humanitarian crisis than the one it is intended to resolve. How can we be certain, or certain enough, that the intervention is not the result of perfidy? How can we know with sufficient certainty that intervention will not simply make the crisis worse?

As to perfidy, the concern is that if intervention is attempted in one case in which the humanitarian crisis giving rise to and justifying the intervention was caused by perfidious action then others will be encouraged, in the future, to engage in such action to further their cause(s). One might think that this should lead us to conclude that the advocate must demonstrate that the humanitarian crisis that justifies the intervention was not a matter of perfidy. Such a standard would, however, place the emphasis on the wrong aspect of intervention. The concern ought to be with how the intervention is carried out, and not whether it is carried out. For that reason, those advocating intervention must demonstrate with reasonable certainty that the intervention will be carried out in such a way that perfidy is not encouraged.

As to the possibility of perverse results, the advocate of intervention must demonstrate that the intervention will alleviate the humanitarian concern without causing a greater one. This condition is more complicated than it may, at first, appear. Intervention, by its very nature, carries with it, not of necessity but a high probability, that violence will be used to accomplish its ends. Harm will be caused. Specifically, harm will be caused to those violating the rights of others, and may place those whom the interveners are seeking to help at greater risk of harm. It is important to recognize, however, that there exists a moral asymmetry between the violators of rights and the victims of such violation.[88] I will not argue that any and all means may be used against the violators, but the concern over perverse results must be understood to be concerned primarily with harm that may befall the intended beneficiaries of the intervention. It would be, at the very least, counterintuitive to argue that an intervention that saved a large number of civilian lives was somehow unjustified because it resulted in additional deaths of genocidaires.

Before moving on, a clarificatory remark about the nature of the considerations identified is in order. One may ask the following: are the considerations delineated necessary conditions for rebuttal of the presumption? Sufficient? Jointly, or individually? Though I do not have a simple answer to these questions, some are likely to be more important than others. For example, the causation of perverse results – the worsening of the humanitarian situation for the victims – ought to be a very weighty consideration in the practical deliberations of a state, and concerns over moral imperialism, less so. However, if there were a situation in which the advocate for intervention were able to demonstrate that each of the considerations in favor of the presumption were rebutted, that would certainly be sufficient for a determination that the presumption had been rebutted, and that the international community had a conclusive practical reason for engaging in a humanitarian intervention. How exactly the international community should make that determination is the focus of the discussion in Chapter 4.

Chapter 4

COMPLETING THE TRANSITION FROM THEORY TO PRACTICE

It has been said that the world is divided among those who make things happen, those who watch things happen, and those who wonder what happened. Too often, when it comes to mass atrocity crimes, too many of us have been left wondering – how could this horror possibly have happened yet again. (Gareth Evans)[1]

INTRODUCTION: FROM THEORY TO PRACTICE

To this point, the discussion has focused on providing the conceptual and moral groundwork justifying the call for the reform of the institutions and principles governing the practical deliberations of states in the international arena. Without more, this project would remain woefully incomplete. To this end, Chapter 4 provides the bridge between the abstract discussion of the previous sections (Chapters 1–3) and the institutional reform that would be involved in the reconstruction of the normative framework of international relations. The approach here is a form of aspirational but practical political philosophy. One of the clearest examples of this philosophical approach comes from John Rawls's *Law of Peoples*.[2] In seeking to provide the moral foundations for international law, Rawls sets his goal as identifying and defending a "realistic utopia."[3] This means that the institutions defended are aspirational, but must also be "practically politically possible."[4]

The discussion begins with an explication of one of the most progressive contemporary views regarding the role the international community *should* play in cases of grave humanitarian crises – the responsibility to protect. The focus of the critical discussion that follows is not on the principle itself, but is primarily focused on the ICISS recommendations for institutionalizing the principle.

There is one additional matter that ought to be addressed before turning to the substantive discussion. The value of thoughtful institutionalization should not be underestimated.[5] When we have identified a norm that should govern the deliberations of certain agents, we could choose to allow those deliberations to be unencumbered by the explicit institutionalization of the norm; in which case the deliberations of the agents within the institution will be ad hoc. The advantage of such an approach is the flexibility it affords to the agents involved in the deliberations, and in an ideal world this would lead to correct answers.

The disadvantages are, however, numerous. Since we do not live in an ideal world, the lack of an institutionalized rule makes the nature of the deliberations unpredictable. As a consequence, the expectations of the deliberating agents and those affected by the outcome will be less certain. In turn, the institution will be less stable. In addition, the ad hoc nature of the deliberations will make the reaction of the international community unpredictable. When passions run high, there may be overreaction. Just as problematic, if apathy reigns there may be no reaction at all.

The alternative is to institutionalize the norm, to make it part of a regular process that governs the deliberations of agents within the institutional system. The disadvantage of such an approach is the loss of flexibility. Since the institutionalization of a norm has to be generally applicable and cannot take every possible circumstance into account, institutionalization renders certain considerations irrelevant within the institutionalized deliberative process that might otherwise be considered relevant.

However, institutionalizing a norm provides a greater degree of certainty over the nature of the deliberations engaged in by agents within the institutional system. This greater degree of certainty makes the behavior of agents within the system more predictable, and helps to support a more stable system. In addition, institutionalizing a norm avoids some of the more egregious actions that might result from ad hoc evaluations; namely, the fact that ad hoc determinations make overreaction or apathy more likely. On this point, institutionalization would result in a structure for deliberations defined by the intentional choice of particular principles and processes at a moment of calm when rational discussion of the merits of different approaches have a better chance of overcoming visceral responses. As a consequence, the deliberations of agents under the institutionalized norm will be forced to operate within a framework that provides some guard against ill-considered and/or reactionary action (or inaction).

One last advantage to be noted is that institutionalizing a norm will provide a common basis for deliberation. This would likely bring about two desirable states of affairs. First, since there would be a common basis for deliberation, states would have a common language through which they could engage and persuade each other. Second, one of the main concerns of many who work in this area is that there is a lack of clarity when it comes to accountability for both action and inaction. In institutionalizing the norm, we construct a basis for assigning and assessing accountability.

It is important to recognize that the advantages listed are dependent on institutionalizing the norm in a way that is thoughtful and focused on the underlying justification. It is certainly possible that a half-hearted commitment to a norm or even a sincere but ill-conceived institutionalization could do more harm than good. Poor institutionalization often results in processes that are ineffective at best and obstacles to effective action at worst. On the other hand, well-considered and thoughtful institutionalization of a norm is likely to result in an effective process that facilitates decisions and action.

EXPLICATION OF THE RESPONSIBILITY TO PROTECT

The first step in completing the transition from theory to practice is the critical assessment of the ICISS recommendations for institutionalizing the responsibility to protect. And, though the principle itself is not at issue, providing an explication of the principle and a brief history of the ICISS's origins will provide the necessary context for understanding the ICISS perspective on institutionalization. Three events motivated the Canadian government to sponsor the creation of the ICISS. First, despite the near universal commitment to the Convention on the Prevention and Punishment of the Crime of Genocide, the international community looked for political cover while 800,000 Rwandan civilians were killed. A year later thousands of unarmed men and boys who were under the *protection* of United Nations peacekeeping forces in Srebrenica (UNPROFOR) were marched outside the town by Serbian military forces and killed.

Rwanda and Srebrenica represent moral failures by the international community. The failure in Rwanda was a failure to act at all. In Rwanda, the reasons offered as a justification for the choice not to intervene were flush with references to traditional notions of sovereignty and the right of nonintervention. In Srebrenica the failure was the impotence of UNPROFOR caused by a commitment to a particularly stringent conception of the principle of neutrality which led to an ill-conceived mandate regarding the use of protective force. In short, Rwanda evinces a failure of the principles affecting the choice to intervene and Srebrenica a failure of willingness to take the actions necessary to fulfill a humanitarian goal.

The last event is not a case of international apathy or failure; rather it is an instance in which an intervention occurred. And, though there was not a global international response, there was little resistance to the intervention carried out by NATO and a willingness by most of the international community to grant the intervention post hoc legitimacy. Specifically, in 1999, NATO engaged in a bombing campaign in Yugoslavia to stop the ethnic-based violence against Kosovar Albanians. The intervention by NATO is considered by many to have had a just cause.

If we take the choice not to intervene in Rwanda and the failure of UNPROFOR to act in Srebrenica and juxtapose them with NATO's intervention in Kosovo, it is reasonable to conclude that there had been a change in the way that the international community viewed humanitarian intervention. At the very least, the complete lack of political will evident in Rwanda and Srebrenica had been replaced with the will to act. In an effort to understand this shift and translate this new-found political will into action, in September 2000, the Canadian government convened an international panel of scholars, diplomats and politicians to interpret these events and the changing nature of the norms governing the practical deliberations of states in cases of grave humanitarian crises.[6]

The ICISS held numerous meetings and forums around the world, seeking a consensus on principles that could be employed by the international community to deal with questions of humanitarian intervention. Then, in 2001, the ICISS issued a report explaining the responsibility to protect principle and setting forth its recommendations regarding the institutionalization of the principle.

The deliberations of the ICISS were governed by two commitments. First, the ICISS sought to avoid becoming embroiled in the intractable debate over the moral permissibility of humanitarian intervention. According to Gareth Evans, one of the ICISS co-chairs, the commission had determined that the debate over humanitarian intervention had become stagnant and that progress was being hampered by the focus on the international community's *right to* intervene in cases of grave humanitarian crisis.[7]

In the developed North there were calls for greater international involvement in the internal affairs of states that proved unwilling or unable to act in the face of humanitarian crises.[8] On the other hand, in the developing South the calls for greater international involvement were met with skepticism. Their opposition was not to the underlying moral belief that individuals should have their basic rights protected, rather the concern was that a right to intervene held by the international community would be used as a pretext to engage in a new form of colonialism.[9]

The ICISS desire to avoid the intransigence of the debate over the right of intervention led to the second methodological commitment; a focus on the apparent consensus around the proposition that the basic rights of individuals ought to be protected and that sovereign states bear primarily responsibility for insuring that their inhabitants' rights are protected. This domestic responsibility is argued by the ICISS to be at the heart of the emerging understanding of what it means to be a sovereign state. As such, the responsibility to protect principle is consistent with respect for state sovereignty.

It is the secondary responsibility assigned to the international community that represents a more significant shift away from the traditional view of state sovereignty. Under the responsibility to protect, if a state fails to fulfill the responsibility it owes to its inhabitants, then the international community has the responsibility to act to insure that the basic rights of individuals are secured against violation.

The primary policy recommendation advanced by the ICISS in furtherance of the responsibility to protect principle was for more proactive efforts by the international community to prevent grave humanitarian crises; not reaction to them. In addition, the commission argued that should international action be required, it must proceed from less intrusive measures to more as necessity demands; employing military force as a last resort only. However, as Gareth Evans admits and Thomas Weis has pointed out, the claims that prevention is preferred over reaction and that less intrusive means should be used first are uncontroversial, and their elucidation does not resolve the controversy over humanitarian intervention.[10]

Turning to the principle itself, the adoption of the just war framework permeates the responsibility to protect. Under traditional just war theory the *jus ad bellum* conditions determine whether a state is justified in going to war, and *jus in bello* conditions place moral constraints on the prosecution of a just war. Under traditional just war theory, there are six conditions that must be met for a state to be justified in choosing to go to war. The choice to use military force must be based on a *just cause*. This is the primary focus of the discussion over the moral nature of humanitarian intervention – can a humanitarian crisis ever justify the use of military force? A state must be motivated by the *right intention*; the just cause must not be a pretext for less admirable purposes. The choice to use military force must be a *last resort.* The use of military forces must also be a *proportionate response* to the circumstances giving rise to the just cause. In the ICISS's delineation of the conditions, they do not seem to distinguish between proportionate response and proportionate means; the latter being a condition of *jus in bello.* In addition, there must be a *reasonable likelihood of success.* This is a consequentialist consideration; to be just, the use of force must be expected to produce a morally good result. Lastly, the declaration of war must be made by a *right authority*, a political institution with the authority to do so.

Returning to the ICISS report, the ICISS lays out four "Principles for Military Intervention" that appeal to traditional just war criteria. First, under the responsibility to protect, humanitarian intervention becomes a viable option only if all less intrusive measures have been exhausted; it must be the last resort. Next, for there to be a just cause,

There must be serious and irreparable harm occurring to human beings, or imminently likely to occur, of the following kind:
A. **large scale loss of life,** actual or apprehended, with genocidal intent or not which is the product either of deliberate state action, or state neglect or inability to act, or a failed state situation; or
B. **large scale 'ethnic cleansing',** actual or apprehended, whether carried out by killing, forced expulsion, acts of terror or rape.[11]

As such, under the ICISS's view the conditions necessary for there to be a just cause are rather stringent.

The second "principle" is a set of side constraints that limit when a just cause should give rise to an intervention. The ICISS refers to these as the "Precautionary Principles". Three of the four precautionary principles are analogues of traditional just war criteria. Like the requirement of a right intention, to be just a choice to intervene must have as its "primary purpose . . ., whatever other motives intervening states may have" resolving the humanitarian crisis providing the just cause.[12] And, there must be reasonable prospects for success.[13]

The last of the four precautionary principles, proportional means, blurs the line between the *jus ad bellum* and *jus in bello* criteria. The position of the ICISS seems to be that the use of military force must be a proportionate response to the crisis *and* that it must be fought within means that are proportionate to the goal; and in this case that goal is humanitarian in nature. Though it is not possible to discuss them here, this latter claim has interesting implications for the means available to soldiers engaged in a humanitarian intervention.

At a general level, the third principle requiring that only those with "Right Authority" can engage in a just war is also taken from traditional *jus ad bellum* conditions. The principle adopted by the ICISS presumes that only one international institution has such authority – the United Nations Security Council (Security Council). This understanding of who/what has been/should be invested with right authority at the international level further evinces the commitment of the ICISS to defending a principle consistent with existing institutional structures.

The final principle, "Operational Principles", provides guidance regarding the mandate authorizing an intervention, the military approach taken by the intervening force, and the means used in carrying out the intervention.[14] This is a departure from the *jus ad bellum* approach, and is an effort to provide a framework for carrying out an effective and just humanitarian intervention.

With this understanding of the principle, the discussion can return to the explication of the ICISS's vision for institutionalizing the principle. The ICISS view is expressed in its statement on the requirement of "Right Authority". On this point, it is worth quoting the report at length:

(3) RIGHT AUTHORITY

A. There is no better or more appropriate body than the United Nations Security Council to authorize military intervention for human protection purposes. The task is not to find alternatives to the Security Council, but to make the Security Council work better than it has.

B. Security Council authorization should in all cases be sought prior to any military intervention action being carried out. Those calling for an intervention should formally request such authorization, or have the Council raise the matter on its own initiative, or have the Secretary-General raise it under Article 99 of the UN Charter.

C. The Security Council should deal promptly with any request for authority to intervene where there are allegations of large scale loss of human life or ethnic cleansing. It should in this context seek adequate verification of facts or conditions on the ground that might support a military intervention.

D. The permanent five members of the Security Council should agree not to apply their veto power, in matters where their vital state interests are not involved, to obstruct the passage of resolutions authorizing military intervention for human protection purposes for which there is otherwise majority support.

E. If the Security Council rejects a proposal or fails to deal with it in a reasonable time, alternative options are:
   I. consideration of the matter by the General Assembly in Emergency Special Session under the "Uniting for Peace" procedure; and
   II. action within area of jurisdiction by regional or sub-regional organizations under Chapter VIII of the Charter, subject to their seeking subsequent authorization from the Security Council.

F. The Security Council should take into account in all its deliberations that if it fails to discharge its responsibility to protect in conscience-shocking situations crying out for action, concerned states may not rule out other means to meet the gravity and urgency of that situation – and that the stature and credibility of the United Nations may suffer thereby.[15]

The ICISS believes that the Security Council is both legally and morally justified in deciding whether and when humanitarian intervention is called for. The ICISS looks to the Charter of the United Nations to construct a legal argument in support of this proposition; noting that one of the purposes of the United Nations is the maintenance and promotion of international peace and security, and that Chapter VII allocates to the Security Council the authority to authorize action "when it 'determine[s] the existence of any threat to the peace, breach of the peace, or act of aggression.'"[16] Under Article 42, such breaches may be dealt with through the use of coercive military force. In addition, the ICISS provides evidence that the Security Council has in recent years employed a broad understanding of what constitutes a threat to international peace and security.

In addition to understanding who has decisional authority, understanding a particular prescription for institutionalization requires that one also understand the deliberative and decision-making processes. Specifically one must have an understanding of the procedural norms that are to govern the operation of the process, and the substantive considerations taken into account in the deliberations.

As to the former, the procedures envisioned by the ICISS are largely ad hoc and informal, but the ICISS does offer a view on the different phases in the decisional process. The process would begin when those advocating for intervention bring the matter before the Security Council.[17] Then the Security Council *should* investigate the matter to "seek adequate verification of facts or conditions on the ground that might support a military intervention."[18] If a reasonable case for humanitarian intervention is made, the five veto-holding members of the Security Council *should* agree "not to apply their veto power, in matters where their vital state interests are not involved."[19]

The last step is, in fact, a catch-all should the Security Council fail to fulfill its responsibility. The Security Council may be the only institution with right authority; however, should the Security Council reject a proposed intervention, two alternative avenues for action are the General Assembly and/or regional/sub-regional organizations, through which some degree of official legitimacy, if not authorization, could be attained.

As noted in the Introduction to Chapter 4, there are a wide range of alternatives for institutionalizing a deliberative process to give practical effect to a particular norm. At one end of the spectrum, we could treat every question in which the norm is implicated as an open one. At the other end, we could explicitly delineate the reasons relevant to and permitted into the deliberations. The process envisioned by the ICISS gives the Security Council a wide range of discretion regarding what reasons to take into account while also highlighting a number of reasons that should be taken into account. The ICISS does not, however, advocate for the delineation to be formalized. Consequently, the deliberative process envisioned is largely ad hoc.

As to the reasons highlighted by the ICISS, first and foremost are those necessary to determine whether there is a just cause for humanitarian intervention. Second, by recommending that the five permanent members of the Security Council agree to withhold their vetoes unless their vital national interests are involved, the ICISS implicitly recognizes vital national interests to be included in the Security Council's deliberations. Lastly, the ICISS believes that the Security Council should consider the impact a choice not to intervene would have on the standing of the United Nations and the Security Council in the eyes of the international community.

CRITICAL PERSPECTIVES ON THE RESPONSIBILITY TO PROTECT

The ICISS's work on the responsibility to protect represents a significant advancement in the international community's understanding of the norms governing humanitarian intervention and the role the international community ought to play in securing the basic rights of individuals against violation. In addition, the responsibility to protect principle is reasonable and likely consistent with the moral obligation of humanitarian intervention defended above. Consequently, the critique that follows is focused on the recommendations for institutionalization made by the ICISS.

Criticisms and Responses

The first task in the critical discussion of the ICISS recommendations for institutionalization is the identification and rejection of a number of more general objections to efforts to institutionalize *any* interventionist principle. Since the ICISS issued its report in 2001, there have been a number of significant events and trends that have shaped current thinking about the responsibility to protect principle and its institutionalization; these give rise to a number of general criticisms applicable to any effort to institutionalize a norm governing and justifying humanitarian intervention.

First, the invasion of Iraq in 2003 has had a tremendous impact on how many people think about any principle that could be used to justify humanitarian intervention. The addition of a new justification for the use of force in the international arena provides additional normative resources that a belligerent could rely upon to hide its less-than-humanitarian reasons for action. The choice by the United States along with a coalition of other states to invade Iraq without explicit Security Council authorization has heightened the concern over the possible illicit use of the responsibility to protect because members of the coalition employed rhetoric (often post hoc) echoing the language of the responsibility to protect to justify their choice to invade Iraq.

Many have come to refer to this as the "Trojan Horse" objection.[20] The concern is that the acceptance of any principle delineating criteria justifying humanitarian intervention increases the possibility that powerful states will invoke such reasons to interfere in the internal affairs of weaker states; a pretextual use of a moral justification. Alex Bellamy has explained why this is a particularly pressing problem with the responsibility to protect.[21] In its effort to reconcile existing institutions and norms with the emerging consensus that the international community should act in cases of grave humanitarian crisis, the ICISS report was ambiguous on a number of important moral and practical considerations regarding the criteria governing the decision to act and the prosecution of the action itself.

This ambiguity allows for confusion over the meaning and intent of the provisions that define when action should be taken, who has the authority to make the decision, and who or what qualifies as a legitimate intervening agent. In addition, the ambiguity allows for the possibility that a unilateral actor could manipulate the principle to justify illicit action under the guise of the responsibility to protect.[22] However, this is a moral hazard that accompanies any new justification for the use of force, and is not unique to justifications for humanitarian intervention.[23] The fact that a rule or principle may be abused by those with less than noble intentions should motivate those designing the institution of the principle to pay special attention to the avoidance of such moral hazards.

As to the 2003 invasion of Iraq in particular, James Pattison argues that the US invasion fails to impugn the justification for humanitarian intervention implied by the responsibility to protect principle's "Just Cause" and "Precautionary Principles" because the invasion of Iraq would not have been consistent with those conditions. As such, the invasion of Iraq is not an example of legitimate action under the responsibility to protect principle.

Though Pattison points out an important conceptual distinction between humanitarian intervention and the pretextual use of humanitarian language in the pursuit of less salutary purposes, as a response to the practical concern regarding the role such principles could play in the practical deliberations of states, this is less than satisfying. If the concern were conceptual accuracy, then drawing such conceptual distinctions would be invaluable. However, here the concern is with making the principle effective as a regulative norm of an institutional structure. Assuming that, as stated, the principle is likely to admit of misunderstanding, abuse, and misuse; then it is a moral imperative that the institutionalization of the principle focuses on limiting the likelihood that this will occur. The invasion of Iraq and its aftermath should help us to realize why proper and effective institutionalization of a principle intended to govern the international community's response to grave humanitarian crises is so important.

The second criticism regarding the institutionalization of the responsibility to protect principle is tied to the 2005 World Summit. In 2005, to commemorate the sixtieth anniversary and sixtieth session of the United Nations General Assembly, the General Assembly met in a high-level plenary session. The purpose of the session was to address some of the most pressing matters of concern facing the international community; including humanitarian intervention.[24] In the end, the proposition that sovereign states had a responsibility to protect the basic rights of their inhabitants was adopted unanimously. Many of the ICISS participants and supporters hailed this as a significant shift in the thinking about the nature of sovereignty.

However, and despite the general commitment to the idea that states are the primary bearers of responsibility for the protection of their inhabitants' basic rights, in the negotiations that led to the outcome document, the responsibility of the international community to act to secure the basic rights of individuals was largely limited to non-coercive measures and much of the bite was taken out of the ICISS recommendations.[25] This has caused some to argue that the international community has managed to create the appearance of reform while changing very little.[26] In the end, as Bellamy notes, in attempting to forge a consensus, nearly all of the key elements of the responsibility to protect were sacrificed.[27]

This should, however, not be understood as a blow against the principle itself nor as a reason for apathy. Rather, as Bellamy concludes,

> It is imperative that states now return to some of the fundamental questions the ICISS raised: *Who,* precisely, has a responsibility to protect? *When* is that responsibility acquired? *What* does the responsibility to protect entail? And *how* do we know when the responsibility to protect has been divested? If they do not, there is a real danger that states of all stripes will co-opt the language of the responsibility to protect to legitimate inaction and irresponsibility.[28]

As such, it is unlikely that the 2005 World Summit version of the responsibility to protect will have a significant practical impact. However, the fact that there exists a (growing) consensus around the underlying proposition that the international community has a responsibility to act in cases of grave humanitarian crisis should motivate those committed to alleviating the suffering of the victims of such crises to continue to seek the effective, just, and fair institutionalization of such a norm.

Lastly, some claim that neither the ICISS explication of the responsibility to protect nor the version of the principle adopted by the General Assembly at the 2005 World Summit has, in fact, had an impact on the behavior of states. If the will to act exists then the international community will act. If it is lacking then the international community won't act. The principle is not playing an independent role in the practical deliberations of states. As an example, Martin Binder notes that the fact that there is a great degree of discretion involved in the determination of which crises calling out for intervention are addressed and which are not is due to the fact that states will act out of their own interests and are not likely to be constrained by a rule imposed by the international community.[29] In short, whether an intervention takes place can be explained without reference to the responsibility to protect principle.

The fact that states continue to act in accordance with their interests and be selective in determining whether and when to intervene does not, however, support a categorical objection to the possibility of effectively institutionalizing a norm intended to govern the practical deliberations of states. It merely demonstrates that the ICISS and the United Nations (at the 2005 World Summit) efforts are lacking. Though these criticisms are intended to stand on their own, it is important to also note that as a general matter, each supports the proposition that efforts to control states through the identification, defense, and institutionalization of normative principles are likely to fail.

This general criticism relies upon a particular understanding of what it means for the institutionalization of a principle to be effective. Namely, that it is effective if, and only if, it has an impact on the deliberations directed at determining a solution to the problem. If the institutionalization of a principle fails to have such an impact, then the principle is not constraining or enhancing the deliberations in any way. This does not mean that states and/or the international community will not, on occasion, act in ways that are consistent with the principle, but it will be the underlying reasons that support the principle that inform their actions, not the principle itself.

There are a number of responses to this general criticism. First, focusing on the claim that the impact of the institutionalization of a principle like the responsibility to protect is doomed to impotence, it is a mistake to confuse a principle with its institutionalization. A successful critique of a particular effort at institutionalization does not impugn the underlying principle nor does it necessarily undermine other designs for the institutionalization of the principle. For example, the failure of the responsibility to protect principle to influence the deliberations of states could be attributed to the desire by the ICISS and the delegates at the 2005 World Summit to seek consensus on the institutionalization of the principle. In which case, the ineffectiveness of the principle could be attributed to the particular approach taken to institutionalization; not on some general inability to effectively institutionalize a norm governing the behavior of states in the international arena.

As to the concern that the adoption of a new norm justifying the use of military force in the international arena will lead to more violence rather than the promotion or protection of humanitarian values, the concern is based on the proposition that states will only act in their own interest. In which case, the availability of a broader range of reasons to which states could appeal to justify the use of force will make military solutions to political problems more available, if not more appealing. The awareness of such concerns should guide those responsible for institutionalizing the norm. Again, this may be a problem with particular efforts at institutionalization, but that is distinct from the underlying principle; and, without more, is separate from the possibility that other approaches to institutionalization will be more effective.

Finally, as to the general proposition that any effort to institutionalize a norm like the responsibility to protect is likely to fail, the underlying argument is based on a particular standard of effectiveness; namely, that to be successful, an institutionalized norm must have a determinative impact on the practical deliberations of states. Beginning with this working definition, and assuming that the arguments pressed regarding either a moral obligation to intervene or the responsibility to protect are correct, the failure resides with the states that could create and abide by an effective institutionalization of a principle. Futility is a justification for inaction only if an agent cannot perform an action. Here, should the international community fail to design an effective institution, it is a matter of choice.

Another response involves adopting an alternative understanding of success. Instead of focusing on the degree to which the institutionalization of the norm has a direct impact on the practical deliberations of states, one might contend that the institutionalization of a norm is successful if it results in a change in the rhetoric surrounding humanitarian intervention. A successfully institutionalized norm would render transparent the considerations relevant to the assessment of the responsibilities of those with the ability to act; thus, laying bare the moral failures of the international community, and making more fundamental reform more likely.

In either case, we are led to the recognition of the need for more reaching reform. The fact that the ICISS recommendations for institutionalization have failed to have a practical impact on the practical deliberations of states does not imply that the project of institutionalization should be abandoned. Rather, what are needed are new ideas for the reform of the institutions and principles that define the normative framework of international relations that render the principle(s) institutionalized effective. If, on the other hand, one adopts the alternative notion of success suggested above, the consensus around the responsibility to protect should compel us to seek out the next step in the reformist project; the ultimate goal being an effective and just institutionalized principle.

Having responded to a number of objections to the project of institutionalization, the critique of the responsibility to protect that follows is an important step in the effort to move beyond the well-intentioned but ineffective effort of the ICISS. Specifically, the critical discussion of the ICISS recommendations for institutionalization focuses on identifying those aspects of the ICISS account that render it unlikely that the responsibility to protect principle will play a significant role in the practical deliberations of states. It is this critical analysis of the ICISS's institutional design that will inform the discussion of an alternative institutional structure.

One might object that the ICISS vision is the best that could be accomplished in a world of sovereign states. Reform, however, should be aspirational in nature. As such, even if states are not at present willing to institutionalize more demanding reforms, there is value in setting our sights on an institutional structure that is likely to be more effective and more just. In addition, by failing to advocate for change in the underlying structures and principles, the ICISS has left intact much of the normative framework that resulted in the humanitarian disasters of the 1990s. Consequently, the ICISS approach may actually hinder the effort to effectively deal with grave humanitarian crises, because the recommendations proposed provide the appearance of international concern without making action any more likely.

Lastly, the underlying assumption is that it is morally wrong for the international community to choose not to intervene in cases where the nature of the humanitarian crisis demands intervention. In which case, the international community has a responsibility to develop and support institutions that would fulfill these moral demands. The fact that other interests prevent states from doing so is not a failing of the institutional design; it is a moral failure of the international community. Even assuming that more extensive reform will not happen, there is value to be gained from the critical perspective an account of a legitimate institution would provide. Rhetoric about human rights and commitments to insure that such horrific events are "never again" allowed to occur could be judged by how far they fall short of what is necessary to make such claims meaningful.

The critical analysis of the ICISS prescription for institutionalization requires a critical standard to be applied. The critical standard developed here is based on the identification of the conditions under which an institution has a justified claim to legitimacy. Those conditions are used to assess the ICISS claim to institutional legitimacy. In the end, the critique of the ICISS recommendations for institutionalization provides a framework for the alternative institutional structure proposed in the next section.

The critical standard should be relevant to the analysis of institutions and not just a general perspective on legitimacy. As such, the critical standard must account not only for the substantive moral or material justification for the institution; it must also provide an understanding of what constitutes a politically legitimate institutional structure. The latter requirement is implied by the fact that there is likely to be (reasonable) disagreement over the facts presented to an institution for its consideration; as well as (reasonable) disagreement over whether an institution should act, and what actions should be taken. In which case, resolution of the matter requires politically legitimate deliberative and decision-making processes.

Consequently, the critical standard is constructed around two distinct aspects of institutional legitimacy, the ability of the institution to advance the underlying material justification and the political legitimacy of the deliberative and decision-making processes of the institution. As to the former, the institution is a means to pursue the goals implied by the principle being institutionalized. As such, the relationship between the institution and the principle being institutionalized is an instrumental one, and the legitimacy of the institution depends on the degree to which the institution advances the goal or purpose of the underlying principle. With regards to the responsibility to protect and humanitarian intervention generally, the underlying principle is that under certain circumstances the international community ought to intervene militarily to prevent grave humanitarian crises from occurring or to stop them once they have begun.

Consequently, for an institution to be instrumentally legitimate, it must make a practical difference in the pursuit of that goal. If the institution merely bends to the will of the agents it is intended to govern rather than adding to or constraining the practical deliberations of those agents, then the institution has no instrumental value. As for those institutions that do make a difference, their relative value or legitimacy is tied to the degree to which the practical deliberations of the agents they are governing are impacted.

There are, however, a number of ways in which an institution could meet the conditions required for instrumental legitimacy. It is not simply the case that to be effective an institution must fulfill the demands of the principle directly. As was discussed in Chapter 2 above, the completion of a norm is directly related to the practical efficacy of the norm. The role this plays in effectiveness is an indirect, but essential one. The responsibility to protect principle is incomplete.[30] It does not implicitly identify with sufficient specificity *who* owes *what* to *whom*.[31] It is essential, especially in instances where humanitarian intervention may be called for, that the norm be completed.

This is not to say, however, that completing a norm will not have a significant impact on the actions taken. Agents (individual and collective) act for reasons, more diffuse reasons render action less likely and make it unreasonable for others to expect that action will be taken. On the other hand, the greater the degree of specificity, the greater our understanding of moral and practical responsibility; thus, there is an increased likelihood that action will be taken.

It would be unreasonable to require that an institution have a determinative impact on the will of the international community. As a moral matter, since the international community is made of independent states, the demands that can be placed on states in the international arena are complicated by the fact that states have special relationships with those living within their political boundaries. The existence of these additional moral demands complicates the practical deliberations of states when deciding whether to act to fulfill their responsibilities within the international arena. One could imagine a case where the domestic considerations are so weighty that it would be unreasonable to expect such a burdened state to act. All that can be reasonably expected is that the institutionalization of the norm makes a difference in the practical deliberations of states.

In addition to these indirect impacts, a relevant consideration in assessing the instrumental value of an institution is the extent to which the institution has a direct impact on the actions taken by the international community. Once a decision by an institution has been reached, the choice of action should be carried out, and there is a practical gap between the determination of what ought to be done and the actual execution of the chosen action(s). The extent to which the institution bridges this gap and plays a causal role in the execution of the chosen action is an important consideration in our assessment of the practical effectiveness and (degree of) instrumental legitimacy of the institution.

We can derive from this discussion three criteria related to the effectiveness of an institution. First, the institution should enhance the ability of the international community to complete the demands of the norm. Second, the institutionalization of the norm should have some impact on the role the norm plays in the practical deliberations of states. And third, the degree to which the institution can aid in the translation of the decision by the institution into action is relevant to our assessment of the institution's claim to efficacy.

Since, agents act based upon the results of their practical deliberations the first two criteria take priority over the third. First, implementation of an institutional decision cannot be justified unless that decision is justified by its relationship to the underlying material justification. This supports the proposition that the correct completion of the norm has normative priority over the translation of the decision into action. Second, the first two criteria have practical priority over the third. It makes little sense to speak of action without an understanding of the mandate to act. In other words, for the translation of a decision into action to be a relevant practical concern, it must be the case that there is a decision to implement.

Some might argue that instrumental legitimacy is all that we need be concerned with. One example of an argument seeking to defend the claim that it is effectiveness alone that matters is given by James Pattison. In his discussion of the legitimacy of humanitarian intervention, Pattison argues that effectiveness is (essentially) the sole criterion for assessing the legitimacy of an intervention.[32] Pattison's project focused on answering, "Who should intervene?" In doing so, he juxtaposes unauthorized versus institutionally authorized intervention, arguing that the fact that an intervention is unauthorized does not, all other things being equal, make it any less legitimate than an authorized intervention.[33]

Pattison's claim is open to two interpretations. First, he might be claiming that under our current institutional framework, the institutions responsible for making such determinations are flawed; consequently, the authorization from such institutions is normatively meaningless. In that case, there is no point to assessing the legitimacy of such institutions. Alternatively he might be arguing that no matter what the nature of the institution making the decision is, authorization is unnecessary for legitimate humanitarian interventions. Though these are significantly different claims, neither implies that effectiveness is the sole criterion of institutional legitimacy. If Pattison is making the former claim, all that is implied is that our current institutional arrangement does not affect the legitimacy of an intervention. It does not imply that *institutional* authorization is irrelevant to our understanding of institutional legitimacy. A full account of institutional legitimacy is still needed.

If, however, the argument is intended to support the latter claim, then I disagree, and find the account of institutional legitimacy incomplete. Though a minimum degree of effectiveness is no doubt necessary to institutional legitimacy, it is not sufficient. Under effectiveness as a standard of institutional legitimacy, whether an institution is legitimate is simply a matter of determining the degree to which the institution advances the morally valuable ends the institution is intended to achieve. This univocal focus on the instrumental value of an institution fails to recognize the significance of the *political* nature of the issues dealt with by most institutions.

An issue is political when reasonable disagreement exists over the correct choice among various alternatives. The institutionalization of a norm governing the decision to use humanitarian military intervention is a political matter, but not necessarily because of disagreement over the norm itself. As the ICISS points out, there is very good reason to believe that a consensus that the international community bears some moral responsibility to secure the basic rights of individuals against violation exists. However, it is likely that there will remain disagreement over the determination of whether the conditions necessary to justify intervention by the international community have been met in a particular circumstance; what Jeremy Waldron calls the "circumstances of politics."[34]

In these moments of disagreement, abstract claims about rightness, permissibility, obligation, and responsibility, though essential to our understanding of what makes a humanitarian intervention legitimate, fail to provide legitimacy to a decision to act because it is the relevance of the principles themselves that is being disputed. Consequently, in addition to requiring that the institution be effective, a legitimate institution must embody deliberative and decision-making *processes* that are politically legitimate such that the decisions rendered by the institution are legitimate, if not correct.

At the very least, political legitimacy requires that all those affected by institutional action should be permitted to participate in the deliberations of the institution. For example, in the case of humanitarian intervention, the burden of the intervention and the impacts of the choice of the institution regarding intervention are going to fall upon many states and communities outside of the target state. As such, and since there is likely to be disagreement about whether a particular intervention is justified, for the choice to intervene to be legitimate, it must be the outcome of deliberative and decision-making processes that provide an opportunity for those affected to participate in the institutional deliberations relevant to the choice.

There are multiple rationales for this requirement of political legitimacy. First, if we assume that those affected by an action have equal moral standing, then to exclude any from the deliberations would fail to respect them as moral equals. One could argue that genocidaires and other violators of basic rights lack equal moral standing, but that would be failing to understand the epistemic priority involved. That is the very question that must be addressed before intervention is permitted; the question the process is intended to answer.

Alternatively, it would be reasonable to assume that participation by all affected by an action is instrumentally valuable. What we want as an outcome of the deliberations is the right answer; or, at least as close to the right answer as possible. Including the perspectives of all who are likely to be affected by an action increases the probability that our deliberations will result in the identification of the right answer. This effort at epistemic accuracy must, however, be balanced against the practical necessity of arriving at *an* answer in a timely fashion. The goal is not perfection, but sufficient correctness to properly assess whether the use of military force is justified.

In addition to the implications the political nature of the institutionalization of a norm has for our understanding of what makes institutional deliberative and decision-making processes legitimate, it is important to recognize that the relationship between the institution's deliberative processes and executive function may be relevant to our account of institutional legitimacy. Specifically, how is the decisional authority of the institution related to its executive function? Returning to Pattison's argument rejecting the relevance of institutional authorization to our assessment of the legitimacy of an intervention, the implication is that a unilateral actor (or coalition of actors) need not seek institutional authorization for the intervention engaged in by the actor(s). In that case, both the decisional and executive authority would lie with the same entity.

In addition to highlighting concerns related to the political legitimacy of the deliberative and decision-making processes, recognition of the political nature of the question of humanitarian intervention highlights the importance of the relationship between the decisional authority and the executive function of the institution(s) authorizing and/or carrying out the intervention. Decisional authority should be separated from responsibility for carrying out the decision because of the equal respect that is owed to all those affected by an action. If decisional authority and executive function are embedded in the same institution, unless the institution has universal membership many who are affected by the institution's choice of action will be treated as political inferiors since they will be subject to the will of those making the decision.

Returning to Pattison, in rejecting prior institutional authorization as irrelevant, he is implicitly endorsing as legitimate an institutional structure that houses decisional authority and executive function within the same body. Whether this is problematic to his account of legitimacy depends on the object of Pattison's claim about legitimacy. Assuming Pattison's argument is about the post hoc evaluation of an intervention, then it may be the case that whether the intervention was authorized is largely irrelevant to our assessment of the intervention's moral legitimacy.

Determining that an unauthorized intervention was legitimate would, however, depend on the truth of a number of factual propositions. For example, it would have to be the case that the cause for the intervention was just, the intervention was motivated by the right reasons (or at least not the wrong ones), and that the intervention in its conduct and outcome accomplished its humanitarian goal. If all of this is true, then it would be reasonable to conclude that *the intervention* was morally legitimate.[35]

If this is accurate, Pattison is assessing the legitimacy of an intervention after the fact; wherein, the standard is employed to distinguish between legitimate and illegitimate interventions post hoc. The ICISS, however, was not focused on the post hoc analysis of interventions, but rather with determining how, within the international arena, the decision to intervene ought to be made and action carried out. As such, setting up an institutional structure that when faced with a humanitarian crisis can effectively and justly decide when such interventions are appropriate is equally important.

Separating decisional authority from the executive function also provides a check on the potential for pretextual use of military force. First, the institution with decisional authority would lack the ability to carry out its own mandate; consequently, it must offer reasons for action sufficient to convince those responsible for carrying out the intervention. Second, separating decisional authority from executive function makes the reasons supplied by the institution making the decision the main motive for action. Pretextual use of humanitarian reasons may still be possible, but the level of covert coordination that would have to go on between the institution holding decisional authority and the entity responsible for carrying out the intervention is unlikely to occur.

There is one final critical point to be raised against a failure to separate decisional authority from executive function. Combining decisional authority with executive function undermines the appearance of impartiality. This may not seem to be a relevant concern since appearance is not the same thing as reality. In that case, the appearance of pretext that arises from a failure to separate decisional authority from executive function could be dismissed as unfounded since it is what is *actually* motivating the intervener and how they are *actually* acting that matters. However, such an understanding unjustifiably disregards the context within which such decisions and actions take place. For most of modern history the international arena has been a venue for states to act upon and further their national interests. Increasingly, international relations have become a rule-governed arena resulting in greater international order. It is important to the stability of a system that depends on the voluntary cooperation of those who it claims to govern that there is an appearance of impartiality in the processes that determine how states may act; especially when it comes to the use of force by one (or some) against another.

To summarize, our understanding of institutional legitimacy should begin with the recognition of two distinct but related categories of conditions. There are those that are concerned with the effectiveness or instrumental value of the institution, and those focused on matters of political legitimacy related to the deliberative and decision-making processes of the institution. It is no doubt true that there are contingent (rather than conceptual) relationships that exist between the two categories. For example, the requirement of political legitimacy that all affected by an action (or inaction) have an opportunity to participate in the deliberative process makes it more likely that the instrumental requirement that the demands of the norm will be completed correctly will be met. However, since fulfilling the political condition does not guarantee that the norm will be completed, the relationship is a contingent one.

As to an explicit delineation of the conditions of institutional legitimacy that will be used to evaluate the ICISS recommendations for institutionalizing the responsibility to protect principle, first are those conditions related to the effectiveness of the institution:

1. *Completion of the demands of the norm*: the content and scope of the demands implied by the underlying material justification for the institution be identified which should include a recognition that completion of any norm governing humanitarian intervention must account for the two phases of humanitarian action and should place decisional authority for both phases within a single institution;
2. *Impact on practical deliberations*: the degree to which the institution impacts the practical deliberations of those responsible for deciding and acting in furtherance of the demands implied by the material justification adds to or detracts from the instrumental legitimacy of the institution; and
3. *Direct impact*: though perhaps less important because of the nature of the international arena, the degree to which the institution plays a direct role in the execution of the plan for the fulfillment of the demands implied by the material justification for the institution is relevant to our assessment of the instrumental legitimacy of the institution.

It is important to note that effectiveness as a measure of legitimacy admits of degrees. The threshold for the legitimacy of an institution based on its effectiveness lies at the point at which the institution makes a practical difference in the role the norm plays in the practical deliberations and actions of those to whom it applies.

Second, there are the conditions of political legitimacy related to the deliberative and decision-making processes of the institution:

4. *Political legitimacy*: in furtherance of the demands of political legitimacy, all who are affected by a potential action (or inaction) should
   have the opportunity to participate in the deliberative process; and
5. *Separation of powers*: decisional authority should be separate from
   executive function.

Whereas the assessment of instrumental legitimacy is determined by
the effectiveness of the institution, the assessment of the legitimacy of
the deliberative and decision-making processes is not tied to the likely
outcomes produced by the institution. As such, an institution may be
highly effective, but fail to be fully legitimate because the deliberative
and decision-making processes of the institution fail to meet minimum
standards of political legitimacy.

Recognizing the fact that instrumental legitimacy is categorically different from political legitimacy highlights an important property of the
dualistic standard for institutional legitimacy being developed. A lack
of legitimacy in one category cannot be made up for by an excess in
the other. For example, if the deliberative and decision-making processes embodied in an institution fail to provide all who are affected
by an action with an opportunity to participate in the deliberations
then the institution lacks political legitimacy to some degree. Its lack
of political legitimacy cannot be compensated for by the fact that the
process is excellent at completing the demands of the underlying norm
– instrumental legitimacy.

CRITICALLY ASSESSING THE ICISS RECOMMENDATIONS FOR INSTITUTIONALIZATION

The critical evaluation of the ICISS recommendations for the institutionalization of the responsibility to protect principle begins with the
assessment of the ability of the ICISS prescription to satisfy the conditions of instrumental legitimacy. As noted above, the ICISS approach
was grounded in an effort to reconcile the responsibility to protect
principle with the existing principles and structures of the normative
framework of international relations. It is not clear, however, that such
reconciliation is possible. As such, it must be demonstrated that the
ICISS is correct in its belief that reconciliation is possible.

The ICISS argument for reconciliation turns on the proposition
that sovereignty has been re-conceptualized by the international

community, and that the contemporary conception of sovereignty implies a protection against outside interference in matters internal to the state but is grounded in the recognition that states have a responsibility to protect the basic rights of their inhabitants. If true, it is argued, the conflict underlying the long-running debate over humanitarian intervention is based on a misunderstanding regarding the nature of sovereignty.

However, the debate over the moral justifiability of humanitarian intervention may have been intractable for so long, not because it was framed improperly, but because there *is* a substantive conflict between humanitarian intervention and state sovereignty. Even assuming the correctness of the ICISS's understanding that sovereignty carries with it a responsibility borne by the domestic political institutions to protect the basic rights of the state's inhabitants does not imply that the international community has a responsibility to intervene when the domestic institutions fail. Consequently, it is not inconsistent for states to concede that they have internal responsibilities owed to their inhabitants while also rejecting the notion that this implies a responsibility to protect borne by the international community that would permit (if not obligate) the international community to intervene. The fact that the 2005 World Summit Outcome Document is only a partial endorsement of the responsibility to protect principle is an indication that agreement regarding the responsibility of domestic institutions should not be taken to imply agreement regarding the existence of a responsibility to protect borne by the international community.

The normative conflict at the heart of the debate over humanitarian intervention is about whether there are circumstances under which humanitarian intervention is permitted. Since the clearest agreement is over the understanding of sovereignty that implies only a responsibility to protect for domestic political institutions, it is unclear that the ICISS approach avoids the conflict between sovereignty and emerging norms regarding the role of the international community in protecting basic rights. For the reconciliation project to be successful, an independent account of the relationship between state sovereignty and the international community's responsibility to protect must be provided. If the reconciliation project is not successful, a resolution of the matter requires taking sides.

Nonetheless, for the ICISS recommendations to satisfy the conditions for instrumental legitimacy, more than reconciliation is necessary.

It must also be the case that the resultant principle and prescription for institutionalization are (or are likely to be) effective at advancing the demands of the underlying material justification. However, it is the ICISS's effort at reconciliation that makes this an unlikely proposition.

In its discussion of the "Sources of Authority Under the UN Charter",[36] the ICISS pays particular attention to Article 2.4 of the Charter which states that

> In order to ensure prompt and effective action by the United Nations, members confer on the Security Council primary responsibility for the maintenance of international peace and security, and agree that in carrying out its duties under this responsibility the Security Council acts on their behalf.[37]

This is an exception to the principle of nonintervention found in Article 2.4 requiring that "All Members shall refrain . . . from the threat or use of force against the territorial integrity or political independence of any state, or in any other manner inconsistent with the Purposes of the United Nations."[38]

The means available to the Security Council to carry out its responsibility to maintain international peace and security are spelled out in Chapters VI and VII of the Charter with the authorization for the use of military force stated in Chapter VII. Specifically, Article 42 states,

> Should the Security Council consider that measures provided for in Article 41 [non-military] would be inadequate or have proved to be inadequate, it may take such action by air, sea, or land forces as may be necessary to maintain or restore international peace and security.[39]

As such, if the actions of a state pose a threat to *international* peace and security, and the only way to avert the threat is through the use of military force then the Security Council has the authority under the Charter to authorize the use of military force.

The ICISS reliance on Article 42 of the Charter may not seem like sufficient justification for the proposition that the Security Council has authority under the Charter to authorize humanitarian intervention, as the humanitarian crises that call out for intervention are often internal to a state, and international peace and security has traditionally been interpreted as the peace and security between states. However, the Charter gives the Security Council discretion to determine what constitutes a threat to international peace and security. Article 39 of Chapter VII states that the

> Security Council shall determine the existence of any threat to the peace, breach of the peace, or act of aggression and shall make recommendations, or decide what measures shall be undertaken in accordance with Articles 41 and 42, to maintain or restore international peace and security.[40]

Thus, what constitutes a threat to international peace and security is a matter of discretion, and is determined by the Security Council's view of the matter.[41]

The ICISS has relied upon the discretion assigned to the Security Council by the Charter to support the contention that the Security Council is within its discretion under Article 42 to authorize humanitarian intervention. In addition, the ICISS looks to a number of Security Council decisions wherein the understanding of international peace and security was expanded to include the destabilizing effect a humanitarian crisis is having on a region. For example, Operation Turquoise was justified because of the threat to regional stability caused by the refugee crisis caused by the genocide. In which case, humanitarian crises that appear internal to a sovereign state fall within the gambit of the authority granted to the Security Council under Chapter VII.

One ought to be skeptical of this argument for the following reasons. First, the fact that the authority for the Security Council to act is based upon a trend in its recent decisions, and not promulgated in any formal rule, means that the authority upon which the ICISS is relying is grounded in the ephemeral will of the Security Council. It is possible that the Security Council's interpretation of international peace and security could change. In which case, its view would be antithetical to the humanitarian concerns underlying the responsibility to protect, and there would be no institutional basis from which to criticize this change in the normative landscape.

Second, relying upon the contingent will of the Security Council undermines the ability of the institutionalization of the norm to make a practical difference in the practical deliberations of the Security Council. Under the ICISS account, the Security Council has the authority to determine what constitutes a threat to international peace and security and the authority based on that determination to authorize humanitarian intervention to re-establish international peace and security; whether the responsibility to protect principle is relevant (determination of what constitutes a threat to international peace and security) and whether it will be enforced (determination of the action the international community is going to take in furtherance of the principles) is left entirely up to the Security Council. It does not influence the will of the Security Council; rather, it is an expression of that will.

As to the specific criteria for instrumental legitimacy discussed above, first, the institution must be able to identify with sufficient specificity the content and scope of the demands implied by the norm. The ad hoc nature of the deliberative process and the influence of political concerns in the deliberations of the Security Council make it unlikely that the completion of the norm will be accomplished satisfactorily. Without a formal delineation of the reasons relevant for consideration, the influence of political concerns will likely hinder the ability of the Security Council to correctly identify with sufficient specificity the content and scope of the norms in question.

The second criterion is perhaps the one most central to the demand that the institution have instrumental legitimacy; namely, the operation of the institution must have an effect on the practical deliberations of those responsible for authorizing action. Owing to the ICISS reliance on existing institutions and principles, it would be unreasonable to expect this sort of impact. It is these very principles and structures that are in need of reform. The only reform sought by the ICISS was a *voluntary* commitment by the veto-holding members of the Security Council to only exercise their vetoes if they had a vital national interest at stake.[42] Despite the fact that this suggestion was not adopted by the Security Council nor by the members of the United Nations at the 2005 World Summit, even if such a commitment were to be gained, the fact that veto-holding states would only exercise their veto in cases of vital national interest does not change the deliberations that one would hope such states would engage in anyway. Rather, the commitment would simply make explicit what states should already be doing.

With regards to the veto, one need not assume that states would exercise their veto in bad faith to understand why the commitment to only use it in cases of vital national interest is unlikely to make much of a difference. The vagaries of language make it reasonable for leaders to differ over a number of important matters. First, they could reasonably disagree over the evaluation of the criteria used to determine whether the responsibility of the international community to act has been implicated. In addition, there could be disagreement over what is considered to be vital and what is considered to be a humanitarian crisis of sufficient moment to justify sacrificing the national interest. In the end, the commitment to withhold their vetoes is unlikely to impact the practical deliberations or alter the decisions reached by the Security Council.

Even if we were to assume that the veto-holding members of the Security Council were to commit to only using the veto when their vital interests were at stake and that this commitment were to make a difference in their practical deliberations and ultimate decisions, there remains a disconnect between the Security Council's decision and the competent execution of that decision. In short, even if the Security Council proves to be an effective decision-making institution, under the ICISS prescription for the institutionalization of the responsibility to protect principle, the execution of the decision is left to the voluntary will of the international community. However, as is discussed below, the United Nations and the Security Council could still play a coordinative role that will aid the effective execution of an intervention.

Additionally, as the Security Council has no official relationship with the various non-governmental organizations (NGOs) that might be best suited, owing to their expertise, to handle post-intervention reconstruction, the coordination necessary to insure that such post-intervention reconstruction is effective is lacking. The lack of coordination takes at least two forms. First, the fact that there is no official relationship between the Security Council and such NGOs increases the likelihood that the actions endorsed by the Security Council may be at cross-purposes with those chosen by the NGOs. And second, there may be numerous NGOs, all well intentioned, engaged in uncoordinated action. The likely result would be inefficient action at best, and may actually cause more problems than they solve.

Finally, the third criterion for the standard of instrumental legitimacy is concerned with the contribution the institution makes (or does not make) to the translation of the decision into action. Much like the standard employed for the evaluation from the second criterion regarding the impact the institution has on the practical deliberations of those deciding whether intervention is authorized, effectiveness on this point is *not* an all-or-nothing proposition. Rather, there is a threshold that must be met, and beyond that threshold, effectiveness is a matter of degree; ranging from merely providing a focal point for the actors to actually commanding a military force.

It is important to note that, at the extreme, is an institution wherein the decisional authority and executive function are embedded within the same institution. For example, one might advocate the creation of an army to serve at the will of the Security Council. This may, at first, appear to be the ideal situation. As a matter of effectiveness, the gap between a decision to intervene and action would not only be bridged; it would no longer exist. Such an institution, one might argue, would be highly effective; and, as a consequence, have a weighty claim to instrumental legitimacy.

The problem, however, arises if we take effectiveness to be normatively unconstrained; that the only thing that matters is the implementation of any decision reached by the institution's deliberative and decision-making processes. However, such an understanding fails to appreciate at least two ways in which normative concerns ought to constrain our understanding of effectiveness as a value. First, the decision being implemented must be a reasonably legitimate one. That would mean that it is a morally correct or defensible completion of the demands of the norm.

A hypothetical may help to understand why this is a problem. Imagine that France, the United Kingdom, and the United States agree that there is a need to intervene in what they claim is a developing humanitarian crisis. These three veto-holding members bring the matter before the Security Council. Under political pressure China and Russia both abstain from the ultimate vote on the resolution. Prior to the deliberations, France, the United Kingdom, and the United States agree (along with other NATO members) to commit NATO military forces to the task of intervention. The resolution passes and NATO intervenes.

In this example, the deliberations by the Security Council are likely to have been heavily influenced (even if with good intentions) by the three veto-holding members. In which case, the larger international community will likely be skeptical of the legitimacy of the decision to intervene. If the decision is suspect, then the fact that the decision is translated immediately into action is not necessarily a fact that adds to the instrumental legitimacy/value of the institution over the long term.

Second, the understanding of effectiveness upon which the argument in favor of embedding decisional and executive authority within the same institution is based is one that has as a logical conclusion the creation of an army and a civilian corps deployable at the discretion of the Security Council. The problems with such a proposal are not new, but bear repeating. In *Perpetual Peace* Kant warned against such a dominant global power. The risk of global tyranny was too great, and could not be overcome by the speculative benefit of an enforced (but authoritarian) peace.[43]

In addition, the existence of such a dominant political, civil, and military power would undermine the freedom of individuals and political communities to determine for themselves how they live. One need only think of Plato's *Republic* to understand this objection.[44] Even if we assume that the Philosopher King was never wrong in his/her judgment, the loss of freedom is not worth the benefits gained. Lastly, such an institution, though conceptually possible, is unlikely now or in the foreseeable future to receive the political support necessary to bring such institutions into existence.

In the end, as a matter of the instrumental legitimacy of an institution intended to implement a norm governing the international community's use of humanitarian intervention, there are two constraints on our understanding and evaluation of that criterion. First, to claim to be effective at translating the decision into action, the institution must make *a* difference in the implementation of the decision reached by the deliberative body of the institution. Second, there is a limitation on the ways in which the institution is permitted to bridge the gap between the decision and action. There must be a degree of separation between the decisional authority of the institution and the executive function of those responsible for carrying out the decision.

One might wonder what this leaves for the institution. There are at least two ways in which an institution could have a (more) direct impact on the implementation of the institution's decision short of commanding its own army and civilian corps. First, an intervention will require multiple levels of coordination. The various participants engaged in and supportive of the military campaign must coordinate their activities. Those engaged in the military campaign must, both during the campaign but more importantly during the transition from a military campaign to a post-intervention phase, coordinate their activities with various political and civil bodies. Lastly, the domestic and regional political bodies will need to coordinate their activities with the international groups providing support both during the military campaign and afterwards during the post-intervention reconstruction. The institution could provide the needed coordination.

Second, since one of the main obstacles to effective action is political will, an institution that influences the willingness of the members of the international community to act or support action by others is one that adds greatly to the translation of the decision to intervene into action. The means by which an institution could have such an influence on the political will of the international community blurs the line being drawn between process-oriented and instrumental legitimacy. Nonetheless, a procedure that appears legitimate and is transparent is likely going to provide a focal point around which the political will to act can be built. It will be easier for the leaders of states to convince their own polities of the rightness of the cause if the institution's deliberative and decision-making procedures are viewed as legitimate.

With that said, the ICISS prescription for the institutionalization of the responsibility to protect principle fails to satisfy this standard. The ICISS reliance on the Security Council is misplaced as the Security Council is both too strong and too weak. Though there is no formal connection between the Security Council and the militaries of the five veto-holding members, few if any interventions are likely to be carried out by militaries not connected to one of the five. As such, the connection between the Security Council and those most likely to carry out its decisions is too strong. On the other hand, the deliberative processes of the Security Council are unlikely to provide a focal point around which political will could be developed. The grossly undemocratic nature of the Security Council undermines its claim to political legitimacy; especially in the case of military action.

In addition, the deliberations of the Security Council and their outcomes are neither sufficiently open nor transparent. As such, there is little record of the rationale behind the decisions and often the resolutions themselves are quite vague. In either case, there is little upon which a state's leaders could rely to build the political will necessary to support or at least not oppose an intervention. In the end, there is little reason to believe that the Security Council, as currently constituted, could satisfy the condition of instrumental legitimacy.

However, even if we assume that the Security Council passes the minimum threshold for instrumental legitimacy, there are two scenarios under which an alternative ought to be preferred. First, in relation to the standard of instrumental legitimacy, if there is an alternative institutional scheme that is practically politically possible,[45] that is more effective at contributing to the fulfillment of the demands of the underlying material justification; then, all other things being equal, the alternative scheme should be preferred. Second, if the two schemes are equally effective and both are achievable, and the alternative has a stronger claim to political legitimacy, then the alternative ought to be preferred on that basis.

However, to assess the latter scenario it is necessary to have an understanding of the extent to which the ICISS recommendation has a justifiable claim to political legitimacy. The evaluation of the political legitimacy of the ICISS's recommendations for institutionalization begins with an assessment of the degree to which the institution provides sufficient opportunities for those likely to be affected by an action to participate in the deliberations leading to the choice of action. What constitutes a sufficient degree of participation to justify an institution's claim to legitimacy will vary. For example, imagine that the United States Senate is voting on a spending bill on the same day that a small village in Scotland is deciding whether to provide public funds for a local Olympic hopeful.

In the vote on the spending bill by the Senate, the requirement of participation would likely be satisfied by the Senators voting after some consultation with and consideration of the interests of their constituents. More direct participation by individual citizens – though perhaps desirable – is not necessary because the vote is of the standard sort for the Senate and is being voted upon by the duly elected representatives of the individuals affected by the action.

On the other hand, the vote in the village regarding the funding of the Olympic hopeful would *require* a greater degree of participation from the individual members of the village to the exclusion of others that may also have an interest in the athlete's training. The individuals in the village have a much greater interest in deciding whether their resources are spent on the Olympic hopeful. In addition, this not likely part of the normal village business and is the sort of decision that should include the whole community in both the deliberations and the ultimate choice.

The level of participation that can be reasonably required for political legitimacy at the international level is likely even more attenuated.

Exactly what level of participation will suffice depends on two aspects of any decision being taken up by the deliberative body. First, is this a matter in the normal course of business or is this a matter of significant moment that may require deeper participation by those most affected by the choice of action (or inaction)? Second, what are the relative interests of those affected by the choice of action (or inaction)?

We can assume that grave humanitarian crises are exceptional matters. However, the interest that various parties have in the choice of action varies greatly. Those with perhaps the greatest interest in the matter are those whose basic rights are being violated and the government allegedly allowing or participating in the violations that is the object of potential military action. Next might be the surrounding states and their populations owing to the fact that the success of the intervention will depend on their cooperation and involvement, and they are likely going to bear the brunt of any resultant refugee crisis. It would be reasonable to presume that the states whose militaries will carry out the intervention, and the NGOs whose staff will carry out the post-intervention reconstruction would likely be the next most affected by the choice to intervene. An exhaustive list would be difficult to set forth here, but at the far end are those who are minimally affected by the choice of action.

By focusing on the exceptional nature of the crisis and the fact that there are certain parties with greater interests in the matter than others, a simple and minimal standard regarding participation can be inferred. An institution intended to decide whether humanitarian intervention should be undertaken should, at the very least, *guarantee opportunities* of participation to those claiming to suffer the violation of their basic rights, the government allegedly allowing or participating in the violation of those rights, the states surrounding the object state, and those likely responsible for carrying out any intervention or post-intervention reconstruction.

It may not be possible for all of these interested parties to participate in a meaningful way. For example, during a genocide it would be difficult for those being killed to find official channels through which to express their voice. In such circumstances, it may be necessary to provide unofficial channels and to make certain reasonable presumptions. In this case, it would be reasonable to presume that those being killed would prefer that their basic right to physical security be respected.

The ICISS assignment of decisional authority to the Security Council fails to meet this minimum standard for participation. The Security Council is a body comprised of fifteen members. Ten seats rotate amongst the members of the United Nations General Assembly. In deciding upon a resolution these members can simply vote in favor or against the resolution. The other five seats are permanently held by China, France, Russia, the United Kingdom, and the United States. Each of these members holds unilateral veto power. Consequently, even if the vote is fifteen to one, provided that the one is one of the veto-holding members, the resolution will not succeed.

Only those with a seat on the Security Council are *entitled* to participate in the deliberations of the Security Council.[46] The representatives of other states may be invited to participate at the discretion of the Security Council.[47] However, there is no provision, not even as a matter of discretion, for the inclusion of a representative of the victims; nor is there a provision for the representation of the NGOs that might be well suited to aid in the post-intervention reconstruction efforts. As a consequence, it is possible for the Security Council to deliberate over the international community's response to a grave humanitarian crisis without the participation of most, if not all, of the most interested parties. Or, as was the case in Rwanda, the Hutu extremist government of Rwanda held one of the rotating seats on the Security Council and (along with France) used that position to exclude from discussion the plight of the victims. Full participation by all who are affected by the decision to intervene may not be possible, but this falls woefully short of an acceptable standard of participation. It should be readily apparent that the Security Council is lacking in its ability to satisfy this foundational criterion of political legitimacy.

One might argue that the Security Council can fulfill the demand of participation by simply taking the interests of all affected into account. There are two reasons for rejecting this claim. First, merely considering the interests of others is not sufficient. The goal of such a deliberative process is to properly assess the circumstances of the situation so that the demands of the underlying norm are fulfilled. The members of the Security Council are biased by their own concerns and need to be presented with the fullest account of the situation possible so that they have the best chance of deciding correctly. Second, the requirement of participation is about respect for those affected by an action. To fail to provide an entitlement to participation to those likely to be most affected by an action is to fail to respect them.

Even if the Security Council regularly decides to exercise its discretion to allow broader participation, this still rests upon a relationship of domination.[48] Those most affected are *entitled* to participate and their participation should not depend on the condescension of the Security Council. A legitimate political institution would insure that such participation is a matter of right. Additionally, the case of humanitarian intervention is, owing to the fact that it is likely an exceptional case, more like the village deciding whether to fund the training of the Olympic hopeful than the United States Senate voting on a spending bill. In which case, those most affected have an even greater claim to participate.

Turning to the final criterion in the standard of legitimacy – the need to separate decisional authority from the executive function – the relationship of this criterion to the standard of instrumental legitimacy has already been discussed. If the previous discussion regarding this criterion is correct, the political bases for this requirement can be found in two underlying principles. First, there is a need for such institutions to appear legitimate. Combining decisional authority with executive function raises the specter of tyranny and abuse. Second, a failure to separate decisional authority from executive function, especially in matters that involve decisions regarding the use of force, places the decision-makers within the institution in a position of dominance over those outside of and subject to the whim of the institution's decision-makers.

As noted above, the ICISS prescription for institutionalization fails to satisfy this criterion, though, in this case, the failure is a contingent one. As a matter of historical fact, proposals for military action taken up by the Security Council have most often been proposed by one (or more) of the five veto-holding members. In which case, if after deliberations the decision is made to intervene, the inequality of the subject state with the members of the Security Council will only be more clearly demonstrated. This is not to say that the intervention is not justified from a substantive moral perspective. Rather, it is the lack of checks and balances that makes the process appear illegitimate, and the way in which the Security Council is being used to authorize military action for its members that further evinces the unjustified nature of the inequality.

NORMATIVE GUIDEPOSTS FOR AN ALTERNATIVE
INSTITUTIONAL STRUCTURE

If we are serious about securing the basic rights of individuals and insuring that grave humanitarian crises are avoided or responded to in the future, more fundamental institutional reform is needed than that offered by the ICISS. The alternative offered below is based on three commitments; two of which have already been developed. The third and final commitment is to the principle of subsidiarity. A brief discussion of the principle and a justification for its invocation are in order.

Subsidiarity is a principle governing political institutions. The principle of subsidiarity privileges political proximity. Simply stated, political tasks should be assigned to the most local political level capable of accomplishing the task at hand.[49] There are various justificatory arguments offered on behalf of the principle.[50] The discussion that follows, however, is neither a critique nor defense of any of these accounts; rather, the justification offered for the invocation of the principle here is independent of, though not inconsistent with, the existing justifications for the principle.

There are at least three justifications that can be offered for the application of the principle of subsidiarity to the design of an institution created (or empowered) to decide when humanitarian intervention is required. First, as one of the primary functions of such an institution is an epistemic one, a principle that facilitates the performance of the epistemic task is, for that reason, valuable. Specifically, the institution will be tasked with the correct completion of the demands implied by the underlying material justification; an epistemic task with normative implications. The principle of subsidiarity would direct that the task be assigned to the lowest (most local) political institutions capable of accomplishing the task.

Assigning the deliberative and decision-making processes to a political level proximate to the situation will likely benefit from the greater cultural, historical, and political knowledge of the matter at hand, and, all other things being equal, result in more accurate decisions. There is, however, an inherent limitation on the downward pressure of the principle of subsidiarity. The institution assigned the task must be capable of accomplishing the task. This has a number of implications for questions of humanitarian intervention. As the humanitarian crises for which military intervention might be considered involve an alleged failure of domestic political institutions, the institution assigned the task of deciding whether military intervention is required cannot reside with those very same domestic institutions that are alleged to have failed. The conflict of interest involved disqualifies the domestic institutions.

In which case, the lowest possible political level is a regional or sub-regional body. There is, however, an important way in which even regional or sub-regional institutions suffer from a significant lack of capacity. Namely, it is unlikely that many regional or sub-regional institutions assigned the task of deciding when humanitarian intervention is required would have the necessary military and civilian capabilities to effectively carry out the intervention (and post-intervention).

Such comprehensive capacity is, however, not necessary for the assignment of decisional authority. If it were, there would not be a single international body to which the task could legitimately be assigned. Even the Security Council relies upon the actions of others to carry out its resolutions – military or otherwise. The solution to this apparent dilemma is one that separates decisional authority from executive function. This is not merely an ad hoc resolution to the problem. For one, the two tasks are categorically different; thus, the determination of whether an intervention is required can be separated from the execution of the decision. In addition, as was discussed above, there are good normative reasons for separating decisional authority from executive function.

This leads to a second virtue of the principle of subsidiarity. Once a determination has been made that humanitarian intervention is required, it becomes necessary to coordinate the activities of the military with other actors and institutions. Perhaps most important is the need to coordinate with the political communities in the areas surrounding the target state. In addition, the activities of the military should be coordinated with and informed by the NGOs and other civil and political institutions responsible for carrying out the post-intervention reconstruction. Regional and sub-regional institutions may lack the capacity for effectively carrying out interventions and the subsequent post-intervention reconstruction; but owing to their proximity to and knowledge of the humanitarian crisis, such regional and sub-regional bodies serve an important coordinative function in the effort to carry out a humanitarian intervention.

One might wonder why coordination is such an important aspect of an institutional structure intended to govern the international community's decision to engage in humanitarian intervention. First, a lack of coordination could do more harm than good. The various military, civil, and political institutions carrying out the intervention and post-intervention reconstruction will need a common source for guidance. The decision reached by a regional or sub-regional body would provide just such a focal point. In addition, the body responsible for making the decision could function as a conduit of communication and place of deliberation for the various groups carrying out the intervention.

Second, as a practical matter, it is fair to assume that, in addition to the cooperation and coordination of the activities of the various military, civil, and political groups engaged in the intervention, most interventions will require the cooperation of the other political communities in the region. If those political communities are involved in the deliberations that led to and are responsible for the decision that intervention is required, it makes it more likely that they will cooperate.

To this point, the justifications for employing the principle of subsidiarity have been instrumental in nature. The instrumental nature of these justifications is, however, also a source of weakness for both. Like any instrumental justification, the truth (or falsity) of the justifications is a matter of contingent fact. The justifications both depend on the truth of the proposition that they, as a matter of empirical fact, provide the sorts of benefits they claim. If they do not, the justification is lost. For example, it would be a problem for such justifications if assigning decisional authority to a regional/sub-regional political body resulted in morally incorrect and/or incomplete understandings of the demands implied by underlying material justification.

There are at least two responses that can be offered on behalf of the principle of subsidiarity. First, if it is the case that regional and/or sub-regional political bodies suffer from deficiencies that make them incapable of fulfilling the task, then application of the principle of subsidiarity would imply that the task should be assigned to a different (and likely less proximate) and more capable institution. Many may find this response less than satisfying. The second response, however, does not rely on such instrumental considerations, and also serves as the third justification for the application of the principle of subsidiarity to the creation (or empowerment) of an institution assigned the task of determining whether and when humanitarian military intervention is required.

Specifically, let us begin with the proposition that a justified claim to political legitimacy is dependent on the ability of the institution to satisfy the demand that those affected by an action (or inaction) have the opportunity to participate in the deliberative and decision-making processes leading to the authorization of the action in question. As noted above, in many cases (if not most in the international arena) full participation by all affected is not possible. Since only limited participation is possible, a principle is needed to determine whose participation should be ensured. It would seem that those with the most at stake, those most affected by the proposed action, should hold a privileged position in the deliberations and decision-making procedures of an institution. Since those likely to be the most affected by the action under consideration are those closest to the situation, the principle should be one that privileges the participation of those closest to the situation. The principle of subsidiarity would assign these institutional functions to the political institutions closest to the situation; as such, the principle of subsidiarity is supported by this demand of political legitimacy.

A REFORMED NORMATIVE FRAMEWORK

The identification of normative guideposts to be considered in the design of an institutional structure, though important, is only one step in the creation of such an institutional structure. A more explicit prescription is needed. Though the discussion that follows is intentionally more aspirational than the ICISS prescription, it is not intended as an idealized utopian vision. Rather, as noted above, it is intended to be aspirational but "practically politically possible."[51]

The first thing to note about the alternative institutional structure being proposed is that it is focused on an alternative operative principle; the presumption of nonintervention. The presumption of nonintervention, though based on the moral obligation of humanitarian intervention, is not inconsistent with the responsibility to protect principle. The main difference is that the presumption is a principle intentionally constructed, and for that reason well suited, to govern institutional deliberative and decision-making processes. Second, the alternative institutional structure proposed will be designed to satisfy the conditions of institutional (instrumental and political) legitimacy.

The third and final commitment is to the principle of subsidiarity which will help to guide the allocation of responsibilities between international, regional, and sub-regional institutions. It is important to emphasize that in a 2011 report issued by the United Nations, both the Secretary General and the President of the General Assembly recognized the need for the Security Council to coordinate and collaborate with regional and sub-regional institutions.[52] The approach endorsed by the United Nations does not, however, advocate full decisional or executive responsibility to be assigned to any single institution. Rather, the report suggests that regional and sub-regional diplomatic efforts to prevent grave humanitarian crises be supported by the international community. As to the use of force, though regional and sub-regional bodies are encouraged to gather information through processes that are independent of but parallel to and collaborative with the investigations by the United Nations, decisional authority to determine the appropriateness of intervention is to remain with the Security Council.[53]

Let us begin with the fact that the standard to be employed in the alternative institutional structure is a rebuttable presumption of nonintervention as opposed to the responsibility to protect principle; the difference between the alternative principle and the responsibility to protect is not necessarily a difference in the underlying moral content. In fact, the presumption of nonintervention is justified by moral reasons similar to those relied upon in the ICISS defense and explication of the responsibility to protect principle. The presumption, though incorporating its moral justification, is not merely a restatement of the underlying moral justification. Rather, it is intentionally constructed to be a practical principle to guide institutional deliberative and decision-making procedures governing whether, when, and how a humanitarian military intervention is carried out.

The responsibility to protect principle, unlike the presumption, treats the question of the appropriateness of humanitarian intervention as an open question. Consequently, under the ICISS recommendation for institutionalizing the responsibility to protect, there is no settled starting point for deliberations. A presumption, on the other hand, sets the stage for deliberations; there is a starting point upon which all involved can rely. Additionally, it assigns burdens of persuasion to the interested parties so that not only can substantive deliberations commence, but the deliberations can proceed in an orderly and principled, rather than ad hoc, fashion.

As to the institutionalization of the presumption of nonintervention, the design for the alternative institutional structure is committed to the proposition that the institutional labor involved should be divided. And, the division of labor begins with the assignment of deliberative and decision-making functions to regional and sub-regional bodies. The assignment of these responsibilities to regional and sub-regional bodies does not absolve the international community of failures that may occur at the regional or sub-regional level. Much like the ICISS prescription, it would remain the case that international bodies would have a secondary (or tertiary) responsibility should the regional/ sub-regional political bodies fail. In the end, the division of labor contemplated here is justified in part by the belief that it will lead to more effective protection of basic rights.

One might be concerned that this empowerment could be abused by regional/sub-regional political bodies with an interest in protecting regional autonomy. For example, it might be the case that a regional/ sub-regional institution conspires to hide atrocities from the international community to protect against the possibility of an intervention into the region.[54] There are a number of reasons that weigh heavily against this concern. If the underlying concern is that the regional/ sub-regional political bodies will have an incentive to abuse their decisional authority, the assignment of decisional authority to regional/ sub-regional political bodies is consistent with respect for regional autonomy, and as such would create an incentive to show that such institutions can be trusted with such responsibility. A betrayal of that trust, through an abuse of the assigned responsibility, is likely to undermine, not advance, respect for regional autonomy.

How the incentives will actually work out is an empirical matter, and cannot be known with certainty until regional/sub-regional political bodies have been assigned decisional authority over such matters. Nonetheless, there is an additional reason weighing against the concern that regional/sub-regional political bodies will abuse their authority. Rarely is it going to be the case that the international community is ignorant of the events at the center of the crisis. As was seen with Rwanda, the international community has access to information about the events unfolding on the ground.

What the regional/sub-regional political bodies have that the international community lacks is an intangible understanding of the culture, religion, history, and so on of the region. This expertise is largely relevant to the identification of solutions; is humanitarian intervention likely to prove successful? Determining whether individual basic rights are being violated will depend very little on regional understanding and nuance. As such, if a regional/sub-regional body denies that violations of basic rights are occurring when it is clear that they are, they have failed in their responsibility; demonstrating they are incapable of performing the task assigned. As a consequence, the international community will be responsible for stepping in to rectify the failures of regional/sub-regional political bodies.

One might object that this implies that international, as opposed to regional/sub-regional bodies have final decisional authority. Consequently, this would mean that there is a risk that any benefits gained by a division of institutional labor will be lost. There are a number of reasons for not being overly concerned about this implication. First, it may, at present, be unavoidable. In most cases military intervention will likely require the assistance of international forces. In which case, the determination that humanitarian intervention is called for is only the first step to action. Those responsible for carrying out the intervention and post-intervention activities must be ready and willing to act based on the determination. In short, the international community simply *is* a check on such determinations by regional or sub-regional bodies.

The second reason why one should not be deeply troubled by the implication that the international community has discretion over action is based in the value of having checks as part of any institutional process. We often take it to be *prima facie* good for there to be checks in our political processes. Without them one political body could exploit a powerful institutional structure for its own ends; or, though not malicious, decide upon actions that are ill advised, or that demonstrate a failure to fully understand the situation.

This is not to deny that the international community has some discretion over whether the regional/sub-regional body's decision should be acted on or rejected. However, the discretion involved is bounded. The decision by the regional/sub-regional body establishes a record to be assessed by the international community; as such, the international community would be put in the position of reacting to a formal record. Consequently, in those instances where the regional/sub-regional decision calls for humanitarian intervention under circumstances where military action would be morally unjustified, the review by the international community allows for a correction. But also, the formal record makes clear the nature of the humanitarian crisis. In which case, the international community could not avoid confronting the facts of the case. To refuse to act under such circumstances would require compelling reasons that override or outweigh the reasons upon which the judgment of the initial decision relied.

On the other hand, in those instances where the regional/sub-regional body decided against humanitarian intervention when there is clear evidence that intervention is necessary, the international community acts as a safety net. The choice not to intervene may have been based on any number of miscalculations or misunderstandings that an international body may be able to correct or clarify. For example, it might be the case that the regional/sub-regional political bodies lack a full understanding of the military capabilities of the major powers and/or the capabilities of the coterie of non-governmental organizations that could be used to fulfill the humanitarian purpose of an intervention. If, however, the decision by the regional/sub-regional body is – for whatever reasons – intractable, the international community would have to consider the risks associated with a humanitarian intervention into a region or sub-region that has expressed a decision disapproving of intervention.

Lastly, as the ICISS pointed out in its initial 2001 report on the responsibility to protect principle, one of the main stumbling blocks to effective action is the lack of political will on the part of the world's major powers. The alternative institutional structure being proposed could significantly alter the political will of the international community. The effect is not a necessary implication of the alternative structure being proposed; rather it is tied to a rhetorical advantage of the alternative structure. When a regional/sub-regional body renders a decision supported by an official record, it forces the leaders of the international community to confront and respond to the decision. It would be difficult for the international community to remain apathetic in the face of an official record and decision; especially if the decision and record are clearly in support of humanitarian intervention.

It may be useful at this point to highlight the impact this would likely have had on the public deliberations engaged in by the international community in relation to the violence in Rwanda. Many on the Security Council claimed ignorance of the events unfolding in Rwanda and uncertainty over the course of action that the international community ought to have taken. So, in the end, nothing was done. If the Security Council had been confronted with an official decision and record regarding the events unfolding in Rwanda, such apathy in the face of the violence unfolding in Rwanda would have been difficult to justify. It may still have been the case that the international community refused to act, but it would have been a choice in which it was clear that the interests of the world's major powers were the reason for inaction, and not the high-minded rhetoric of respect for sovereignty.

The assignment of deliberative and decision-making responsibility, though important, only accounts for a portion of the institutional labor involved in an effort to carry out a humanitarian intervention. There are also a number of executive functions essential to carrying out a humanitarian intervention. The division of executive labor must begin by recognizing that the executive function is complex in nature. There are three primary functions and a number of overlapping phases that must be taken into consideration.

As to the functions involved, the institutional structure must account for the assignment of responsibility for the military action, the post-intervention reconstruction, and the coordination of all activities needed to insure that the intervention is carried out effectively and future humanitarian crises avoided. The functions need to be coordinated within and across overlapping phases of a humanitarian intervention ranging from the initial military campaign to the post-intervention reconstruction of civil and political society; and lying between the two is a transitional period where the primacy of the military campaign gives way to the reconstruction effort.

In light of the complexity involved, it may be tempting to assign all executive responsibility to a single entity. Though, in the end, I believe this to be an unjustified allocation of executive responsibility, there are a number of reasons in favor of such an approach. Under ideal circumstances, this would lead to more effective humanitarian action because the coordination of actions between functions and across phases will be part of a single institution's coherent plan. Even in the less-than-ideal world, assigning the executive labor to a single entity decreases the likelihood that action taken pursuant to one function will be at cross-purposes with other essential functions.

The practical value of such an assignment of executive labor should be clear. It would be a mistake, however, to fail to understand the moral significance of these practical advantages. In the case of humanitarian intervention, where the underlying justification and goal of action is moral in nature, any increase in the ability of the institutional structure to effectively carry out the humanitarian task is morally valuable. As such, all other things being equal, an institutional structure that increases effectiveness ought to be morally preferred over other alternatives that are clearly less effective.

These advantages are only realized if an institution with the capabilities necessary to carry out all of the executive functions required in a humanitarian intervention is possible; and, that all things considered, the allocation of such comprehensive executive responsibility to such an entity is morally desirable. A complete explication of the capabilities such an institution would have to possess is not possible here, but it would likely have to be a global institution with the ability to carry out military campaigns and engage in the reconstruction of civil and political society.

There is little doubt that such an institution is possible. However, this is to understand possibility in the weakest sense, and one that tends towards utopian accounts rather than attainable institutional structures. The goal of this discussion is to identify an institutional structure that is not merely possible in this weak sense, but practically politically possible. As such, we must ask what the likelihood is that such an institutional structure is attainable taking into consideration the existing institutional structure of the international arena and political considerations that might hamper efforts to create such an institutional structure.

Though this question cannot be answered with certainty, it is my considered judgment that the creation of a single entity with the responsibility for and ability to carry out all of the executive labor involved in a humanitarian intervention is not practically politically possible. First, setting aside the political considerations that are likely to weigh heavily against the creation of such an institution, there is little reason to believe that the creation of such an institution is practically possible from where we are now. The level of coordination and institution-building necessary is not the sort of task that could be completed in a timely manner, if at all. For example, it would be necessary to provide an institutional mechanism for the institution created to control the activities of an independent military force and various civil and political institutions with the ability to reconstruct civil and political society. Neither of which currently exist.

As to the political obstacles, the sort of institution to be created must be an effective one. As such, to attain the advantages of effectiveness that an assignment of executive labor to a single entity promises, the entity must be independent and not subject to the control of outside forces. For example, the Security Council would not suffice as it is an institution under the control of the five veto-holding members. However, it is also unlikely that many, if any, sovereign states would be willing to endorse the creation of a politically independent institution with the ability to command military forces and civil and political services. Underlying this political obstacle is the unwillingness of sovereign states to surrender the very functions that define their sovereignty. In the end, it would be unreasonable to expect that such an institution could be created.

One might disagree with this assessment and contend that not only is such an institution possible, but that in light of the significant advantages that could be gained by its creation, such an institution could garner enough support for it to be practically politically possible. Even if we assume for the sake of argument that this is true, the possibility of such an effective institution does not settle the matter. It remains to be seen whether such an assignment of executive labor is morally preferable to the alternatives. Before comparing the unitary institutional structure under consideration with a more divided structure, it is essential to understand what, if any, moral reasons weigh against the creation of, and assignment of executive labor to, such an institution.

As noted above, in *Perpetual Peace* Immanuel Kant warns against seeking to advance global peace through the creation of a global institution with the power to enforce such a peace.[55] Kant believed that an institution with such power may be capable of providing peace, but the cost was too great as the peace attained would be the "peace of a graveyard." In short, all things considered, the potential instrumental value of a global institution was not worth the risk of global tyranny that would likely accompany such a powerful political institution.

One might argue that what is needed is merely the creation of a military with sufficient capacity to effectively carry out humanitarian interventions, and that this does not imply the need for a military with capacities sufficient to support a global tyrant. The assignment of all executive functions related to humanitarian intervention to a single independent institution would, however, still have moral costs. First, though creating an independent institution with the capacity to act militarily does not necessarily run the risk of global tyranny, it would likely add to the uncertainty that exists in the international arena. A new and independent military force with the resources capable of engaging in a humanitarian intervention could be used in ways that create greater tensions in areas already on the brink of conflict. As such, there is a risk of actually worsening the global security situation.

In addition, though perhaps less of a concern, the institution would have to be created with the capacity to effectively engage in the reconstruction of political and civil society. There is a risk that since the institution is independent, it may substitute its judgment for that of those who it is seeking to help. In which case, the creation and empowerment of such an institution runs the risk of moral and cultural imperialism. In the end, though the creation of an institution capable of carrying out all of the executive labor required for a humanitarian intervention and assignment of such functions to that institution has the potential advantage of increasing the effectiveness of humanitarian interventions, it is not clear that the overall instrumental value of such an assignment of executive labor supports a unitary model.

Assuming, however, that on balance there is some instrumental value in a unitary model, the question becomes whether that value is superior to the overall value of a model that divides the assignment of executive labor amongst a number of institutions. In large part the answer to this question will depend on the specific division of executive labor proposed. There are significant and decisive moral reasons to prefer a divided model. The primary reason for this belief is based on the fact that the main advantage the unitary model is presumed to have is related to its effectiveness.

As the advantage is one that relies on the instrumental value of the institutional division of labor proposed, there is nothing inherently valuable about the unitary model. Consequently, if there is an alternative that is roughly equally effective, the determination of which model should be preferred will be based on non-instrumental moral considerations. There is a wide degree of latitude regarding the construction of a divided model, and it is my considered judgment that the model proposed is one that is arguably as effective as a unitary model and more likely to become a reality. The divided model ought to be preferred over the unitary model because of moral reasons not directly related to effectiveness.

There is more than one way to approach the development of an institutional structure that divides the executive labor required for a humanitarian intervention. Here, the development of such a model is built around recognition of the complex relationship(s) that exist between the overlapping phases, functions, and shifting functional priorities involved as the intervention progresses from one phase to the next. In addition, it is essential to identify the agents and/or institutions with the capabilities to effectively carry out the executive labor.

To begin with the latter first, there are at least five different types of institutions with capabilities relevant to the effective execution of the functions required for a humanitarian intervention. There are three different types of political institutions that ought to be included – individual states, regional/sub-regional political bodies like the African Union, and international political institutions like the Security Council. There are also those institutions that have security as their primary function; for example, NATO. Lastly, there are the various NGOs with wide-ranging capabilities. No single institution identified is capable of individually carrying out a humanitarian intervention. As such, an institutional structure that divides the executive labor amongst multiple institutions must be based on more than the identification of the separate pieces of the functional puzzle. It is essential that the puzzle be put together to form a coherent whole.

It is important to understand the difference between capabilities and functions. The terminology may seem familiar to those who have been introduced to the work of Amartya Sen;[56] and though there are some similarities, the use of the terminology here is not a reference to Sen's work. In the present discussion, capabilities refer to the abilities possessed by an institutional agent to engage effectively in certain activities. Functions, on the other hand, are not exercises of those abilities; rather, functions are the goals of the institutional structure that the capabilities are used to carry out.

The next step in the development of the divided model is the identification of the specific capabilities needed during various phases of an intervention, and the normative priorities that should govern the coordination of action by various institutions across phases and between functions. Though a more complete explication is preferable, here the focus is on providing a general understanding of the needs and priorities involved. The conceptual framework for thinking about these matters provided here should be able to account for the inclusion of functions that may not have been specifically taken into account.

Understanding how the executive labor should be divided in a particular phase requires first that we have an understanding of the functions that need to be taken into account. The functions to be considered fall within three general categories. The first two categories are concerned with action of one sort or another. First, there are those functions related to the use of force; the initial military campaign to secure the basic rights of individuals against (further) violation, the protection of those providing humanitarian and other services to the population, and the provision of security for the general population during the reconstruction of civil and political society. Second, there are many non-military functions essential to a humanitarian intervention, ranging from the provision of basic health services to those suffering to the reconstruction of civil and political society.

The third functional category is based on the need to coordinate activities both within and across phases of an intervention. Within a particular phase, it may be essential to make sure that efforts to provide humanitarian services do not get in the way of, or are not hampered by, military activities essential to the protection of basic rights. Coordination across phases must also be accounted for; for example, how should one coordinate the actions engaged in by various institutions when the normative priorities that will be involved in the transition from the initial military campaign to the reconstruction effort change?

The first phase of any humanitarian intervention is going to include the military campaign to secure the basic rights of individuals against (further) violations. In addition, there will be a need to provide basic services to those impacted by the intervention; including refugees fleeing combat areas and those whose rights had been violated prior to the intervention. There is also a need to provide security for the refugees and for those providing basic humanitarian services. It is also important to recognize that the use of force in a humanitarian intervention is significantly different from the use of military force in a traditional war; the use of force in a humanitarian intervention is primarily concerned with protection and stability, not the defeat of an armed enemy.

The second phase is a transitional phase. Its beginning is not marked by easily discernible events. Rather, it is the long transition from the initial phase where the use of military force to secure basic rights and provide protection for a victimized population gives way to forward-looking efforts to reconstruct civil and political society. Determining whether the intervention has moved into this transitional phase will be a matter of judgment based on the shifting normative priorities. During this phase many of the functions relevant to the initial phase will continue to have a significant role to play. Apart from the shifting normative priorities, which are discussed below, the main functional difference between the initial phase and this transitional phase is that the intervening institutions must begin to lay the groundwork for the reconstruction of civil and political society. This will include, at a minimum, providing security for the population at large and initial efforts to create the foundations for civil and political institutions.

The final phase of a humanitarian intervention is defined largely by the effort to reconstruct civil and political society, but should also recognize that there must be a coordinated withdrawal of all intervening institutional actors with the goal of insuring long-term stability and protection against future humanitarian crises. With that said, there will remain, until the completion of the humanitarian project, a need for a military (or security) presence of some sort to provide logistical and other support for the provision and protection of security within the reconstructed society. What will no longer be needed is a continued military campaign.

Allocating executive responsibility to particular institutional agents requires that we identify the specific capabilities respective institutions have and divide the executive labor accordingly. Beginning with individual states, states though presumed equal within the international arena, have different capabilities. Some will have standing armies with significant military capabilities. Others, owing to their geographic proximity to the site of the proposed intervention, will have unique abilities to provide logistical support and coordination for the intervention. Others, owing to their diplomatic and cultural ties to the state in which the intervention is to occur, have capabilities related to the coordination and planning necessary for the reconstruction to be effective.

Regional/sub-regional political bodies like the African Union are uniquely situated geographically, politically, and culturally. This position translates into special capabilities related to the coordination of various functions across phases of an intervention. From a military standpoint, regional/sub-regional political bodies will be able to help coordinate military activities across a region. It is likely that any humanitarian intervention will create refugees and a need for services to be provided, members of the regional/sub-regional political bodies are going to bear the brunt of any refugee crisis, and responding to the needs of the refugees will require a coordinated effort that is as close to the situation on the ground as possible. Lastly, with regards to the reconstruction of civil and political society, regional/sub-regional political bodies are well situated to coordinate those efforts as well as provide support for the transition to an independent and stable state.

International political bodies like the Security Council, though often far from the actual intervention, have capabilities that no other institution can bring to bear. They do not directly command military forces, but they do have other capabilities relevant to both the military campaign and the effort to reconstruct civil and political society. First, the United Nations and its agencies possess a level of expertise and logistical knowledge that is unrivaled. For example, specific agencies within the United Nations are dedicated to understanding the demographics of particular areas of the world. That information will be essential to the initial planning of the use of military forces needed for an intervention and will also aid in tracking the impact of the intervention on particular populations so that the reconstruction will be based on an understanding of the nature of the communities that existed prior to the intervention. Owing to its unique position, it could also serve as a clearing-house for NGOs with capabilities valuable to the intervention.

Having discussed the capabilities of various political bodies, the discussion now turns to two distinct types of nonpolitical institutions (in the sense that they are not intended as part of their mission(s) to be political bodies in the sense of governance structures). First, there are security organizations like NATO. Though primarily military in nature, such institutional agents possess a wide range of capabilities that are likely distinct from those possessed by (most) states. For example, NATO has at its disposal the ability to engage in surveillance, the disruption of radio and television broadcasts, air power, and logistical support that is not available to most states. This would not require NATO to put a single "boot on the ground" to aid in a humanitarian intervention.[57]

Lastly, there are the innumerable NGOs with specific missions related to the alleviation of suffering around the world. It would be a near Sisyphean task to try to explain in any complete and coherent way the abilities possessed by the world's NGOs; nonetheless, I think there are a number of specific capabilities that are extremely important to a humanitarian intervention. For example, some organizations are dedicated to delivering medical services to those suffering in areas of conflict. There are other organizations focused on educational reform and development; and others on political and economic reform.[58] In addition, many NGOs have a regional orientation that may enhance their knowledge of a region's problems and make them better suited for work in a particular region. Harnessing the capabilities of these NGOs in the most effective way possible is essential to the success of a humanitarian intervention.

Now to connect the three phases and functions with the capabilities possessed by the types of institutions identified. As to the initial phase of any humanitarian intervention, the military campaign will require the services of the standing armies of individual states, logistical support provided by security organizations like NATO, and regional coordination. In addition, there will be the need to provide basic services to those suffering from the humanitarian crisis as well as those impacted by the intervention; implicating NGOs, regional bodies, and the United Nations due to the expertise it possesses. Lastly, some military/security forces will be needed to provide protection to NGO staff, and those impacted by the intervention.

As the intervention transitions from a military campaign to an effort to lay the groundwork for reconstruction and then from that preparatory transitional phase to active reconstruction, though there are new functions to be fulfilled, many of the functions involved in the initial phase will remain, but the normative priorities will change. The need to lay the foundations for the reconstruction to come will require additional security services focused on securing existing population centers. This task should fall, to the extent possible, to local security forces under the direction of, and with the support of, external advisors. However, if the local police are implicated in the humanitarian crisis, it may be necessary to call on outside forces (preferably civilian or military police). The service of additional NGOs and support by regional/ sub-regional political bodies will also likely be required because the functions required by the reconstruction are fundamentally different from those focused on the provision of humanitarian services.

In the final phase, the military campaign will have wound down, the reconstruction will be under way, and the focus will be on producing a stable civil and political environment where the likelihood of another humanitarian crisis emerging is greatly reduced. The military should have little to no role except in helping to plan the departure of all intervening forces. NGOs should be well into their efforts to reconstruct civil and political society and should be working alongside the United Nations and the relevant regional/sub-regional political bodies to plan for their eventual departure. This should include the development of mechanisms within the regional/sub-regional political bodies backed by the United Nations that will help to insure the stability of the reconstructed civil and political society.

Coordinating the Intervention

In addition to these more direct executive functions, it is essential to identify an institution(s) with responsibility for coordinating the actions of those responsible for carrying out the intervention. The suggestions that follow range from the general allocation of responsibility for coordinating activities within a phase to some specific suggestions regarding the allocation of coordinative labor. Before discussing the assignment of coordinative responsibilities, it may be useful to have an understanding of what would be involved in carrying out the coordinative functions. There is a working assumption that the various institutions involved are committed to the same goal – successfully carrying out the humanitarian intervention. As such, the problem is not a typical collective action problem where agents have different interests and acting on individual interests leads to a less than optimal result. Rather, what is needed are institutions with the capacity to insure that *within a particular phase* normative priorities are understood by all involved, and that none of the functions is carried out at cross-purposes with either the other functions or the normative priorities; and that *across phases* the functions are part of a coherent plan.

There are two types of institutions uniquely positioned to carry out these coordinative functions. Though neither could satisfactorily perform these functions alone, regional/sub-regional political bodies and the United Nations working together have the capabilities to effectively coordinate a humanitarian intervention. This is different from the parallel processes discussed in the report recently issued by the President of the United Nations General Assembly on the need for coordination between the United Nations and regional/sub-regional institutions.[59] In that report the coordination between the United Nations and the relevant regional/sub-regional political bodies would be, much like the entire process envisioned by the ICISS, ad hoc and informal, created on a case-by-case basis as a reaction to a humanitarian crisis. It would be better to construct formal institutional mechanisms for collaboration and coordination for reasons of efficiency as well as the stability of expectations.

One challenge to developing such mechanisms is that the political environment of the international arena does not lend itself to coordination by compulsion. Rather, the institutions responsible for coordinating the interventionist effort are going to need to provide those delivering the military, humanitarian, and reconstruction services with focal points and plans that are justified. Though this may at first seem like a significant obstacle, with the right sort of division of coordinative labor this challenge can be overcome.

With that said, in the international arena, what is needed is not compulsion or inducements to act; rather the coordinating institutions need to gain the trust of those responsible for and committed to carrying out the intervention. Gaining such trust can be attained by a coordinating institution with special knowledge or expertise in areas relevant to the intervention and the leadership abilities necessary to maintain the trust and commitment of those carrying out the work of the intervention.

The specialized knowledge relevant to building the trust necessary to coordinate a humanitarian intervention includes understanding the local history and culture, the logistical and military support necessary and available, the likely impact on the region, and the relevant capabilities of the participating institutions. Regional/sub-regional political bodies proximate to the intervention are in the best position to provide much of this information as it is dependent on localized knowledge and understanding.

Whereas the particular expertise of regional/sub-regional political bodies is based on the depth of their experience locally, there are other informational matters that require a broader perspective. It is in these matters that the United Nations may have special expertise. For example, the United Nations has the ability to see the larger humanitarian picture. The intervention will often be one amongst any number of competing humanitarian causes. The ability to see the bigger humanitarian picture is useful for understanding which NGOs might be overstretched and which might be underutilized. In addition, having such a broad perspective allows for a broader and longer-term view; both of which are valuable to insuring that the humanitarian crisis resolved in one region does not ignite or exacerbate a crisis elsewhere.

To understand what is needed for leadership based on trust to be successful, we need only consider the fact that when those who are being led trust those who are leading, those being led are willing, based on their trust, to suspend their own practical judgment. No matter its expertise or its excellence, an institution is unlikely to develop relationships of trust if it fails to act in ways that lend credence to the view that it is worthy of the suspension of judgment that goes along with placing trust in another.

With this in mind, there are a number of qualities we would want in an institution with the responsibility for leading the coordinative effort. First, the institution should have little or no interest in the intervention other than successfully achieving its humanitarian goals. Second, the institution should have a justified claim to a degree of political legitimacy. In the international arena this would mean that the relevant institutional processes are transparent, participatory, and representative.

The United Nations, if taken as a whole, fulfills to an adequate degree the conditions necessary to be a trustworthy leader. In addition, as the ICISS points out, the United Nations is perceived by the international community as the ultimate source of political legitimacy in the international arena; and though perceptions do not always match reality, perceptions are extremely important to relationships of trust. In the end, the United Nations should work with regional/sub-regional bodies through formal mechanisms that take advantage of their relative strengths to coordinate the execution of a humanitarian intervention.

Before turning to the discussion of the priorities involved, I want to offer a specific suggestion regarding a coordinative function that the United Nations would be well suited to perform. Throughout the intervention there will be a need to identify non-governmental organizations with specific skill sets. In addition, the effectiveness of an intervention would likely be undermined by multiple NGOs with the same capabilities competing with one another on the ground. The United Nations has extensive institutional knowledge regarding NGOs, their respective capabilities, and regional affiliations. As such, participation in an intervention by an NGO should be allowed only by invitation from the United Nations. Those acting outside the auspices of an invitation from the United Nations should be subject to official sanctions of some sort because their refusal to abide by the mandates of the coordinating institution(s) undermines the likely success of the intervention.

Effective coordination requires more than merely identifying the functions to be coordinated and the institutions capable of coordinating the functions identified. It is also necessary to delineate the normative priorities involved within each phase and have an understanding of how those priorities are likely to change across phases. The importance of delineating the normative priorities should not be underestimated. Within a particular phase the institution(s) responsible for coordinating the activities involved will often be forced into making decisions in the face of tension or conflict between the functions involved in that particular phase.

For example, different institutions may be engaged in conflicting functions that are both important to the ultimate success of the intervention but cannot be carried out simultaneously; or at least cannot be carried out effectively if both are being carried out at the same time. In addition, as the intervention progresses from one phase to the next, the coordinating institution(s) will be responsible for redirecting resources based on the shift in normative priorities. There are a number of significant practical advantages that can be gained if the normative priorities are understood prior to the intervention. First, it will aid the coordinating institution(s) in deciding between competing functions. Second, the institutions being coordinated will be able to have established expectations when they act in furtherance of their responsibilities in the intervention.

Determining the normative priorities in any phase must be understood in relation to the overarching humanitarian goal(s) of the intervention. Priorities should be set such that the allocation of resources and action in accordance with the delineated priorities advance the humanitarian goals of the intervention. Initially, it will almost certainly be the case that advancing the humanitarian goals of the intervention will require the use of military force as the primary goal will be to secure the basic rights of individuals against further violation. As such, the priorities at this initial phase are clear. The use of force to secure the basic rights of individuals must take precedence over other functions.

However, once the initial military intervention has occurred, there will be an immediate need for humanitarian services, and at this point the tension between the various functions begins to arise. To a large extent, where priorities lie will be based on the facts on the ground.

If after the initial intervention, there continue to be armed factions engaged in widespread violence against segments of the civilian population and the provision of security for humanitarian services would be a significant burden on the ability of the military to stop the violation of basic rights, then even though humanitarian services are needed if there is a conflict between the ability to carry out the military campaign and the provision of such services, the military campaign must take priority.

It is important to remember that the goal is the overall success of the intervention; not individual achievements. This is an additional reason for allocating coordinative responsibility to an institution not directly involved in carrying out the functions that may be in conflict. There is much to be said for the greater independence such institution(s) would, under these circumstances, likely possess. When faced with such conflicts, they would be in the best position to ignore the short-term gain that might be found in sacrificing the military effort and to focus instead on the overarching goals of the intervention.

At some point, however, the military campaign will have to give way to the provision of humanitarian services and efforts to lay the groundwork for the reconstruction of civil and political society. The transitional phase is not a single moment within a humanitarian intervention. Rather, the transition is a complex progression in the shifting focus of functions and priorities that is necessarily involved in any successful humanitarian intervention. Here again the independence of the coordinating institution(s) is of utmost importance. The responsible institution will have to make judgments that are as much about wisdom as they are about principle; balancing competing interests, all of which are necessary for a successful humanitarian intervention.

Nonetheless, and despite this complexity, there are going to be at least two competing sets of functions involved in this transitional phase. First, there are those tied to the primary goals of the initial military intervention – the protection of basic rights and the provision of humanitarian services. To borrow a medical metaphor, this is about stopping the bleeding and saving the patient's life. On the other hand, there will now be pressure to consider what is needed to lay the groundwork for the reconstruction of civil and political society. Returning to the metaphor, this is about helping the patient to fully recover and thrive. It is my considered judgment that the presumption at this point should weigh in favor of the goals of the initial phase. If, however, it can be demonstrated that continued focus on the remaining armed factions and allocation of scarce resources for security is providing only minimal humanitarian benefit while risking the overall success of the intervention, then the priorities should shift.

An example may help to understand this presumption in operation. One could imagine an instance where the military phase of the intervention has been, to a large degree, successful, but there remain stubborn pockets of armed resistance where the violation of basic rights continues and it is extremely difficult to provide humanitarian services in those areas without a significant commitment of resources. Those same resources may be needed to start to provide the foundation for the reconstruction of civil and political society. One might contend that so long as the international community is committed to remain involved for the long term, even though it is a significant drain on resources and interferes with moving the reconstruction effort forward, the effort to completely eradicate the violation of basic rights should take precedence.

Such an understanding of the example fails to account for the fact that a successful intervention is also likely the shortest one possible. The intervener, once seen as savior and provider of necessary aid, may come to be viewed as an occupier and imperialist. In the end, this could threaten the ability of those involved to achieve the humanitarian goals of the intervention. In which case, it would be appropriate to give greater priority to those laying the groundwork for the reconstruction of civil and political society.

Lastly, in the reconstruction phase the main function of the intervention will be completing the successful reconstruction of civil and political society. Though international forces may continue to provide some security, the brunt of that effort should be carried out by domestic forces. Though it may seem like there are few, if any, points of tension in the waning stages of an effective humanitarian intervention, there is at least one significant point of possible tension that might exist between the coordinating institution(s) and those carrying out the functions in this final phase. At some point, the priorities of this final phase will have to shift from reconstruction to withdrawal. Here again, this final shift in priorities should be governed by a rebuttable presumption that favors complete reconstruction, as the prevention of future humanitarian crises will depend on how well civil and political society has been reconstructed.

To insure that the reconstructed civil and political society is stable over the long term, it is likely that regional/sub-regional bodies are going to be involved in and monitor the affairs of the subject state for a long while. As such, since the regional/sub-regional political bodies involved could have significant conflicts of interest during this final phase (for example, the humanitarian goal of a complete reconstruction versus the desire to have international institutions withdraw from the region), it would be wise to allocate coordinative responsibility for this final phase to the United Nations. This does not mean that the United Nations should act without the input of the relevant regional/sub-regional political bodies. Rather, it would avoid the impression that the regional/sub-regional political bodies were acting solely on their own interest rather than in the interests of the reconstructed society.

CONCLUSION: APPLICATION OF THE REFORMED NORMATIVE FRAMEWORK AND CONCLUDING REMARKS

I told him that I did not believe that they could burn people in our age, that humanity would never tolerate it . . . (Elie Wiesel)[1]

Out of our memory . . . of the Holocaust we must forge an unshakable oath with all civilized people that never again will the world stand silent, never again will the world . . . fail to act in time to prevent this terrible crime of genocide . . . we must harness the outrage of our own memories to stamp out oppression wherever it exists. We must understand that human rights and human dignity are indivisible. (Jimmy Carter)[2]

We wish to inform you that we have heard that tomorrow we will be killed along with our families. (Pastor Ezekiel Semugeshi et al.)[3]

Despite the increase in world attention toward Sudan in the past months, the genocide in Darfur has continued without any serious attempt by the Sudanese government to do what governments primarily exist to do, protect their citizens. (Tom Allen)

Would the outcome have been different if the alternative institutional structure proposed here had been in effect in 1994? In response, the discussion that follows will focus on the decisional process; including the transitional phase between the decision of the regional/sub-regional body and action taken (or not) by the international community in furtherance of that decision. I will not speculate on the manner in which an intervention in Rwanda would have been carried out. There are a number of reasons for the choice to refrain from such speculation. First, there are two practical reasons. I do not have the necessary expertise in these matters, and my speculations regarding how an intervention would have or should have been carried out add little to our understanding, and would be better addressed by those with the relevant expertise. In addition, a satisfactory assessment would require a more detailed analysis than I can provide here.

Second, apart from these practical reasons, though the analysis I am engaging in is based on a counterfactual, there is something categorically different about using a counterfactual to assess the way in which an alternative institutional structure would evaluate reasons and impact choices over time as opposed to a counterfactual analysis that seeks to revisit a particular decision. For example, imagine that an individual is choosing between two options. S/he fails to consider a significant moral reason against one choice of action. As a consequence s/he chooses the morally wrong action and engages in a long series of actions, each one flowing from the previous action. It is one thing to point out that had s/he taken the ignored reason into consideration then s/he would likely have chosen the morally correct option. It is completely different to provide an analysis of the chain of events that would likely have flowed from that proper decision. In the former case, the counterfactual is a source critical analysis of an actual decision. In the latter, the counterfactual is a process of world-creation.

APPLICATION OF THE REFORMED NORMATIVE FRAMEWORK

Turning our attention to the application of the alternative institutional structure to Rwanda, we must begin with the identification of a candidate regional/sub-regional body with responsibility for making the initial determination. Presently, regional affairs fall under the auspices of the African Union. In 1994, the Organization of African Unity (OAU) would have been the most likely candidate to fill this decisional role. The task before the OAU would have been to determine whether the events unfolding in Rwanda were sufficiently egregious to rebut the presumption against intervention.

The presumption is rebutted if it can be demonstrated that the conditions related to the existence of an all-things-considered moral obligation of humanitarian intervention have been met. The order has been revised to reflect the fact that some conditions are related to the initial phase of the decision-making process and others to the transitional phase of the decision-making process.

1. The circumstances must be a violation of the basic right to physical security thus giving rise to the moral obligation of humanitarian intervention;
2. Intervention would not irreparably harm the existence of a community of moral significance;
3. Intervention would not unjustifiably compromise international peace and security;
4. Intervention would not worsen the situation that the intervention is intended to resolve;
5. Those bearing the obligation are capable of effectively fulfilling the obligation of humanitarian intervention;
6. Fulfillment of the moral obligation of humanitarian intervention does not require the obligation-bearing states to make substantial internal sacrifices; and
7. Intervention would not undermine the presumption against intervention or reward provocateurs that use violence in their efforts to cause the circumstances that trigger humanitarian intervention.

As noted above, the decisional phase is comprised of an initial phase in which the relevant regional/sub-regional political body determines if humanitarian military intervention is called for, and a transitional phase in which the relevant political bodies of the international community determine whether the decision by the regional/sub-regional body will be acted upon. Looking at the criteria governing the presumption against intervention, conditions 1, 2, 3, and 4 ought to be assessed in the initial phase of the decisional process owing to the special knowledge and expertise of the regional/sub-regional political bodies. However, conditions 5, 6, and 7 ought to be assessed by international political bodies because of the broader perspective required for proper evaluation of these criteria.

As to these latter criteria, this is not to say that the relevant regional/sub-regional bodies should not address these criteria in their evaluation, but that the regional/sub-regional views would be merely advisory. One might contend that *all* determinations by the regional/sub-regional political bodies are merely advisory. Such an understanding fails to understand the distinction between the nature of review involved in the evaluation of either set of criteria. Much like appellate review in the legal realm, the international community is like an appeals court determining whether the lower court has abused its discretion. If not, the appellate court (and here the international political bodies) should defer to the lower court (the regional/sub-regional political bodies). As to the evaluation of the criteria assigned to the international political bodies, the analogy would be an appellate court taking up the matter *de novo*. The appellate court in such instances is taking a fresh look at the issue, without any deference owed to the lower court.

As to the first condition, the Security Council sought to characterize the violence in Rwanda as the unfortunate cost of civil war. For the argument here, whether this was a sincere claim or not is irrelevant. The distance of the Security Council from the facts on the ground put it in a position of informational dependence and discretion. The Security Council had discretion because it could choose to believe those whom it wished to believe and claim ignorance of troublesome facts. An organization like the OAU, however, would not have the same sort of dependence or discretion. Its proximity to Rwanda and the eyewitness accounts of refugees would limit the degree to which it has to rely on officials from Rwanda for information, and this lack of dependence and greater firsthand knowledge would also limit the discretion it has over the information relevant to the assessment of the nature of the human rights violations involved.

The second condition is tied to a normative judgment that should apply to all political communities; however, determining whether a particular political community is a community of moral significance and whether a humanitarian intervention is likely to cause irreparable harm to such a community ought to be made by those most familiar with the culture and history of the community. Regional/sub-regional bodies are in the best position to evaluate the nature of the community and, assuming that the community is one that is worth preserving, whether military intervention is going to irreparably harm it. In the case of Rwanda, even if Rwanda was a community of moral significance, it is clear that intervention would have helped rather than undermined the flourishing of that community.

As to the third criterion, that humanitarian military intervention should not pose an unreasonable threat to international peace and security, those closest to the situation are in the best position to assess the nature of the threat. In Rwanda in particular, it was the refugee crisis that served as the justification for the – too little, too late – French backed intervention, Operation Turquoise. The OAU would likely have anticipated more quickly the fall-out of renewed violence in Rwanda. This is due in part to its greater awareness of the initial signs of trouble and the interest it would have had in maintaining regional stability.

One might think that international political bodies like the Security Council are in a better position to make this determination. However, if we accept that in most instances international peace and security is about peace and security within a region, there is good reason to assign the evaluation of this criterion to the relevant regional/sub-regional body. For example, during the Rwandan genocide a claim that was being made within the Security Council by a Rwandan official was that the outbreak of violence was an internal matter. Those within the OAU would likely have been intimately aware of the fact that this claim was false.

The fourth condition is about insuring that the intervention will not be futile or produce perverse results. In other words, to rebut the presumption, one of the things that must be demonstrated is that a humanitarian intervention will produce the humanitarian results that justify the use of military force. A specific example may help to understand why assigning this to a regional/sub-regional political body would likely have made a difference in the decision regarding intervention in Rwanda.

One of the claims relied upon by many in the international com-munity to support the choice not to intervene in Rwanda was the claim that the genocide was based on ethnic hatred that was centuries old and any effort to resolve the violence between these ethnic factions would, in the end, be futile. Besides the fact that this claim failed to recognize that moderate Hutus were being slaughtered alongside Tutsis, the claim of a centuries-old hatred that would undermine the long-term humanitarian goals of an intervention is not historically accurate. As many historians have pointed out, prior to the colonization of Rwanda by European powers in the nineteenth century, Tutsis and Hutus lived together, and the distinction was more a matter of socio-economic class than ethnicity. With the sensitivity African nations have to their colonial history, the falsity of the claimed ethnic divide would likely have been known to those within the OAU.

If these four conditions are met, one could reasonably claim, and the regional/sub-regional political body ought to find, that humanitarian intervention would be called for. It is my considered judgment that the OAU would likely have decided that four conditions had been met, and it would have, under the alternative institutional structure proposed, issued an official decision and report advocating intervention to which the Security Council would then have to respond.

This, however, does not settle the matter. There are two distinct bases upon which the international community might rely to reject the decision to intervene. First, the international community may find that the regional/sub-regional body has failed to properly evaluate whether the presumption has been rebutted; either because the regional/ sub-regional body failed to adequately evaluate the facts known, or because it failed to include relevant facts in its evaluation. Second, as noted above, there are certain considerations that international political institutions like the United Nations are in a much better position to evaluate; consequently, the international community might reject the regional/sub-regional call to action for reasons related to these broader considerations.

One might be concerned that this would simply provide additional normative resources to be used by the international community to avoid its responsibility. This concern is based on a failure to recognize the sequence of deliberative/decisional processes. In the case of Rwanda, assuming that the OAU called for an intervention, to reject the call for intervention, the United Nations would have to state explicitly its reasons for choosing not to act. The United Nations would be reacting to a record and would have to provide the underlying rationale for its rejection of the call to action. Herein is the difference. If nothing else, the alternative institutional structure being proposed would require the United Nations and the international community to confront the matter at a substantive, rather than merely rhetorical, level.

We can now turn to the decisional responsibilities of the international community. The fifth condition is about assessing the ability of the international community to successfully carry out the intervention. We are assuming that an intervention, if properly resourced, could achieve the humanitarian goals that justify the call to action. Here the question is whether the necessary resources exist. The United Nations is in the best position to make this determination. As noted previously, Romeo Dallaire estimated that the Rwandan genocide could have been stopped with roughly 5,000 well-supported troops. As for the likely long-term success of a humanitarian intervention in Rwanda, the fact that nearly two decades after the genocide Rwanda remains stable is good reason to believe that the reconstruction of social and political society would have been successful.

The fifth condition does not account for the fact that in using resources to carry out a humanitarian intervention, there are opportunity costs for those political communities supplying the resources. The sixth condition is about assessing whether the opportunity costs to those political communities are unreasonable. Does carrying out a successful humanitarian military intervention require those political communities to make unreasonable moral sacrifices domestically? Again, there seems little reason to think that a humanitarian intervention in Rwanda would have made unreasonable demands on those political communities supplying the necessary resources. In any case, under the alternative institutional structure being proposed, any state claiming otherwise would have been forced to publicly justify this claim. In Rwanda this would have been an unenviable position for many of the major powers; especially since what was being asked was so small.

Lastly, there is the concern that the presumption against intervention could be undermined, and with it international order. If humanitarian military intervention became the rule rather than the exception, there is the possibility that secessionist movements would create humanitarian crises in order to draw the international community in to aid in their effort to become independent. As such, in order to rebut the presumption, one would need to demonstrate that the proposed intervention is not a threat to the presumption against intervention. The United Nations is likely in the best position to assess whether this criterion has been met.

In addition, when deciding upon the strategy for the military campaign as well as for the post-military intervention reconstruction, those institutions responsible for such decisions should be cognizant of this criterion. If the concern is that humanitarian efforts do not become a tool for secessionists and other provocateurs, then the intervention itself as well as the reconstruction should be focused, to the extent that there are not compelling moral reasons to the contrary, on reconciliation and repair. This is not to say that under certain circumstances, the best alternative available for insuring against future humanitarian crises may be to support aspirations for political self-determination or secession, but that should only be supported in the most exceptional of circumstances.

In the end, the proposed alternative institutional structure, if it had existed at the time of the Rwandan genocide, would have made at least two significant differences in the international community's practical deliberations over what to do about the violence in Rwanda. First, there is little reason to doubt that the initial decision about whether humanitarian intervention was called for would have been different. In fact, throughout the genocide one of the most ardent supporters of intervention was one of Rwanda's neighbors and one of the political communities most impacted by the refugee crisis caused by the genocide, Uganda. The voice of the Ugandans in the Security Council was largely ignored. It is safe to presume that their influence in the OAU would have been greater.

The second difference has less to do with the ultimate outcome, and more to do with affecting the rhetoric of political discourse in the international arena. In many cases, the ad hoc nature of international relations allows for institutions – largely states – to appeal to principle in defense of unprincipled and at times morally unjustified action. The alternative institutional structure proposed here is intended to provide procedural mechanisms that force those institutions to provide substantive reasons, and not merely normative rhetoric laced with platitudes about "never again" if they are going to choose inaction in the face of grave humanitarian need.

CONCLUDING REMARKS

There are at least four general propositions that have been defended here that are worthy of restatement. First, despite various skeptical objections, a moral obligation of humanitarian military intervention is possible, and the growing consensus that the international community was wrong to choose not to intervene in Rwanda is justified. Second, not only is such an obligation possible, but the Rwandan genocide presented an instance in which the international community was the bearer of such an obligation. Third, the normative framework of international relations that governed the practical deliberations of states provided the international community with the rhetorical and normative resources to choose not to intervene, and was in need of significant reform. Finally, to date the efforts at institutional reform are wanting and more fundamental reform is needed.

With that said, these concluding remarks are not intended to be a summary of the arguments presented. Such an effort would not only be practically difficult, but would likely be unwise; as providing such an extensive summary would involve missing an opportunity. Rather, in the remarks that follow, the focus is twofold. First, it is essential to understand the importance of continued engagement by the international community in the ever-evolving discussion over the responsibilities borne by the international community when grave humanitarian crises arise. Second, the arguments presented have a number of significant implications for how we ought to think about the role of justice in the practical deliberations of states and the international community.

As to the former, many would likely contend that there are more pressing matters with which the international community ought to be concerned, and that the issues surrounding humanitarian intervention have already received a thorough investigation. The quotes introducing these concluding remarks, however, demonstrate how naïve it would be to believe that the work regarding the development of institutional capacities to respond to humanitarian crises like Rwanda or Darfur is complete. More than 50 years after Wiesel offered his mistaken faith in the will of humanity, Jimmy Carter uttered the simple, yet powerful and now (in)famous phrase "never again". These two words represent the appropriate attitude to have towards such horrific actions, but less than fifteen years later a pastor sought protection against acts no less vile, and then again more than ten years later a United States senator condemned the brutal violence sponsored by the government of Sudan against its own people. In short, recent history indicates the need for new thinking about how to create institutional structures to protect basic rights.

It would be remiss not to recognize that there has been significant progress in our thinking about the responsibilities that states and the international community have to those suffering the violation of their basic rights. The formation of the ICISS, the development of the responsibility to protect principle and its continued presence in discussions occurring at the highest levels in international politics should provide us with reason to hope that the international community remains amenable to the substantial reform necessary for fulfilling the moral responsibility the international community has to insure that individual human rights are respected and protected. However, if we are committed to protecting basic rights against violation, these efforts at reform have not gone far enough.

Even if one rejects the specific conclusions defended in this discussion, recognizing the continued relevance and importance of the ongoing discussion over the responsibilities of the international community to protect basic rights should lead to more rather than less engagement by those with the ability to influence the design and construction of the institutional structures necessary for protecting basic rights. To that end, the arguments presented in this discussion should help to frame the conversation. In short, the discussion contained here provides a critical perspective through which the issue and possible institutional structures can be viewed. Anyone who would defend the status quo or offer an institutional structure less demanding than the alternative proposed should be prepared to respond to the arguments contained here.

More specifically, as to the alternative institutional structure and reformed normative framework proposed here, they will no doubt have detractors. Nonetheless, the alternatives defended here – the presumption of nonintervention as the governing normative principle and the alternative institutional structure intended to implement the presumption – provide a framework for an approach to institutional reform that is more aspirational than the reforms envisioned by the ICISS but still practically politically possible.

In addition to the importance of the continuing discussion over the responsibilities of the international community to provide and protect the basic rights of individuals and the relevance of the arguments presented above to that discussion, these arguments have significant implications for our thinking about the role of justice in the practical deliberations of states. First and foremost, the understanding of justice defended here implies that as a conceptual matter justice is not limited to negative duties. And, if we take it to be a basic moral proposition that we ought to fulfill the demands of justice and that our social and political institutions are mediating agents through which we can accomplish tasks that would be impossible for us to accomplish as a collection of isolated moral agents, then – all other things being equal – we ought to design our political and social institutions to fulfill these demands. As a consequence, this means that we should reform our social and political institutions to fulfill the demands of justice, including those that are foundationally positive and owed to distant others.

Second, the arguments presented have implications for the public discourse over what can be justifiably demanded of social and political institutions in the international arena. In the best case, this understanding will inform the positions of policy makers with the ability to reform the relevant social and political institutions. At the very least, the understanding presented provides a basis from which to evaluate claims made by diplomats and officials regarding the demands that can be made of international social and political institutions. Objections to the construction of or reform of institutions that would require states and other institutions to take responsibility for moral demands that are foundationally positive could no longer be based on a claim that such demands are supererogatory. Such rhetoric would be revealed for what it is; or those objecting would have to provide good substantive reasons as to why the proposed action is unjustified.

One might wonder how this is related to the practical deliberations of states and/or the international community. Simply put, the practical deliberations of states and the other actors that make up the international community are found in the specific institutional structures through which the international community deliberates, decides, and acts. The construction and reform of those structures are justified by the normative principles they are intended to institutionalize, and the principles being institutionalized become the principles that govern the practical deliberations of the institutions themselves. As such, since we should be seeking to construct and/or reform institutions and institutional structures such that the demands of justice are met, and the demands of justice include foundationally positive moral obligations; then in our effort to construct and/or reform institutions we will implicitly be affecting the way in which states and the international community deliberate about the demands of justice.

There are at least two additional implications for how we ought to understand the normative framework of international relations. First, echoing the claims made by the ICISS, our understanding of what is required for legitimate claims to sovereignty needs to be reevaluated. To the extent that sovereignty will continue to imply a certain type of normative/moral standing for those political communities claiming it, the international community should seek to construct institutions that demand a closer tie between internal political legitimacy and the rights ascribed to sovereign states. Second, the approach taken to evaluate the moral justifiability of the rules of the normative framework of international relations governing the international community's responsibility with regards to humanitarian intervention provides a framework for assessing the moral justifiability of other rules and principles governing the actions of states and the international community.

The last point is not an implication of the arguments presented. In fact, it is based on the recognition of a serious limitation in my capabilities; and, as a consequence, the arguments presented. Though the theoretical and conceptual critiques and the specific suggestions for the design of an alternative institutional structure were the result of significant thought and critical evaluation, in the end, I am relying on the expertise of others. This does not necessarily mean that those with the expertise that I lack will agree with the views I have defended, nor does it imply that they will endorse the alternative institutional structure I have proposed. But I hope to have provided a normative framework around which those with expertise in institutional design can build their own discussion.

In the end, the arguments presented in this discussion are a challenge to traditional thinking about global justice, the moral responsibilities of the international community, and the institutional structure of and principles governing the normative framework of international relations. To say that the underlying issues and relationships here are complicated is an understatement. As such, it would be foolish to think that any individual discussion, including this one, is going to provide finality or resolution to the problems facing the international community. Nonetheless, the critical views expressed and defended here should encourage recognition of the importance of the suffering of distant others and an understanding of what we can do about such suffering if we act through the social and political institutions that make up the international community. In addition, this discussion should engender a broader discussion amongst academics across various disciplines and new thinking by policy makers about how we can act together to resolve rather than exacerbate humanitarian crises. As the world becomes more and more interconnected, it is morally imperative that we begin to think beyond the conventional boundaries that rely on anachronistic thinking about the value of the traditional state system. If the system no longer serves humanity, then we ought not to hesitate to change it so that it does.

NOTES

INTRODUCTION

1. See Samantha Powers, *"A Problem from Hell": America and the Age of Genocide* (New York: Perennial, 2003); Philip Gourevitch, *We Wish to Inform You that Tomorrow We Will be Killed with Our Families: Stories from Rwanda* (New York: Farrar, Straus, and Giroux, 1998); and see Lt-Gen. Romeo Dallaire, *Shake Hands with the Devil: The Failure of Humanity in Rwanda* (Toronto: Random House Canada, 2003).
2. See Gourevitch, pp. 294–8. See also Dallaire, p. 518.
3. Gourevitch, pp. 26–8.
4. Ibid. pp. 26–8.
5. The Rwandan Patriotic Front was a rebel army comprised of Tutsis and moderate Hutus led by Paul Kagame.
6. Dallaire, p. 53.
7. Ibid. pp. 54–5. See also Powers, pp. 340–1.
8. Dallaire, p. 96.
9. Ibid. pp. 141–4, 146.
10. Ibid. p. 146.
11. Ibid. p. 359. See also Powers, p. 378.
12. Dallaire, pp. 374–6.
13. Ibid. pp. 222–5.
14. Ibid. pp. 145, 195.
15. UN Convention on the Prevention and Punishment of the Crime of Genocide (1948).
16. See Powers, pp. 358–64.
17. Ibid. p. 359; quoting a memo from the Office of the Secretary of Defense, "1. Genocide Investigation: Language that calls for an international investigation of human rights abuses and possible violations of the genocide convention. *Be Careful. Legal at State was worried about this yesterday – Genocide finding could commit [the U.S. government] to actually 'do*

something'" Office of the Secretary of Defense, "Secret Discussion Paper: Rwanda," 1 May 1994; *emphasis added by Powers.*

18. See Powers, p. 364.
19. Ibid. pp. 377–80.
20. See Dallaire, pp. 431–6.
21. Ibid. pp. 463–4, 471–2,
22. See L. R. Melvern, *A People Betrayed: The Role of the West in Rwanda's Genocide* (London: Zed Books Ltd, 2004), pp. 210–11.
23. See Powers, pp. 380–2. See also Melvern, p. 214.
24. See Clea Koff, *The Bone Woman: A Forensic Anthropologist's Search for Truth in the Mass Graves of Rwanda, Bosnia, Croatia, and Kosovo* (New York: Random House, 2004), p. 21.
25. UN Convention on the Prevention and Punishment of the Crime of Genocide (1948).
26. See Powers, pp. 370–1. See also Gourevitch, pp. 99–100.
27. See Powers, pp. 370–3.
28. See Noam Chomsky, "Humanitarian imperialism: the new doctrine of imperial right," *Monthly Review*, September (2008). And see Michael Walzer, *Just and Unjust Wars: A Moral Argument with Historical Illustrations*, 3rd edn (New York: Basic Books, 2000).
29. See Jeremy Rabkin, *The Case for Sovereignty: Why the World Should Welcome American Independence* (Jackson, TN: AEI Press, 1994). And see Michael Chertoff, "The responsibility to contain: protecting sovereignty under international law," *Foreign Affairs*, vol. 80 (2009), 130.
30. Stephen A. Garrett, *Doing Good and Doing Well: An Examination of Humanitarian Intervention* (Westport, CT: Praeger Publishers, 1999), p. 1.
31. J. L. Holzgrefe, "The humanitarian intervention debate," in J. L. Holzgrefe and Robert O. Keohane (eds), *Humanitarian Intervention: Ethical, Legal, and Political Dilemmas* (New York: Cambridge University Press, 2003), p. 18.
32. Jovana Davidovic, "Are humanitarian military interventions obligatory?" *Journal of Applied Philosophy* 25 (2008), pp. 134–44.

CHAPTER 1

1. Ernest J. Weinrib, "The case for a duty to rescue," 90 *Yale Law Journal* 247 (1980).
2. Roger D. Spegele, *Political Realism in International Theory* (Cambridge: Cambridge University Press, 1996), p. 19.
3. Thucydides, *History of the Peloponnesian War* (London: Penguin Classics,

1954), pp. 400–8. See also Mervyn Frost, *Ethics in International Relations: A Constitutive Theory* (Cambridge: Cambridge University Press, 1996), pp. 53–4.

 4. Hans Morgenthau, *Politics Among Nations* (New York: Alfred A. Knopf, Inc., 1968), p. 5. See also Frost, p. 53.

 5. Frost, p. 54 (that Kenneth Waltz argues that international relations is a "spontaneous system" beyond the control of individual agents and states). See also Morgenthau (that the rejection of normative theory is inevitable), p. 245.

 6. Gerald Elfstrom, *Ethics for a Shrinking World* (New York: St. Martin's Press, 1990) (that agents that comprise institutions can change the goals, policies, and actions of the institution), p. 31.

 7. See Kenneth Arrow, *Social Choice and Individual Values*, 2nd edn (New York: Wiley, 1963).

 8. Spegele, p. 19.

 9. Marshall Cohen, "Moral skepticism and international relations," *Philosophy & Public Affairs*, vol. 13, no. 4 (Autumn, 1984), p. 319. See also Gordon Graham, *Ethics and International Relations* (Oxford: Blackwell Publishers, 1997).

10. Thomas Hobbes, *Leviathan* [1651] (Oxford: Oxford University Press, 1996), pp. 82–5.

11. Ibid. p. 86–9.

12. Ibid. p. 84.

13. Ibid. pp. 86–9.

14. Ibid. p. 87.

15. See Charles R. Beitz, *Political Theory and International Relations* (Princeton, NJ: Princeton University Press, 1999), p. 32. See also Cohen, p. 319. See also Graham.

16. Hobbes, p. 85.

17. Ibid. pp. 86–7.

18. Ibid. pp. 86–7.

19. Beitz, p. 36.

20. Ibid. p. 36.

21. Ibid. p. 37.

22. Ibid. (that it is obvious that there have been "coalitions, alliances, and secondary associations"), p. 37.

23. Ibid. p. 40–2.

24. Ibid. p. 41.

25. Ibid. pp. 42–3.

26. Ibid. pp. 46–7.

27. David Hume, *A Treatise of Human Nature* [1737] (Oxford: Oxford University Press, 2000), p. 315. See also Hume, *An Enquiry Concerning*

the Principles of Morals [1751] (La Salle, IL: Open Court Publishing Co., 1966) (no justice in a society of ruffians), pp. 18, 19.

28. Hume [1737], pp. 307–9.
29. Ibid. p. 322. See also Hume [1751], pp. 18, 19.
30. Hume [1737], pp. 308–9.
31. Ibid. pp. 308–9.
32. Ibid. pp. 362–4. See also Cohen, pp. 329–31.
33. Cohen, p. 329.
34. Ibid. pp. 330–1. See also Hume [1737], p. 362–4.
35. See Saladin Meckled-Garcia, "On the very idea of cosmopolitan justice," *Journal of Political Philosophy* vol. 16, no. 3 (2008), pp. 245–71. And see Thomas Nagel, "The problem of global justice" *Philosophy & Public Affairs*, vol. 33, no. 2 (2005), pp. 113–47.
36. Nagel (2005), p. 128.
37. See Nagel (2005), pp. 125, 129, 131. And see Meckled-Garcia, p. 246.
38. Fernando Teson, "The liberal case for humanitarian intervention," in J. L. Holzgrefe and Robert O. Keohane (eds), *Humanitarian Intervention: Ethical, Legal, and Political Dilemmas* (Cambridge: Cambridge University Press, 2003), pp. 93–129, p. 95.
39. The instrumental argument is that international law is intended to provide international peace and security, and such goals are best served by a prohibition on intervention. See Michael J. Smith, "Humanitarian intervention: an overview of the ethical issues," in Joel H. Rosenthal (ed.), *Ethics & International Affairs* (Washington, DC: Georgetown University Press, 1999), p. 274.
40. Teson (2003), p. 111.
41. See Leslie Green, "Legal obligation and authority", *The Stanford Encyclopedia of Philosophy (Spring 2004 edition)*, Edward N. Zalta (ed.), *http://plato.stanford.edu/archives/spr2004/entries/legal-obligation/*, p. 3. See also H. L. A. Hart, "Legal and moral obligation," in A. I. Melden (ed.), *Essays in Moral Philosophy.* (Seattle: University of Washington Press, 1966), pp. 82–107; and see H. L. A. Hart, *Essays on Bentham* (Oxford: Clarendon Press, 1982), pp. 254–5.
42. Green, p. 3.
43. Ibid.
44. Ibid. p. 3.
45. Teson (2003), p. 111.
46. See International Commission on Intervention and State Sovereignty (ICISS), *The Responsibility to Protect* (Ottawa: International Development Research Center, 2001).
47. Teson (2003), pp. 108–9.

48. Green.
49. Ibid. p. 7.
50. Hobbes, ch. 17.
51. John Locke, *Two Treatises of Government* [1698] (Cambridge: Cambridge University Press, 1988), ch. 8.
52. H. L. A. Hart, "Are there any natural rights?" *The Philosophical Review*, vol. 64, no. 2 (April 1955), pp. 175–91, 185.
53. Green, p. 12.
54. See James Rachels, *The Elements of Philosophy*, 3rd edn (Boston: McGraw-Hill College, 1999), pp. 22–5. See also Chris Gowans, "Moral relativism", *The Stanford Encyclopedia of Philosophy (Spring 2004 edition)*, Edward N. Zalta (ed.), *http://plato.stanford.edu/archives/spr2004/entries/moral-relativism/*.
55. H. L. A. Hart, *The Concept of Law*, 2nd edn (Oxford: Oxford University Press, 1994), pp. 56–7.
56. T. M. Scanlon, *What We Owe to Each Other* (Cambridge, MA: Harvard University Press, 1998), pp. 191–7.
57. Michael Walzer, *Thick and Thin: Moral Argument at Home and Abroad* (Notre Dame: University of Notre Dame Press, 1994).
58. See Jean Hampton, *Political Philosophy* (Boulder, CO: Westview Press, 1997), p. 170. See also Michael Sandel, *Liberalism and the Limits of Justice* (Cambridge: Cambridge University Press, 1982), p. 187.
59. Hampton, p. 183. See also Alasdair MacIntyre, *After Virtue* (Notre Dame: Notre Dame University Press, 1981), p. 187.
60. Michael Walzer, "The moral standing of states," *Philosophy & Public Affairs*, vol. 9, no. 3 (Spring 1980), pp. 209–29, p. 210.
61. Ibid. p. 211.
62. Ibid. p. 228.
63. Ibid. p. 212.
64. Ibid. p. 212.
65. Ibid. p. 212.
66. Ibid. p. 214.
67. Ibid. pp. 216–18.
68. Ibid. p. 217.
69. David Luban, "The romance of the nation-state," *Philosophy & Public Affairs*, vol. 9, no. 4 (Summer 1980), pp. 392–7.
70. Ibid. p. 395.
71. Ibid. p. 395.
72. Mark W. Janis, *An Introduction to International Law*, 3rd edn. (New York: Aspen Law & Business, 1999), ("that the key actor on the world's stage was the sovereign state"), p. 161.
73. Immanuel Kant, *Toward Perpetual Peace*, in Immanuel Kant, *Practical*

Philosophy, ed. Mary J. Gregor (Cambridge: Cambridge University Press, 1996), pp. 311–51, p. 319.
74. UN Charter ch. I, art. 1, para. 1.
75. UN Charter ch. I, art. 2, para. 4.
76. For a similar example, see Peter Singer, *One World* (New Haven, Connecticut: Yale University Press, 2002), pp. 186–7.
77. Wesley Newcomb Hohfeld, *Fundamental Legal Conception as Applied in Judicial Reasoning* (Westport, CT: Greenwood Press Publishers, 1978).
78. Hohfeld, pp. 35–6.
79. Ibid. pp. 35–6.
80. Cicero, *On Obligations*, tr. P. G. Walsh (Oxford: Oxford University Press, 2000).
81. Ibid. Bk I, p. 5.
82. Ibid.
83. Ibid.
84. Ibid.
85. Hohfeld, p. 35.
86. Ibid. p. 36.
87. Ibid.
88. Ibid. pp. 36–8, 44–5.
89. Ibid. pp. 44–5.
90. Ibid. pp. 36–8.
91. Cicero, p. 5 (that obligations provide moral guidance derived from the conceptual aspect of the obligation).
92. Joseph Raz, *Practical Reason and Norms* (Oxford: Oxford University Press, 1999), p. 36.
93. Ibid.
94. Ibid.
95. Ibid. pp. 35, 46–7.
96. Ibid. p. 35.
97. Ibid. pp. 46–7.
98. Ibid.
99. Ibid. (that "in most situations [the second-order reason's] weight is not in question. It prevails in virtue of being an exclusionary reason."), p. 79.
100. Ibid. pp. 46–7.
101. Ibid. p. 77.

CHAPTER 2

1. See Sumner's discussion of the constitutive elements of rights serving as existence conditions: L. Wayne Sumner, *The Moral Foundation of Rights* (Oxford: Oxford University Press, 1986), pp. 11, 13.

2. John Stuart Mill, *Utilitarianism* (Indianapolis, IN: Hackett Publishing Co., Inc., 1979), pp. 7, 11.
3. Ibid. pp. 23–5.
4. See Brad Hooker, "Rule consequentialism", *The Stanford Encyclopedia of Philosophy (Spring 2004 edition)*, Edward N. Zalta (ed.), *http://plato. stanford.edu/archives/spr2004/entries/consequentialism-rule/*.
5. Sumner, ch. 6.
6. Thomas Pogge, *World Poverty and Human Rights* (Oxford: Blackwell Publishing, 2002), p. 13.
7. Ibid.
8. Ibid. See also Richard A. Epstein, "A theory of strict liability," 2 *The Journal of Legal Studies* (1973), pp. 160–89.
9. The name of the state in the example, Kundu, may be familiar to some readers. It was the name of a fictional state used in an episode of *The West Wing.*
10. Sumner, pp. 174, 189–98, 201–3.
11. Ibid.
12. Ibid. p. 191.
13. Ibid. ("Since we have settled on the model of rights as protected choices . . ."), p. 203.
14. Henry Shue, *Basic Rights: Subsistence, Affluence, and U. S. Foreign Policy,* 2nd edn (Princeton, NJ: Princeton University Press, 1996), pp. 13–20.
15. Ibid. pp. 21, 37–8.
16. Ibid. p. 19. Sumner makes a similar argument regarding the periphery of the core of rights. One might think of basic rights as the periphery that is necessary for the core to be fulfilled. See Sumner, p. 202.
17. Shue, p. 13.
18. Pogge (2002), p. 13.
19. Shue, pp. 37–8.
20. Ibid. p. 18.
21. Ibid. p. 19.
22. David Rodin, *War and Self-Defense* (Oxford: Oxford University Press, 2002), pp. 122–32.
23. Ibid. p. 123.
24. Ibid. pp. 122–7.
25. Ibid. pp. 127–32.
26. Ibid. pp. 131–2.
27. See Gerald Elfstrom, *Ethics for a Shrinking World* (New York: St. Martin's Press, 1990), p. 163.
28. Shue, p. 135.
29. Ibid.
30. Ibid. pp. 131–9.

31. Ibid. pp. 142–4.
32. Michael Walzer, "The moral standing of states," *Philosophy & Public Affairs*, vol. 9, no. 3 (Spring 1980).
33. David Luban, "The romance of the nation-state," *Philosophy & Public Affairs*, vol. 9, no. 4 (Summer 1980), pp. 395.
34. Elfstrom, p. 143.
35. Ibid.
36. Shue, pp. 30–1.
37. Ibid. p. 31.
38. Ibid. pp. 32–3.
39. Ibid. p. 33.
40. Ibid. pp. 16–18.
41. Joseph Raz, *Engaging Reasons: On the Theory of Value and Action* (Oxford: Oxford University Press, 1999), footnote 4, p. 22.
42. One could argue that not only must the moral value being protected be of sufficient moral weight, but that the person being harmed or threatened with harm must be the cause of, or be contributing to, the threat to the moral value being protected. See David Rodin's discussion of "innocent aggressors": Rodin, pp. 80–3.
43. Raz (1999), pp. 37–45.
44. Cicero, *On Obligations*, tr. P. G. Walsh (Oxford: Oxford University Press, 2000), Bk I, pp. 5, 23.
45. Ibid. p. 23.
46. Raz (1999), pp. 139–41.
47. Ibid. p. 144.
48. Ibid. pp. 46–7.
49. H. L. A. Hart, *The Concept of Law*, 2nd edn (Oxford: Oxford University Press, 1994), pp. 56–7.
50. See Ian Brownlie and Guy S. Goodwin-Gill (eds), *Basic Documents on Human Rights* (Oxford: Oxford University Press, 2002).
51. Onora O'Neill, "The great maxims of justice and charity," *Constructions of Reasons: Explorations of Kant's Political Philosophy* (1989), pp. 219–21. See also Allen Buchanan, "Justice and charity", *Ethics* 97 (1987), pp. 558–75, 561–2.
52. O'Neill, "The great maxims," pp. 219–21.
53. O'Neill, "The great maxims," pp. 219–21. See also Robert Nozick, *Anarchy, State, and Utopia* (New York: Basic Books, Inc., 1974), pp. 32–4, 47. And see Pogge (2002), p. 13.
54. O'Neill, "The great maxims," pp. 219–21. See also Michael Sandel, *Liberalism and the Limits of Justice* (Cambridge: Cambridge University Press, 1982), pp. 1–7. And see Isaiah Berlin, *Four Essays on Liberty* (Oxford: Oxford University Press, 1969), pp. 118–72.

55. O'Neill, "The great maxims," pp. 224–5.
56. Ibid. p. 224.
57. Shue, pp. 18–22.
58. Shue advances a similar argument regarding our understanding of basic rights. See Shue, pp. 21, 37–8.
59. John Hospers, "What libertarianism is," in Tibor R. Machan (ed.), *The Libertarian Alternative: Essays in Social and Political Philosophy* (Chicago, IL: Nelson Hall Co., 1974), pp. 3–20. See also Shue's discussion of the libertarian conception of justice: Shue, p. 19.
60. Hospers. See also Nozick, pp 32–4, 47. And see Pogge (2002), p. 13.
61. Emphasis in original: Nozick, p. 47.
62. I have not discussed the issue of conscription in order to fulfill the moral obligation of humanitarian intervention, as it bears little on the claims defended here.
63. Shue, p. 18.
64. Raz (1999), p. 21.
65. Buchanan, pp. 558–75, 561–2.
66. This is an often raised objection to Singer's principle in "Famine, affluence and morality": Peter Singer, "Famine, affluence, and morality", pp. 231–2. Some versions of this objection include the following: Samuel Scheffler, "Relationships and responsibilities", *Philosophy & Public Affairs*, 26 (1997), pp. 189–209; and see Garrett Hardin, "Life boat ethics" from *Psychology Today* (September 1974).
67. Ernest J. Weinrib, "The case for a duty to rescue," 90 *Yale Law Journal* 247 (1980).
68. O'Neill, "The great maxims," pp. 224–5.
69. Samantha Powers, *"A Problem from Hell": America and the Age of Genocide* (New York: Perennial, 2003), pp. 461–73.
70. Ibid. pp. 463–6.
71. Ibid. pp. 461–3.
72. Ibid. pp. 466–8.

CHAPTER 3

1. Charter of the United Nations, art. 2 paras 1 and 4.
2. For a discussion of the special importance of this problem to political philosophers, see Onora O'Neill, *Faces of Hunger* (London: Allen & Unwin Publishers Ltd, 1986), ch. 7.
3. O'Neill (1986), p. 123.
4. David P. Forsythe, *Human Rights in International Relations* (Cambridge: Cambridge University Press, 2000), p. 3.

5. Michael Byers, *Custom, Power and the Power of Rules* (Cambridge: Cambridge University Press, 1999), p. 75.
6. Charles R. Beitz, *Political Theory and International Relations* (Princeton, NJ: Princeton University Press, 1999), pp. 36–7.
7. Forsythe, p. 3.
8. See Mark W. Janis, *An Introduction to International Law*, 3rd edn (New York: Aspen Law & Business, 1999), p. 157. See also *Treaties of Peace Between Sweden and the Holy Roman Empire and Between France and the Holy Roman Empire* (Peace of Westphalia, 14 October 1648), 1 C.T.S. 119–356. The Charter of the United Nations also provides some guidance here, as chapter 7 interventions are conducted to preserve or establish international peace and security. And see Michael J. Smith, "Humanitarian intervention: an overview of the ethical issues," in Joel H. Rosenthal (ed.), *Ethics & International Affairs* (Washington, DC: Georgetown University Press, 1999), p. 274 (that establishment of sovereignty converted chaos of pre-Westphalian world into order).
9. See Michael Chertoff, "The responsibility to contain: protecting sovereignty under international law," *Foreign Affairs* January/February 2009.
10. Thomas Hobbes, *Leviathan* [1651] (Oxford: Oxford University Press, 1996), chs 17–18.
11. Ibid. pp. 111–15.
12. Ibid. pp. 135–9.
13. Ibid. p. 114.
14. Ibid. pp. 115–20.
15. Robert O. Keohane, "Political authority after intervention: gradations in sovereignty," in J. L. Holzgrefe and Robert O. Keohane (eds), *Humanitarian Intervention: Ethical, Legal, and Political Dilemmas* (New York: Cambridge University Press, 2003), p. 282.
16. Christopher W. Morris, *An Essay on the Modern State* (Cambridge: Cambridge University Press, 1998), p. 172.
17. Ibid.
18. Roger Scruton, "Sovereignty," in *A Dictionary of Political Thought* (London: Macmillan Press, 1982), p. 441.
19. Morris, p. 14.
20. Ibid. p. 178.
21. Scruton, p. 441.
22. Hobbes, pp. 115–20.
23. See Morris, p. 41.
24. Wesley Newcomb Hohfeld, *Fundamental Legal Conception as Applied in Judicial Reasoning* (Westport, CT: Greenwood Press Publishers, 1978), pp. 35–39. See also David Rodin, *War and Self-Defense* (Oxford: Oxford University Press, 2002), p. 18.

25. L. Wayne Sumner, *The Moral Foundation of Rights* (Oxford: Oxford University Press, 1986), pp. 11, 13.
26. For Mill's discussion of the harm principle, see John Stuart Mill, *On Liberty*, from *On Liberty and Other Essays* [1859] (Oxford: Oxford University Press, 1991), p. 14.
27. For a discussion of second-order reasons, see Joseph Raz, *Engaging Reasons: On the Theory of Value and Action* (Oxford: Oxford University Press, 1999), pp. 39–45.
28. See Janis, p. 157. See also *Treaties of Peace Between Sweden and the Holy Roman Empire and Between France and the Holy Roman Empire*, 1 C.T.S. 119–356.
29. Janis, pp. 159–60.
30. Hans Morgenthau, "To intervene or not to intervene," *Foreign Affairs*, vol. 45, no. 3 (April 1967), pp. 425–36.
31. Beitz, p. 65–6.
32. Hobbes, pp. 82–4.
33. Hobbes, pp. 82–6. See also David Hume's discussion of "Justice." Hume, *An Enquiry Concerning the Principles of Morals* [1751] (La Salle, IL: Open Court Publishing Co., 1966), pp. 15–38. For a more contemporary version of the Humean argument regarding the nature of morality, see David Gauthier, *Morals by Agreement* (Oxford: Oxford University Press, 1986).
34. Hobbes, pp. 85, 86.
35. Ibid. chs 15–17.
36. Hobbes, ch. 21, p. 142.
37. Mill (1859), pp. 5–130.
38. See S. I. Benn and R. I. Peters, *The Principles of Political Thought: Social Principles and the Democratic State* (New York: Free Press, 1965), pp. 429–31. And see R. J. Vincent, *Nonintervention and International Order* (Princeton, NJ: Princeton University Press, 1974), p. 345.
39. Mill (1859), p. 14.
40. See Benn and Peters, pp. 429–31. And see Vincent, p. 345.
41. See Michael Walzer, *Just and Unjust Wars: A Moral Argument with Historical Illustrations*, 3rd edn (New York: Basic Books, 2000), pp. 87–91. See also John Stuart Mill, "A few words on nonintervention," in *Dissertations and Discussions, Vol. III* (London: Longmans, Green, Reader, and Dyer, 1867).
42. Michael Walzer, "The argument about humanitarian intervention," *Dissent* (Winter 2002), pp. 29–37, 29–31.
43. Walzer (2000), p. 87. See also Beitz's discussion of Walzer's argument, Beitz, p. 85.
44. Walzer (2000), p. 88.

45. For a detailed discussion, see Beitz, pp. 83–92.
46. Mill (1859), pp. 83–103.
47. Walzer (2000), p. 89.
48. See Benn and Peters, pp. 429–31.
49. See Vincent, p. 345.
50. Benn and Peters, p. 431. See also Beitz, p. 84.
51. Mill (1859), pp. 91–6.
52. Ibid.
53. Beitz, p. 84.
54. I am relying on Beitz's account of Hall's argument: Beitz, p. 88. But see William E. Hall, *International Law*, 8th edn (Oxford: Clarendon Press, 1924), p. 347.
55. See Beitz, p. 88.
56. Jovan Babic, "Foreign armed intervention: between justified aid and illegal violence," in Aleksandar Jokic (ed.), *Humanitarian Intervention: Moral and Philosophical Issues* (Peterborough, ON: Broadview Press, 2003), pp. 45–70, 52–4.
57. Ibid. pp. 53–4.
58. Ibid. pp. 52, 64–6.
59. Janis, p. 159.
60. Smith, p. 274.
61. UN Charter, art.1, para. 1. See also Smith, p. 274.
62. Michael Taylor, *Community, Anarchy, and Liberty* (Cambridge: Cambridge University Press, 1982), pp. 44–5.
63. Ibid. p. 44.
64. Ibid. p. 45.
65. Stanley Hoffman, *The Ethics and Politics of Humanitarian Intervention* (Notre Dame, IN: University of Notre Dame Press, 1996), p. 19. See also Smith (that a rule against intervention is necessary because the costs of intervention when it should not occur are too high), pp. 284–5.
66. Beitz, pp. 36–7.
67. Mill (1859), p. 83.
68. Ibid. pp. 91–6.
69. See David Luban, "The romance of the nation-state," *Philosophy & Public Affairs*, vol. 9, no. 4 (Summer 1980), pp. 392–7, p. 395.
70. Mill (1859), pp. 83–6.
71. Ibid.
72. Michael Walzer (1980), pp. 209–29, p. 211.
73. Walzer (2000), p. 87.
74. For a discussion of Hall's argument, see Beitz, p. 84.
75. Ibid. pp. 52–4.
76. See Smith, p. 274.

77. Hoffmann, p. 19 (that a rule is needed to prevent states from using humanitarian concerns as a pretext for aggressive war). See also Smith, pp. 284–5 (that a rule against intervention is necessary because the costs of intervention when it should not occur are too high).
78. See Walzer (2002), pp. 29–31.
79. Brian Orend, "War," in *The Stanford Encyclopedia of Philosophy (Winter 2005 edition)*, Edward N. Zalta (ed.), *http://plato.stanford.edu/archives/win2005/entries/war/*.
80. See the International Commission on Intervention and State Sovereignty (ICISS), *The Responsibility to Protect* (2001). And see Gareth Evans, *The Responsibility to Protect: Ending Mass Atrocity Crimes Once and for All* (Washington, DC: The Brookings Institution, 2008).
81. Luban (1980), p. 395. See also Walzer (1980), p. 214.
82. Babic, pp. 64–6. See also Smith, pp. 284–5.
83. Jeff McMahan, "Humanitarian intervention, consent and proportionality", in N. Ann Davis, Richard Kershen, and Jeff McMahan (eds), *Ethics and Humanity: Themes from the Philosophy of Jonathan Glover* (Oxford: Oxford University Press, 2010), pp. 44–72.
84. Ibid.
85. Ibid.
86. Ibid.
87. Ibid.
88. For a detailed analysis of the moral status of agents, see Jeff McMahan, *Killing in War* (Oxford: Clarendon Press, 2009).

CHAPTER 4

1. Gareth Evans, *The Responsibility to Protect: Ending Mass Atrocity Crimes Once and for All* (Washington, DC: The Brookings Institution, 2008), p. 241.
2. John Rawls, *The Law of Peoples* (Cambridge, MA: Harvard University Press, 1999).
3. Ibid.
4. Ibid.
5. For a more thorough discussion, see Joshua J. Kassner, "Deliberating about justice: the role of social justice in the practical deliberations of states," *Contemporary Political Theory*, vol. 5, no. 2, 2011, pp. 210–31.
6. International Commission on Intervention and State Sovereignty (ICISS), *The Responsibility to Protect* (Ottawa: International Development Research Center, 2001).
7. Evans.
8. Ibid.

9. Ibid.
10. Ibid. And see Thomas Weiss, *Humanitarian Intervention: Ideas in Action* (Cambridge: Polity Press, 2007).
11. ICISS, XII.
12. Ibid.
13. Ibid.
14. Ibid. XIII.
15. Ibid. XIII.
16. Ibid. p. 47, quoting art. 39 of the Charter of the United Nations.
17. ICISS (2001), XIII.
18. Ibid.
19. Ibid.
20. See James Pattison, "Humanitarian intervention and international law: the moral importance of and intervener's legal status," *Critical Review of International Social and Political Philosophy* vol. 10, no. 3 (2007), 301–19. And see Alex J. Bellamy, "Responsibility to protect or Trojan Horse? The crisis in Darfur and humanitarian intervention after Iraq," *Ethics & International Affairs*, vol. 19, issue 2 (September 2005), pp. 31–54.
21. Alex J. Bellamy, "Whither the responsibility to protect? Humanitarian intervention and the 2005 World Summit." *Ethics & International Affairs*, vol. 20, issue 2 (June 2006), pp. 143–69.
22. Ibid.
23. As James Pattison notes, this problem is not just related to new justifications for the use of force. It is common for states to rely on the rhetoric of self-defense to justify what, in the end, proves to be self-interested action. See James Pattison, *Humanitarian Intervention and the Responsibility to Protect: Who Should Intervene?* (Oxford: Oxford University Press, 2010).
24. 2005 World Summit.
25. See Bellamy (2006).
26. Ibid.
27. Ibid. p. 169.
28. Ibid.
29. Martin Binder, "Humanitarian crisis and the international politics of selectivity," *Human Rights Review* vol. 10 (2009), 327–48.
30. Onora O'Neill, "The great maxims of justice and charity," *Constructions of Reasons: Explorations of Kant's Political Philosophy* (Cambridge: Cambridge University Press, 1989).
31. See Pattison.
32. Pattison.
33. Ibid.

34. Jeremy Waldron, *Law and Disagreement* (Cambridge: Cambridge University Press, 1999), p. 154.
35. Pattison.
36. ICISS, ch. 6.
37. Charter of the United Nations, ch. V, art. 24.
38. ICISS (2001) quoting Charter of the United Nations, art. 2.4, p. 47.
39. Charter of the United Nations, ch. VII, art. 42.
40. Charter of the United Nations, ch. VII, art. 39.
41. This does not mean that the Security Council has unbounded discretion. The meaning of "international peace and security" requires interpretation because, to borrow a phrase from H. L. A Hart, the language employed is "open-textured," H. L. A. Hart, *The Concept of Law*, 2nd edn (Oxford: Oxford University Press, 1994). One could interpret this narrowly, as it has often been interpreted, to refer only to open conflict between two sovereign states. On the other hand, the phrase could be interpreted to include any action that might threaten cross-border stability. In any case, there must be some connection between the act and international peace and/or security.
42. ICISS.
43. Immanuel Kant, *Toward Perpetual Peace*, in Immanuel Kant, *Practical Philosophy*, ed. Mary J. Gregor (Cambridge: Cambridge University Press, 1996).
44. Plato, *The Republic* (Oxford: Oxford University Press, 1993).
45. Rawls.
46. Provisional Rules of Procedure of the Security Council, ch. III, rule 13, available at *http://www.un.org/en/sc/repertoire/93–95/93–95_01.pdf*.
47. Ibid. rule 14.
48. For a detailed discussion of non-domination, see Philip Pettit, *Republicanism: A Theory of Freedom and Government* (Oxford: Oxford University Press, 1997).
49. Andreas Føllesdal, "Survey article: Subsidiarity," *The Journal of Political Philosophy*, vol. 6, issue 2 (June 1998), pp. 190–218.
50. Ibid.
51. Rawls.
52. See President of the United Nations General Assembly, "The role of regional and sub-regional arrangements in implementing the responsibility to protect" (12 July 2011), available at *www.un.org*. And see Report of the Secretary General, "The role of regional and sub-regional arrangements in implementing the responsibility to protect" (12 July 2011), available at *www.un.org*.
53. Ibid.

54. I would like to thank Hillel Steiner for bringing this potential objection to my attention.
55. Kant.
56. Amartya Sen, *Development as Freedom* (New York: Anchor Books, 2000).
57. For example, recall that many of the victims of the Rwandan genocide were killed because their names had been read out during daily broadcasts by Radio Mille Collines. Blocking the radio station's airwaves would have saved many lives.
58. For a list of NGOs recognized by the UN, visit the following website: *http://www.unodc.org/ngo/list.jsp.*
59. See President of the United Nations General Assembly, "The role of regional and sub-regional arrangements in implementing the responsibility to protect" (12 July 2011). And see Report of the Secretary General, "The role of regional and sub-regional arrangements in implementing the responsibility to protect" (12 July 2011).

CONCLUSION

1. Elie Wiesel, *Night* (New York: Hill and Wang, 2006), p. 33.
2. Jimmy Carter, 39th President of the United States, "Remarks at the Presentation of the Final Report of the President's Commission on the Holocaust," 27 September 1979.
3. Letter from Pastors Ezekiel Semugeshi, Isaka Rucondo, Seth Rwanyabato, Eliezer Seromba, Seth Sebike, Jerome Gakwaya, and Ezekias Zigirinshuti to Pastor Elizaphan Ntakirutimana; quoted in Philip Gourevitch, *We Wish to Inform You that Tomorrow We Will be Killed with Our Families: Stories from Rwanda* (New York: Farrar, Straus, and Giroux, 1998), p. 42.

BIBLIOGRAPHY

Howard Adelman, "Theory and humanitarian intervention," in Michael Keren and Donald A. Sylvan (eds), *International Intervention: Sovereignty versus Responsibility* (Portland, OR: Frank Cass & Co. Ltd, 2002).

Sharon Anderson-Gold, *Cosmopolitanism and Human Rights* (Cardiff, Wales: University of Wales Press, 2001).

Raymond Aron, *Peace and War: A Theory of International Relations*, translated by Richards Howard and Annette Baker Fox (Garden City, NY: Doubleday & Co., 1966).

Kenneth Arrow, *Social Choice and Individual Values*, 2nd edn (New York: Wiley, 1963).

Jovan Babic, "Foreign armed intervention: between justified aid and illegal violence," in Aleksandar Jokic (ed.), *Humanitarian Intervention: Moral and Philosophical Issues* (Peterborough, ON: Broadview Press, 2003).

Brian Barry, "Humanity and justice in global perspective," in Robert E. Goodin and Philip Pettit (eds.), *Contemporary Political Philosophy: An Anthology* (Oxford: Blackwell Publishing, 1997).

Charles R. Beitz, *Political Theory and International Relations* (Princeton, NJ: Princeton University Press, 1999).

Charles R. Beitz, Marshall Cohen, Thomas Scanlon, and A. John Simmons (eds), *A Philosophy and Public Affairs Reader: International Ethics* (Princeton, NJ: Princeton University Press, 1985).

S. I. Benn and R. I. Peters, *The Principles of Political Thought: Social Principles and the Democratic State* (New York: Free Press, 1965).

Jeremy Bentham, *An Introduction to the Principles of Morals and Legislation* (Amherst, NY: Prometheus Books, 1988).

Isaiah Berlin, *Four Essays on Liberty* (Oxford: Oxford University Press, 1969).

Alex J. Bellamy, "Whither the responsibility to protect? Humanitarian intervention and the 2005 World Summit," *Ethics & International Affairs*, vol. 20, issue 2 (June 2006), pp. 143–69.

Alex J. Bellamy, "Responsibility to protect or Trojan Horse? The crisis in Darfur and humanitarian intervention after Iraq," *Ethics & International Affairs*, vol. 19, issue 2 (September 2005), pp. 31–54.

Martin Binder, "Humanitarian crisis and the international politics of selectivity," *Human Rights Review*, vol. 10 (2009), 327–48.

Luigi Bonanate, *Ethics and International Politics* (Columbia, SC: University of South Carolina Press, 1995).

Chris Brown, "International affairs," in Robert E. Goodin and Philip Pettit (eds), *A Companion to Contemporary Political Philosophy* (Oxford: Blackwell Publishing, 1995).

Ian Brownlie (ed.), *Basic Documents in International Law* (Oxford: Oxford University Press, 2002).

Ian Brownlie (ed.), *Basic Documents on Human Rights* (Oxford: Oxford University Press, 2002).

Allen Buchanan, "From Nuremberg to Kosovo: the morality of illegal international legal reform," in Aleksandar Jokic (ed.), *Humanitarian Intervention: Moral and Philosophical Issues* (Peterborough, ON: Broadview Press, 2003).

Allen Buchanan, "Justice and charity", *Ethics* 97 (1987), pp. 558–75.

Michael Byers, *Custom, Power, and the Power of Rules* (Cambridge: Cambridge University Press, 1999).

Deen K. Chatterjee, *The Ethics of Assistance: Morality and the Distant Needy* (Cambridge: Cambridge University Press, 2004).

Deen K. Chatterjee and Don E. Scheid, *Ethics and Foreign Intervention* (Cambridge: Cambridge University Press, 2003).

Michael Chertoff, "The responsibility to contain: protecting sovereignty under international law," *Foreign Affairs*, vol. 80 (2009).

Cicero, *On Obligations* (Oxford: Oxford University Press, 2000).

Marshall Cohen, "Moral skepticism and international relations," *Philosophy & Public Affairs*, vol. 13, no. 4 (Autumn 1984), pp. 299–346.

Jean-Marc Coicaud and Daniel Warner (eds), *Ethics and International Affairs: Extent and Limits* (New York: United Nations University Press, 2001).

Gustav Daniker, "Intervention as a challenge for the military," in Michael Keren and Donald A. Sylvan (eds), *International Intervention: Sovereignty versus Responsibility* (Portland, OR: Frank Cass & Co. Ltd, 2002).

Jovana Davidovic, "Are humanitarian military interventions obligatory?" *Journal of Applied Philosophy* 25 (2008), pp. 134–44.

Michael C. Davis, Wolfgang Dietrich, Bettina Scholdan, and Dieter Sepp (eds), *International Intervention in the Post-Cold War World* (Armonk, NY: M. E. Sharpe, Inc., 2004).

Michael C. Davis, Wolfgang Dietrich, Bettina Scholdan, and Dieter Sepp (eds), "The emerging world order: state sovereignty and humanitarian intervention," from Michael C. Davis et al. (eds), *International Intervention in the Post-Cold War World* (Armonk, NY: M. E. Sharpe, Inc., 2004).

Declaration on Principles of International Law Concerning Friendly Relations, NewYork, 24 October 197, available at *http://untreaty.un.org/cod/avl/ha/dpil-frcscun/dpilfrcscun.html*.

Jack Donnelly, *Universal Human Rights: In Theory and Practice* (Ithaca, NY: Cornell University Press, 2003).

Patrick Dunleavy, "The state," in Robert E. Goodin and Philip Pettit (eds), *A Companion to Contemporary Political Philosophy* (Oxford: Blackwell Publishing, 1995).

Gerald Elfstrom, *Ethics for a Shrinking World* (New York: St. Martin's Press, 1990).

Gerald Elfstrom, *International Ethics: A Reference Handbook* (Santa Barbara, CA: ABC-CLIO, Inc., 1998).

Anthony Ellis, "War, revolution, and humanitarian intervention," in Aleksandar Jokic (ed.), *Humanitarian Intervention: Moral and Philosophical Issues* (Peterborough, ON: Broadview Press, 2003).

Richard A. Epstein, "A theory of strict liability," 2 *The Journal of Legal Studies* 160–89 (1973).

Toni Erskine (ed.), *Can Institutions Have Responsibilities? Collective Moral Agency and International Relations* (New York: Palgrave Macmillan, 2003).

Joel Feinberg (ed.), *Moral Concepts* (Oxford: Oxford University Press, 1969).

Joel Feinberg, *Doing and Deserving* (Princeton, NJ: Princeton University Press, 1970).

Mary Gore Forrester, *Persons, Animals, and Fetuses: An Essay in Practical Ethics* (Boston, MA: Kluwer Academic Publishers, 1996).

David P. Forsythe, *Human Rights in International Relations* (Cambridge: Cambridge University Press, 2000).

Mervyn Frost, *Ethics in International Relations: A Constitutive Theory* (Cambridge: Cambridge University Press, 1996).

Alton Frye (Project Director), *Humanitarian Intervention: Crafting a Workable Doctrine* (New York: Council on Foreign Relations, 2000).

Stephen A. Garrett, *Doing Good and Doing Well: An Examination of Humanitarian Intervention* (Westport, CT: Praeger Publishers, 1999).

Raymond D. Gastil, "Beyond a theory of justice", *Ethics*, 85:3 (1975).

David Gauthier, *Morals by Agreement* (Oxford: Oxford University Press, 1986).

General Assembly Resolution 1803 (XVII) of 14 December 1962, "Permanent Sovereignty over Natural Resources, available at *http://www.un.org/en/sc/repertoire/93–95/93–95_01.pdf*.

Robert E. Goodin and Philip Pettit (eds), *A Companion to Contemporary Political Philosophy* (Oxford: Blackwell Publishing, 1995).

Robert E. Goodin and Philip Pettit (eds), *Contemporary Political Philosophy: An Anthology* (Oxford: Blackwell Publishing, 1997).

Philip Gourevitch, *We Wish to Inform You that Tomorrow We Will be Killed with Our Families: Stories from Rwanda* (New York: Farrar, Straus, and Giroux, 1998).

Pablo De Greiff and Ciaran Cronin (eds), *Global Justice and Transnational Politics: Essays on the Moral and Political Challenges of Globalization* (Cambridge, MA: The MIT Press, 2002).

Gordon Graham, *Ethics and International Relations* (Oxford: Blackwell Publishers, 1997).

Leslie Green, "Legal obligation and authority", *The Stanford Encyclopedia of Philosophy (Spring 2004 edition)*, Edward N. Zalta (ed.), *http://plato.stanford. edu/archives/spr2004/entries/legal-obligation/*.

William E. Hall, *International Law*, 8th edn (Oxford, Clarendon Press, 1924).

Jean Hampton, *Political Philosophy* (Boulder, CO: Westview Press, 1997).

Garrett Hardin, "Life boat ethics," in *Psychology Today* (September 1974).

H. L. A. Hart, "Are there any natural rights?" *The Philosophical Review*, vol. 64, no. 2 (April 1955), pp. 175–91, 185.

H. L. A. Hart, "Legal and moral obligation," in A. I. Melden (ed.), *Essays in Moral Philosophy* (Seattle, WA: University of Washington Press, 1966), pp. 82–107.

H. L. A. Hart, *Essays on Bentham* (Oxford: Clarendon Press, 1982).

H. L. A. Hart, *The Concept of Law*, 2nd edn (Oxford: Oxford University Press, 1994).

Thomas Hobbes, *Leviathan* [1651] (Oxford: Oxford University Press, 1996).

Stanley Hoffman, *The Ethics and Politics of Humanitarian Intervention* (Notre Dame, IN: University of Notre Dame Press, 1996).

J. L. Holzgrefe, "The humanitarian intervention debate," in J. L. Holzgrefe and Robert O. Keohane (eds), *Humanitarian Intervention: Ethical, Legal, and Political Dilemmas* (Cambridge: Cambridge University Press, 2003).

J. L. Holzgrefe and Robert O. Keohane (eds), *Humanitarian Intervention: Ethical, Legal, and Political Dilemmas* (Cambridge: Cambridge University Press, 2003).

Brad Hooker, "Rule consequentialism", *The Stanford Encyclopedia of Philosophy (Spring 2004 edition)*, Edward N. Zalta (ed.), *http://plato.stanford.edu/archives/ spr2004/entries/consequentialism-rule/*.

John Hospers, "What libertarianism is," in Tibor R. Machan (ed.), *The Libertarian Alternative: Essays in Social and Political Philosophy* (Chicago, IL: Nelson Hall Co., 1974), pp. 3–20.

David Hume, *An Enquiry Concerning the Principles of Morals* [1751] (La Salle, IL: Open Court Publishing Co., 1966).

David Hume, *A Treatise of Human Nature* [1737] (Oxford: Oxford University Press, 2000).

Micheline R. Ishay (ed.), *The Human Rights Reader: Major Political Essays, Speeches, and Documents from the Bible to the Present* (New York: Routledge, 1997).

Mark W. Janis, *An Introduction to International Law*, 3rd edn (New York: Aspen Law & Business, 1999).

Aleksandar Jokic (ed.), *Humanitarian Intervention: Moral and Philosophical Issues* (Peterborough, ON: Broadview Press, 2003).

Charles Jones, *Global Justice: Defending Cosmopolitanism* (Oxford: Oxford University Press, 1999).

Immanuel Kant, *Practical Philosophy*, ed. Mary J. Gregor (Cambridge: Cambridge University Press, 1996).

Joshua J. Kassner, "Deliberating about justice: the role of social justice in the practical deliberations of states," *Contemporary Political Theory*, vol. 5, no. 2, 2011, pp. 210–31.

Robert Keohane, "Introduction," in J. L. Holzgrefe and Robert O. Keohane (eds), *Humanitarian Intervention: Ethical, Legal, and Political Dilemmas* (Cambridge: Cambridge University Press, 2003).

Robert Keohane, "Political authority after intervention: gradations in sovereignty," in J. L. Holzgrefe and Robert O. Keohane (eds), *Humanitarian Intervention: Ethical, Legal, and Political Dilemmas* (Cambridge: Cambridge University Press, 2003).

Michael Keren and Donald A. Sylvan (eds), *International Intervention: Sovereignty versus Responsibility* (Portland, OR: Frank Cass & Co. Ltd, 2002).

Clea Koff, *The Bone Woman: A Forensic Anthropologist's Search for Truth in the Mass Graves of Rwanda, Bosnia, Croatia, and Kosovo* (New York: Random House, 2004).

Anthony F. Lang Jr, *Agency and Ethics: The Politics of Military Intervention* (Albany, NY: State University of New York Press, 2002).

Paul Gordon Lauren, *The Evolution of International Human Rights: Visions Seen* (Philadelphia, PA: University of Pennsylvania Press, 1998).

Lauren E. Lomasky, *Persons, Rights, and the Moral Community* (Oxford: Oxford University Press, 1987).

David Luban, "The romance of the nation-state," *Philosophy & Public Affairs*, vol. 9, no. 4 (Summer 1980), pp. 392–7.

David Luban, "Just war and human rights," reprinted in Charles R. Beitz et al. (eds), *A Philosophy and Public Affairs Reader: International Ethics* (Princeton, NJ: Princeton University Press, 1985), pp. 195–216.

David Luban, "Intervention and civilization: some unhappy lessons of the Kosovo War," in Pablo De Greiff and Ciaran Cronin (eds), *Global Justice*

& Transnational Politics: Essays on the Moral and Political Challenges of Globalization (Cambridge, MA: The MIT Press, 2002).

Alasdair MacIntyre, *After Virtue* (Notre Dame, IN: Notre Dame University Press, 1981).

Mahmood Mamdani, *When Victims Become Killers: Colonialism, Nativism, and the Genocide in Rwanda* (Princeton, NJ: Princeton University Press, 2002).

Jeff McMahan, *Killing in War* (Oxford: Clarendon Press, 2009).

Jeff McMahan, "Humanitarian intervention, consent and proportionality," in N. Ann Davis, Richard Kershen, and Jeff McMahan (eds), *Ethics and Humanity: Themes from the Philosophy of Jonathan Glover* (Oxford: Oxford University Press, 2010), pp. 44–72.

Saladin Meckled-Garcia, "On the very idea of cosmopolitan justice," *Journal of Political Philosophy*, vol. 16, no. 3 (2008), pp. 245–71.

L. R. Melvern, *A People Betrayed: The Role of the West in Rwanda's Genocide* (London: Zed Books Ltd, 2004).

John Stuart Mill, "A few words on nonintervention," in *Dissertations and Discussions, Vol. III* (London: Longmans, Green, Reader, and Dyer, 1867).

John Stuart Mill, *On Liberty*, from *On Liberty and Other Essays* [1859] (Oxford: Oxford University Press, 1991).

Hans Morgenthau, *Politics Among Nations* (New York: Alfred A. Knopf, Inc., 1968).

Christopher W. Morris, *An Essay on the Modern State* (Cambridge: Cambridge University Press, 1998).

Thomas Nagel, "The problem of global justice" *Philosophy & Public Affairs*, vol. 33, no. 2 (2005), pp. 113–47.

Jan Narveson, *Respecting Persons in Theory and Practice: Essays on Moral and Political Philosophy* (Lanham, MD: Rowman & Littlefield Publishers, Inc., 2002).

Robert Nozick, *Anarchy, State, and Utopia* (New York: Basic Books, Inc., 1974).

Onora O'Neill, *Faces of Hunger* (London: Allen & Unwin (Publishers) Ltd, 1986).

Onora O'Neill, "The great maxims of justice and charity," *Constructions of Reasons: Explorations of Kant's Political Philosophy* (Cambridge: Cambridge University Press, 1989).

Onora O'Neill, "Agents of justice," in Thomas Pogge (ed.), *Global Justice* (Oxford: Blackwell Publishing, 2001).

Claus Offe and Volker Ronge, "Theses on the theory of the state," in Robert E. Goodin and Philip Pettit (eds), *Contemporary Political Philosophy: An Anthology* (Oxford: Blackwell Publishing, 1997).

Brian Orend, "War," in *The Stanford Encyclopedia of Philosophy (Winter 2005 edition)*, Edward N. Zalta (ed.), *http://plato.stanford.edu/archives/win2005/entries/war/*.

Thomas L. Pangle and Peter J. Ahrensdorf, *Justice Among Nations: On the Moral Basis of Power and Peace* (Lawrence, KA: University Press of Kansas, 1999).

James Pattison, "Humanitarian intervention and international law: the moral importance of and intervener's legal status," *Critical Review of International Social and Political Philosophy* vol. 10, no. 3 (2007), 301–19.

James Pattison, *Humanitarian Intervention and the Responsibility to Protect: Who Should Intervene?* (Oxford: Oxford University Press, 2010).

Michael Philips, "Humanitarian intervention and moral theory," in Aleksandar Jokic (ed.), *Humanitarian Intervention: Moral and Philosophical Issues* (Peterborough, ON: Broadview Press, 2003).

Thomas Pogge (ed.), *Global Justice* (Oxford: Blackwell Publishing, 2001).

Thomas Pogge, "Introduction: global justice," in Thomas Pogge (ed.), *Global Justice* (Malden, MA: Blackwell Publishing, 2001).

Thomas Pogge, *World Poverty and Human Rights* (Oxford: Blackwell Publishing, 2002).

Thomas Pogge, "Human rights and human responsibilities," in Pablo De Greiff and Ciaran Cronin (eds), *Global Justice and Transnational Politics: Essays on the Moral and Political Challenges of Globalization* (Cambridge, MA: The MIT Press, 2002).

Thomas Pogge, "Preempting humanitarian interventions," in Aleksandar Jokic (ed.), *Humanitarian Intervention: Moral and Philosophical Issues* (Peterborough, ON: Broadview Press, 2003).

Samantha Powers, *"A Problem from Hell": America and the Age of Genocide* (New York: Perennial, 2003).

Jeremy Rabkin, *The Case for Sovereignty: Why the World Should Welcome American Independence* (Jackson, TN: AEI Press, 1994).

John Rawls, *The Law of Peoples* (Cambridge, MA: Harvard University Press, 1999).

Joseph Raz, *Practical Reason and Norms* (Oxford: Oxford University Press, 1999).

Joseph Raz, *Engaging Reasons: On the Theory of Value and Action* (Oxford: Oxford University Press, 1999).

Joseph Raz, *The Morality of Freedom* (New York: Clarendon Press, 1986).

David Rodin, *War and Self-Defense* (Oxford: Oxford University Press, 2002).

Joel H. Rosenthal, *Ethics and International Affairs: A Reader*, 2nd edn (Washington, DC: Georgetown University Press, 1999).

Alfred P. Rubin, "Humanitarian intervention and international law," in Aleksandar Jokic (ed.), *Humanitarian Intervention: Moral and Philosophical Issues* (Peterborough, ON: Broadview Press, 2003).

Michael Sandel, *Liberalism and the Limits of Justice* (Cambridge: Cambridge University Press, 1982).

T. M. Scanlon, *What We Owe to Each Other* (Cambridge, MA: Harvard University Press, 1998).

Roger Scruton, "Sovereignty," in *A Dictionary of Political Thought* (London: Macmillan Press, 1982).

Amartya Sen, *Development as Freedom* (New York: Anchor Books, 2000).

Samuel Scheffler, "Relationships and responsibilities", *Philosophy & Public Affairs*, 26 (1997), pp. 189–209.

Henry Shue, *Basic Rights* (Princeton, NJ: Princeton University Press, 1996).

Henry Shue, "Limiting sovereignty," in Jennifer M. Welsh, *Humanitarian Intervention and International Relations* (Oxford: Oxford University Press, 2004).

Henry Sidgwick, *The Methods of Ethics* (London: Macmillan, 1907).

Peter Singer, "Famine, affluence, and morality," *Philosophy & Public Affairs*, 1: 2 (1972), pp. 231–2.

Peter Singer, *One World* (New Haven, CT: Yale University Press, 2002).

Peter Singer, "Outsiders: our obligations to those beyond our borders," *The Ethics of Assistance: Morality and the Distant Needy* (Cambridge: Cambridge University Press, 2004), pp. 11–32.

Quentin Skinner, "The state," in Robert E. Goodin and Philip Pettit (eds), *Contemporary Political Philosophy: An Anthology* (Oxford: Blackwell Publishing, 1997).

Michael J. Smith, "Humanitarian intervention: an overview of the ethical issues," in Joel H. Rosenthal (ed.), *Ethics & International Affairs* (Washington, DC: Georgetown University Press, 1999).

Roger D. Spegele, *Political Realism in International Theory* (Cambridge: Cambridge University Press, 1996).

L. Wayne Sumner, *The Moral Foundation of Rights* (Oxford: Oxford University Press, 1986).

Fernando Teson, *Humanitarian Intervention* (Irvington-on-Hudson, NY: Transnational Publishers, Inc., 1996).

Fernando Teson, *A Philosophy of International Law* (Boulder, CO: Westview Press, 1998).

Fernando Teson, "The liberal case for humanitarian intervention," in J. L. Holzgrefe and Robert O. Keohane (eds), *Humanitarian Intervention: Ethical, Legal, and Political Dilemmas* (Cambridge: Cambridge University Press, 2003), pp. 93–129.

Kenneth W. Thompson (ed.), *Ethics and International Relations: Ethics in Foreign Policy, Vol. 2* (New Brunswick, NJ: Transaction, Inc., 1985).

Thucydides, *History of the Peloponnesian War* (London: Penguin Classics, 1954).

Treaties of Peace Between Sweden and the Holy Roman Empire and Between France and the Holy Roman Empire (Peace of Westphalia, 14 October 1648), 1 C.T.S. 119–356.

United Nations, Charter of the United Nations, 24 October 1945, 1 UNTS XVI.

R. J. Vincent, *Nonintervention and International Order* (Princeton, NJ: Princeton University Press, 1974).

Gregory Vlastos, "Human worth, merit, and equality," in Joel Feinberg (ed.), *Moral Concepts* (Oxford: Oxford University Press, 1969).

Michael Walzer, "The moral standing of states," *Philosophy & Public Affairs*, vol. 9, no. 3 (Spring 1980), 209–29.

Michael Walzer, *Thick and Thin: Moral Argument at Home and Abroad* (Notre Dame, IN: University of Notre Dame Press, 1994).

Michael Walzer, *Just and Unjust Wars: A Moral Argument with Historical Illustrations,* 3rd edn (New York: Basic Books, 2000).

Michael Walzer, "The argument about humanitarian intervention," *Dissent* (Winter 2002), pp. 29–37.

Michael Walzer, *Arguing about War* (New Haven, CT: Yale University Press, 2004).

Mary Anne Warren, *Moral Status: Obligations to Persons and Other Living Things* (Oxford: Oxford University Press, 1997).

Ernest J. Weinrib, "The case for a duty to rescue," 90 *Yale Law Journal* 247 (1980).

Thomas G. Weiss and Cindy Collins, *Humanitarian Challenges and Intervention* (Boulder, CO: Westview Press, 2000).

Jennifer M. Welsh, *Humanitarian Intervention and International Relations* (Oxford: Oxford University Press, 2004).

Jennifer M. Welsh, "Taking consequences seriously: objections to humanitarian intervention," in Jennifer M. Welsh, *Humanitarian Intervention and International Relations* (Oxford: Oxford University Press, 2004).

Nicholas J. Wheeler, *Saving Strangers: Humanitarian Intervention in International Society* (Oxford: Oxford University Press, 2000).

C. H. Whitley, "On duties," in Joel Feinberg (ed.), *Moral Concepts* (Oxford: Oxford University Press, 1969).

Burleigh Wilkins, "Humanitarian intervention: some doubts," in Aleksandar Jokic (ed.), *Humanitarian Intervention: Moral and Philosophical Issues* (Peterborough, ON: Broadview Press, 2003).

Rudiger Wolfrum, "The UN experience in modern intervention," in Michael Keren and Donald A. Sylvan (eds), *International Intervention: Sovereignty versus Responsibility* (Portland, OR: Frank Cass & Co. Ltd, 2002).

Veronique Zanetti, "Global justice: is interventionism desirable?" in Thomas Pogge (ed.), *Global Justice* (Oxford: Blackwell Publishing, 2001).

INDEX